Letters from California

Monterey, June 5, 1847. A General View from Jones' Fort by William R. Hutton. Garner's balconied house is at the far right; the chute for carrying drinking water to the ships is seen in the center foreground; Larkin's wharf with hoist is at the far left. The pole tripods were probably for cutting up beeve for the new butchershop, which is the odd double building near the Customhouse.

William Robert Garner

Letters from California 1846-1847

EDITED, WITH A SKETCH OF THE
LIFE AND TIMES OF THEIR AUTHOR,
BY DONALD MUNRO CRAIG

University of California Press
Berkeley, Los Angeles, and London
1970

University of California Press
Berkeley and Los Angeles, California
University of California Press, Ltd.
London, England

CONTENTS

ILLUSTRATIONS

This sketch by Garner's guest shows the relationship of Garner's house to the rest of Monterey. Cf. the same view in an early photograph in the plate section. (Courtesy of the Henry E. Huntington Library and Art Gallery.)

From the National Archives, Record Group 49. (Courtesy of the National Archives.)

This engraving shows one method of cutting and the use of oxen in Garner's time. From W. H. Rideing, *Boys in the Mountains* (New York, D. Appleton & Co., 1882).

From the Castro Papers, Bancroft Library, University of California, Berkeley. (Reproduced by permission of the Director of The Bancroft Library.) It reads:

San Francisquito
Feb. 17, 1844

Don Manuel Castro

My dear sir,

    I sent to your ranch for the cattle as we agreed, and they were turned over to me according to your promise. But I must tell you they did not put your sale brand on them, for José María said the brand was not on the ranch. It is very necessary that you have branded for me the hides I am disposing of and also those cows I do not intend to kill.

Three hides from these cattle leave today for Monterey, going to Salvador Munras. I beg you to go to the marker's house and tell him about these three hides so that my business not suffer arrears.

I hope you will come or send someone to brand the remaining cattle.

I remain your devoted servant,
William R. Garner

Custom House, Built 1814, Monterey, California.
From photograph taken around 1875. (Courtesy of The Bancroft Library.)

Ruins of Old Mexican Jail, Monterey, California, 1875
This was the disreputable *calabozo* that held the prisoners taken in the Graham Affair of 1840. Sheriff Garner and Alcalde Colton had their office in this building. (Courtesy of The Bancroft Library.)

ACKNOWLEDGMENTS

Most of my free time since 1958 has been spent pursuing fragmentary information in widely separated archives. I am grateful to all who have helped me, especially to Mr. Emmet McMenamin, County Clerk, for permission to use the archives of Monterey County; to the late Mrs. Helen H. Bretnor and to Mr. Cecil L. Chase for aid during years of research at the Bancroft Library, University of California, Berkeley; to Mr. Robert O. Dougan, Librarian of the Henry E. Huntington Library and Art Gallery, San Marino, Calif., for many past kindnesses and for present permission to reproduce the drawings by William Rich Hutton; to Mrs. Marjorie Hancock, Deputy Librarian, The Mitchell Library (Sydney, N. S. W., Australia); to the Public Record Office (London), the National Maritime Museum (Greenwich, England), the Ministry of Transport's General Register and Record Office (Cardiff), and the Admiralty's Historical Section (London), and to Dr. William B. Williams of Carmel for tracking down the answers to innumerable small questions of fact; to Mrs. Maxine Shore for encouragement, and to Mrs. Amelie Elkinton for her expert knowledge of old Monterey and to Mr. Jay Margulies, and Mrs. Margery Riddle of the University of California Press.

[Illustrations were made possible through the financial assistance of the Monterey History and Art Association, of which Donald Craig was a long and valued member and editor of its historical bulletin.]

INTRODUCTION

IN APRIL 1847, almost exactly one year after the outbreak of the Mexican War, an extraordinary series of letters from Monterey, California, was published as a special supplement to the Philadelphia *North American and United States Gazette*. They were signed *W. G.* The editor of the newspaper prefaced them by explaining that he had asked his friend the Reverend Walter Colton, when he sailed as chaplain of the California-bound frigate *Congress*, to select for him "able and accomplished correspondents who could not only furnish graphic accounts of the passing news of the day, but render their letters valuable by the introduction of historical, statistical, agricultural and political information in relation to countries of which we now know little."

He congratulated Mr. Colton on his choice of the Monterey correspondent. "His letters afford, to our view, the best description of California we have yet seen." Today they still have a freshness, a frankness, and intimacy that is astonishing. Unlike the travelers' tales of the period, the letters cater neither to sensationalism nor to the desire to be picturesque; they are advertisements, honest propaganda. Their unfeigned intent was to draw to California a solid body of American farmers, craftsmen, and merchants who would develop the land, break the trading monopolies, and forestall any idea of returning the territory to Mexico after the war. For this reason they teem with facts illustrated by the author's personal experiences over a period of twenty-two years.

In fact, the letters are the most authoritative and complete de-

scription of the customs and life of the Californians and the resources and economic prospects of the country to reach the general
American public before the Gold Rush. The rare supplement to
the *North American* was only brought to light in 1924 by William
Abbatt as Extra No. 103 of his long-defunct *Magazine of History*,
but he missed an equal amount of correspondence by *W. G.* in
other issues of the Philadelphia *North American* and the New
York *Journal of Commerce*. These previously undiscovered letters are an integral part of the series, and the entire text is now
collated and presented here as a unit for the first time.

Who was *W. G.*, and why was he peculiarly fitted to record the
California scene? When William Abbatt published the *North
American* supplement letters, he did not identify their author. It
is now clear that he was William Robert Garner, an Englishman
who came to California in 1824 and in 1846 was secretary-
interpreter-guide to Walter Colton, the American alcalde of Monterey. He was a rancher, a lumberman, a miner, a constable, an
officer in the recurrent and bloodless revolutions that distracted
Mexican California. He worked hard, shone briefly in the world
of letters, fought to clear his name of libelous charges, and died of
Indian arrows in the Sierra Nevada, aged forty-six. Unlike most
other writers of the period on California, he was linked by ties
of marriage and citizenship to the native Californians. He was
privy to their councils, their fraternal bickering and political intrigues, their social and religious customs, their ambitions and
fears for the future of California.

Inspection of Garner's letters immediately brings up a question.
If Colton chose him as correspondent for the *North American*,
why did Garner also contribute to the New York *Journal of Commerce?* From the tone of the *Journal of Commerce*'s opening
statement on July 21, 1847, "the voluminous correspondence" came
to it unsolicited. None of the material duplicates the letters received three months earlier by the *North American*. Did Garner
decide on his own initiative after reading a copy of the *Journal*
brought out by a ship, or did he discuss his hopes for California
with Colton and get advice to spread his advertisements through
a wider territory? Colton's hand seems evident in this, for Garner

wished to reach manufacturers and investors, and Colton knew that the *Journal* was the organ of these groups.

There seem to have been three shipments of letters to the *North American* and two to the *Journal of Commerce*. The *North American* received dispatches in late April and July 1847 and January 1848; the *Journal of Commerce* received its share only in July 1847 and January 1848. If parcels were lost in an October 1847 shipment, this would account for the gap in the letter sequence from March 6, 1847, to October 4, 1847. Conceivably, Garner may have sent that sheaf to a third newspaper or even to England, but search in the sources at hand has not revealed it.

It is difficult to recognize any system in Garner's division of letters between his two publishers. The *North American* printed an almost unbroken run from November 1 to December 16, 1846. The *Journal of Commerce* confesses that it threw away many letters, presumably covering the period July–September 1846, because they dealt with the military occupation of Monterey and had "lost their interest by delay." However, it did print one, or a combination of several letters, that antedates the *North American* series, and three more that fill in dates left blank in the Philadelphia columns.

Initially, there was probably a spate of letters for September, October, and November 1846, as Garner, excited about the stirring events in California, tried his hand at the new field of journalism. The stream dwindled in mid-December and almost dried up in January, 1847, either because of severe editorial cutting in Philadelphia and New York or a lack of inspiration on their author's part once he had made clear his basic points for immigration. February again gives a good flow into the first week of March, then a drought for six months, a freshet in October including three on October 10, and then — nothing. Garner had tired of the unaccustomed task, or he was distracted by his libel suit and other business.

William Robert Garner and his role in California's history have been almost forgotten. There is neither monument nor plaque commemorating him; his fine two-story adobe home was razed years ago; no portrait gives us his lineaments; no family letters

survive to illuminate his private life. Despite the dramatic circumstances of his life, William Robert Garner has never been the
subject of a biography. His aloof self-sufficiency, the lack of personal, intimate correspondence, and the difficulty of checking
archives in England and Australia have kept him a shadowy figure in the wings of history. Therefore, to give perspective and
background to the California Letters, a sketch of his life precedes
them, and to unravel the tangled web of mystery that clings about
the man, a thorough investigation has been made of the sensa-
tional charges in the unresolved *Garner* v. *Farnham* suit for libel.

BIOGRAPHICAL SKETCH

In 1803, when William Robert Garner was born in London, England was girding herself for the long struggle against Napoleon. The great ports of the island hummed with preparations for war. The shipyards never turned out fighting ships so fast as from 1803 to 1815, for on the strength of those "wooden walls" depended the safety of England. William Garner's life was to be fatefully linked to the sea and to a warship readied for launching in 1804.

William's father had come to London from a quiet Norfolk hamlet, Massingham, halfway between Norwich and Lynn. Work was scarce, the crops were poor, and the cost of food very high. In the towns there were food riots. Charity kitchens, where hot pease soup was ladled into the plates of the poor three times a week, were set up in the streets of Lynn by the town council in 1801. Not in all Norfolk was there a future or even a present for a newly-married young clerk. Like many others, Henry Gardner and his wife Anne moved to the great city.[1]

In London government offices burgeoned under the heat of war like plane trees in spring. Henry Gardner settled into place on one

---

1. William Richards, *History of Lynn*, 2 vols. (Lynn, England, 1812), II, 243; London, Admiralty Archives, Historical Section. The Admiralty records spell the name "Gardner." William may have dropped the "d" in California because the Spanish-speaking people pronounced his name "Gar'na," or he may have changed it to hide his identity without actually taking a pseudonym. His Mexican father-in-law spelled it "Cane" [Kah-neh] in phonetic Spanish on his *diseño* in 1837. English usage varied between "Garner" and "Gardner."

of the high stools in the Office of Seamen's Wages at the Admiralty. The unimposing brick building on Parliament Street was only a short ten minutes' walk from his lodgings on Southampton Street in the Strand, where his son William was born. Henry Gardner did his work competently but not brilliantly; in 1824 he was still in the same office, a junior clerk.

Anne was of different metal. She was proud of her connections with the merchant Godfreys of Norfolk. She was an expert seamstress and milliner. Years later William told his son José that she was not only needlewoman to Queen Caroline, but her confidante as well. The story is difficult to verify, but it has the ring of truth. Although Anne Gardner's name appears on no list of palace servants, her claim to acquaintance with the queen in those chaotic times is very likely valid. Many a humble Londoner could say as much.

Caroline of Brunswick, the "injured queen" of George IV, was lonely, unconventional, and warm-hearted. She had all fashionable London whispering behind its fans at her free and easy manner, her unaffected kindness to common people, and habit of stopping to chat affably with anyone. The humble citizens of London adored their queen, and upon George's insulting attempt to divorce her and force her abdication in 1820, mobs rose ready to defend her cause. With pride William Garner related how his mother had loyally sewed for Queen Caroline both before and after the great trial in the House of Lords.[2]

The fact that lends credence to his boast is that Southampton Street was then famous for its dressmakers and milliners. Caroline, who loved elaborate hats and fine clothes as much as she did the theater, must often have looked in at her seamstresses before going to a new play at her favorite Covent Garden or at those just beyond in Drury Lane. The flying needles would then have paused for a few moments while the queen walked among the flattered women to inspect their work. Little wonder, when all London

---

2. The information on Garner's parents comes from two brief California sources and corroborative material in English archives. In the *San Jose Pioneer* (April 27, 1878) José Garner states that his father's parents were Henry Garner, a clerk in the Admiralty (verified from Admiralty records), and a Godfrey of Norfolk. The

gossiped about the royal scandal, that Mrs. Gardner treasured her intimacy with the unfortunate queen and that her son never forgot it.

There are no intimate personal papers in the archives or in the possession of Garner's descendents to give further detail to this sketch of his early life. It is obvious, however, from his beautiful penmanship, his meticulous spelling, his choice of words, ability to use legal terms correctly, and the organization of his writing that he had received far more schooling than most English boys of his day. Despite the modest place in London society of William's family, it evidently had influential friends.

Young Garner's education did not run its full course. An anonymous note in the Vallejo documents states that the boy got into mischief while at school and, as a punishment, his father put him aboard a whaler to learn the trade. José Garner remembered his father's telling him that at an early age he was apprenticed to Mr. Bennett, a shipowner and whaler. The records of apprentice indentures kept by the Registrar General of Shipping and Seamen date only from 1824 and therefore do not contain the name of William Garner, who entered into service at least five years earlier. However, in the lists available from 1824 to 1835, a number of boys were apprenticed to a Mr. William Bennett. In the archives of Lloyd's of London, William Bennett and Son is noted not only as a well-established whaling firm but also as the owner in 1824 of the *Royal George*, a whaler bound for the South Seas with William Robert Garner serving aboard her as an experienced apprentice.

At this period the most prosperous whaling grounds were in the South Seas and the great rendezvous for the ships was the Bay of Islands on the northern tip of New Zealand. In the 1820's, this area was a no-man's-land, truly the end of the earth. Whalemen were a hard breed; they numbered among them the vilest of men. Rigid as was the discipline aboard ship, ashore debauchery

other California source is the baptismal record in the Mission of San Juan Bautista of Garner's conversion to Catholicism, which is reproduced as Appendix I along with additional genealogical information.

and brutality reigned. No government kept order; on the loveliest of islands cannibal tribes waged incessant warfare. The most frightful accounts can be found in the log books of whalers and trading ships. Nothing was allowed to stand in the way of a profitable voyage.[3]

There was a little-known side line to British whaling in the South Seas. Many English vessels made the long journey down under Africa and east to Australia for a special reason: the first convicts transported to the penal colonies went out in South Seas whalers, and for years thereafter thrifty shipowners made a profit not only on the oil and whalebone carried home but also on each condemned man and woman they brought out on contract for the crown. The fee of £17/7/6 per head and sixpence a day for food made many an owner and ship's captain close his nostrils to the stench of prisoners confined below decks in foul weather.[4]

There is a strong likelihood that young Garner served as apprentice aboard such a whaler-transport. His memories could not have been wholly unpleasant. A hostile witness in Garner's later libel suit swore that he "spoke of a passage made by himself and . . . convicts from England to the Penal Colonies on the Island of New Holland [Australia]. And that during his conversation that time, Garner boasted much of the favors of a very special character which were shown him by his fellow passengers the convict women on board."[5] (Garner may have been merely tale-swapping. In any case, this would have been a whaler other than the *Royal George*, which did not call at the penal colonies between 1816 and 1824, according to the *Australian Almanac*.) On the transports such dissolute behavior was commonplace. In 1806 Captain Bertram reported, "The captain and each officer enjoy

---

3. For example, in 1831 the English trader *Elizabeth*, in exchange for a cargo of flax, carried one hundred bushel baskets of human flesh from a Maori battlefield to the victorious tribe's feasting place. William John Dakin, *Whalemen Adventurers: The Story of Whaling in Australian Waters and Other Southern Seas*, 2d rev. ed. (Sydney: Angus & Robertson, 1938), pp. 50–68.

4. Charles White, *Early Australian History: Convict Life in New South Wales* (Bathurst, Australia, 1889), pp. 79–130; Dakin, p. 12.

5. Deposition of Isaac Graham, in Monterey County Archives, County Court-

right of selection. Each sailor and soldier is allowed to attach himself to one of the females. . . . As regards the crew themselves, poor Jack is planted in a perfect garden of temptation when among probably a hundred of such fair seducers, and is more an object of pity than of wrath." On one vessel which brought out 226 women from English prisons, the voyage lasted fifteen months. With less interesting passengers the trip ordinarily took from five to nine months, depending on stopovers at Cape Town and other ports. Unencumbered four-masters averaged 127 days from London to Sydney in the mid-1800's.[6]

The transport-whalers unloaded their miserable "live lumber" at Port Jackson or Botany Bay and proceeded to New Zealand to take on water and firewood before cruising the coasts of the Americas and the wide reaches of the Pacific off Japan. They returned to England only after every cask had been topped with oil and every corner stacked with baleen.

From 1800 to 1810 a whaling venture from London to the South Seas fisheries lasted only two years and three months on the average. By the decade 1820 to 1830 the figure had risen six months because of the competition and the need to go farther and farther to make a cargo.[7] Monthly wages did not enter into the scheme of whaling. A whaling voyage was a speculation, and captain and crew shipped "upon the lay," or a share of the value of the cargo at market in London. According to the usual practice, the owners were entitled to one-half the profit to recompense them for assuming all expenses. The captain would claim between 1/11th and 1/15th share, each officer and harpooner proportionately less, and the man before the mast hoped for anything from a 1/110th to 1/200th share. From the sailor's share, of course, was deducted the

---

house, Salinas, California, XIII, 761–781. This is the main document in the *Garner* v. *Farnham* libel suit. It is given in full, with a discussion of its claims and related documents, as Appendix II below.

6. White, p. 124; *A Voyage Through the Islands of the Pacific Ocean* (Dublin, 1824), p. 136.

7. Dakin, p. 132; Thomas Beale, *The Natural History of the Sperm Whale, To Which Is Added a Sketch of a South-Sea Whaling Voyage . . . in Which the Author Was Personally Engaged*, 2d ed. (London, 1839), pp. 150–154.

cost of the exorbitantly priced articles he had purchased on credit while at sea.[8]

Apprentice boys like William Garner had little but experience in seamanship and accounting to show for a three-year voyage. The period for which they were bound ranged from five to seven years. They messed and berthed near the officers' quarters, but traditionally the apprentice led a dog's life, being neither child nor man, fo'c's'le hand nor gold braid. Some were serving at twelve years of age; most began between thirteen and fifteen and took their place as officers in their early twenties.

Although the records do not show when William Garner was apprenticed to Mr. Bennett, it must have been before the age of fifteen. The 1824 voyage of the *Royal George* bears this out. It was clearly not his first nor his second, for a shipmate, James Watson, later testified that "the captain remarked that Mr. Garner's apprenticeship would expire in two or three months and that he was so satisfied with his work that he would then put him on the 'lay.' "[9] Since the *Royal George* sailed from Gravesend on the Thames about the first of January 1824 and Garner left her in November at the age of twenty or twenty-one, he must have served at least five years as apprentice and made two previous trips to the South Seas.

The *Royal George* was a fine looking little ship. She had been built at Cowes, Isle of Wight, in 1804 as an eighteen-gun, two-decked, ship-rigged sloop-of-war. After Waterloo many such a small ship was retired from the naval list. At 250 tons the *Royal*

---

8. Frederick Debbell Bennett, *Narrative of a Whaling Voyage Round the Globe*, 2 vols. (London, 1840), I, 191–192. Albert Church, *Whaleships and Whaling* (New York: W. W. Norton, 1938), appendix, gives the "lay" for the whaler *Milton* of New Bedford in 1836. The master drew 1/17th of a cargo worth about $100,000 ($5,882); the first mate, 1/22nd ($4,545); the second mate, 1/50th ($2,000); the third mate, 1/65th; the boatsteerers, 1/75th to 1/90th; the carpenter, 1/110th; the cook, 1/115th; and the seamen, 1/120th to 1/220th (about $454).

Despite the hardship and risk, a seafarer's wages compared favorably with those of the landsman: $.75 a day for a laborer in 1840 in New York, Boston, or Philadelphia equals $234 per year for an eleven- to thirteen-hour day. Skilled mechanics and carpenters were paid $1.50 for the same hours, totaling $468 for the year. Out of this they paid board and room; the sailor had them furnished, bad as they were. The best study of this period is John Rogers Commons, et al., *History of*

George was somewhat small for a whaler — most were 300 to 400 tons burthen and carried a crew of 28 to 33 men — however, she was bought about 1817 by William Bennett, who refitted her, raised the upper deck, and sent her off to the southern whaling grounds in 1818 under a hell-roaring master, Captain William Buckle. Within three years she was back in London with a fat profit, and Captain Buckle sailed her out again in 1821. He brought her back toward the end of 1823, deep in the water with a full cargo of oil, and was rewarded with the command of a larger ship, the *Daniel IV*.[10]

Captain D. Barney replaced Buckle on the *Royal George*. Once again repairs were made, iron cables bent on, and her bottom sheathed with shining copper for the 1824 cruise. But the *Royal George* was getting old, and her costs were rising. Bennett and Son cut them by economizing on her provisioning. The beginning of the cruise promised well. She made the run to the Pacific with a bone in her teeth all the way, took up station on the new grounds south of Japan, and then, for seven months, through fair weather and foul, her boats pursued whales without bringing one alongside.

In his haste to make a fast and profitable voyage Captain Barney had not anchored the ship anywhere long enough to give the men recreation or to supplement the skimped and poor provisions taken aboard in London. Now, with such a run of ill fortune, he did not dare turn about and sail for some island where fresh food might be procured and the water casks refreshed. He could not spare the time nor take the risk; whaling captains were

---

Labor in the United States, 4 vols. (New York: Macmillan, 1918–1935), vols. I and II.

9. Monterey County Archives, XIII, 707–708.

10. *Lloyd's Register of Shipping* (London, 1804–1828). Captain Buckle proceeded to win a notorious niche in Hawaiian history. The *Daniel IV* anchored at Lahaina on October 3, 1825, and the crew found that the missionaries had called a halt to drunken revelry and prostitution. With the approval of Captain Buckle forty of the whalers raised a black flag, armed themselves with knives and pistols, and threatened the Reverend Mr. Richards and his wife with death if they did not relax the blue laws. There was hell to pay for a short time until the native converts rallied to the support of the missionaries and patrolled the town. Captain Buckle bought a girl for $160 and sailed off with her.

notoriously reluctant to allow sailors to leave the ship on the voyage for fear that they would never see them again. Desertion was as common as accidents and sickness on a cruise, especially if the hunting was bad and prospects of a good "lay" poor.

Neither could Captain Barney put into a Japanese port for relief. Japan was closed to foreigners. The shogun had prohibited intrusions by whalers, and those who violated the edict lived to rue it. So month after weary month the whaleboats were rowed away on their fruitless chases, and aboard ship the discouraged officers and men morosely ate shortened allowances of the whaler's fare. A whaleman of the period feelingly described such food:

salt junk [beef] or pork, often putrid, and as dry and with about as much nourishment as a rope-yarn; biscuits so alive with maggots and weevils as to crumble into dust between the fingers; black, stinking water, in such a state of decomposition that upon a lighted candle being applied to the bunghole of a cask, the ignited pestiferous hydrogen gas would blaze out like gunpowder.[11]

The lack of proper food aboard the *Royal George* took its toll. The officers and crew fell ill with scurvy. They grew weak and listless, blood vessels broke beneath the skin and formed great purple weals, their bodies so tender that the least touch was torment and it was torture to move. In their mouths the gums swelled so that the teeth could not touch but became so loose that the sailors spat them out with the saliva. Captain Barney reluctantly turned the *Royal George* and let the sails fill with the fresh westerly wind blowing toward California and health.

At the end of October or the first of November, 1824, Captain Otto von Kotzebue of the Russian frigate *Predpriatie*, anchored in San Francisco Bay while her corps of scientists explored the region, was astonished to see a boat, rowed in from the open sea

---

11. William Bowers, *Naval Adventures during Thirty-five Years Service* (London, 1835), I, 94.

12. Otto von Kotzebue, *A New Voyage Round the World, in the Years 1823, 24, 25 and 26,* 2 vols. (London, 1830), II, 128–130. The use of lime juice in the 1770's had proved an effective antiscorbutic; Captain James Cook had no scurvy at all on his second voyage, 1772–1775. There was little excuse for it on the *Royal George* in 1824.

by six men, lay to alongside his vessel. It belonged to the scurvy-stricken English whaler, which was tacking back and forth outside the strait unable to cope with the contrary winds. As a last resort, the rowers said, the captain had sent the ship's boat for the fresh provisions so desperately needed aboard. Von Kotzebue noted:

> I immediately furnished the boat with an ample supply both of fresh meat and vegetables, and having completed its little cargo, it proceeded again to sea forthwith. The next day the whaler succeeded in getting into the bay, and came to anchor close alongside. It was evident, from their manner of working the vessel, that she had but few hands on board capable of labour. The captain, who shortly afterwards visited me, was himself suffering severely, and his mates were all confined to their beds. . . . The scurvy with which the crew was afflicted was mainly attributable to unwholesome food, selected on a principle of unpardonable economy, and to the want of cleanliness; a vice not usual among the English, but which, during so long an absence from land, is scarcely to be avoided.[12]

How long the *Royal George* lay at anchor while the men drew strength back into their bodies is uncertain. There is evidence that she sent eight men ashore for treatment, and William Garner has been counted as one of these, but however long the empty whaler idled there, it was too long for the anxious captain and not long enough for the crew. In a scant two weeks she was at sea again, the sailors sullen and glowering, Captain Barney chafing at the loss of time. The great whales were migrating along the California coast from the cold North Pacific to their spawning grounds in the tropics. Finback, gray, humpback and spermwhale, sulphur-bottom and right whale rolled and spouted off the Faralones, each one worth from 60 to 150 barrels of oil.[13]

The *Royal George* turned south with the favoring wind, but she had only been under way a few days when the resentment

13. Jack Swan, "Monterey in 1843 — By a Pioneer," *Monterey Weekly Herald,* August 1, 1874, describes the whaling in Monterey Bay in the 1840's and 1850's. See also James Colnett, *A Voyage to the South Atlantic and Round Cape Horn into the Pacific Ocean, for the Purpose of Extending the Spermaceti Whale Fisheries* (London, 1798), pp. 92–93. Colnett was one of the first to trace the migration of the innumerable whales down the coast of Baja California (November 1793).

of the crew broke through the surface discipline. They complained angrily about the quality and quantity of the food and
refused to obey commands until their demands were met. Garner,
an officer by now, championed them and spoke for them. It must
have been tantamount to open mutiny, for Captain Barney took
an exceedingly unusual step.

José Garner remembers his father's telling him that he and his
friends deserted the ship at Santa Barbara. He was glossing over
a humiliating memory: James McKinley, testifying on oath
twenty-three years later, said: "They were manacled and put on
shore." He knew of what he spoke; he was one of those five ringleaders marooned at Santa Barbara on November 16, 1824.[14]

The deserted five — two London lads, William Garner and
James Watson, two Scots, James McKinley and Thomas Stewart,
and a Negro named either Dixon or Robinson — were reported
to the *comandante*, Don José de la Guerra y Noriega, and taken
into custody for unlawful entry. After a brief preliminary examination by Don José, the sailors were packed off to Monterey, the
capital of Upper California, for official disposition. As in other
such cases where no ship's captain offered a reward for runaway
sailors, the men were given a hearing and allowed to stay in
California and earn their living. Garner, Watson, and McKinley
chose to remain in Monterey; Stewart and Dixon (Robinson?)
drifted back to southern towns.

*   *   *

14. Monterey County Archives, XIII, 711–712.

If they had only known it, their punishment was a blessing. The *Royal George*
drove on in pursuit of the whales. In the next five months off Lower California
she filled about 550 barrels of oil, and at the end of March the captain headed her
for Honolulu to get supplies. On Friday, April 8, 1825 the Reverend Charles S.
Stewart wrote in his journal:

> I was awakened this morning by the exclamation, "The *Royal George* is lost!"
> and on reaching the window, regretted exceedingly to see the fine English
> ship — formerly a sloop-of-war — of that name high on the reef a mile or two
> west of the mouth of the harbor, a complete wreck, without a mast standing.
> It appears that she was run ashore through the carelessness of the first officer
> while the captain was on board another vessel. The night was not very dark
> and the wind fresh off the land; so that the person having charge of the ship
> seems to be inexcusable.

Andrew Bloxam, the naturalist aboard the H.M.S. *Blonde,* was blunter: "lost

What William Garner did immediately after he was released by the authorities is uncertain. He was only twenty-one. Tall, blue-eyed, and blond, with long lanky legs, he soon acquired the nickname of *Patas Largas* or *Long Shanks*.[15] Such nicknames were indispensable in a sparsely settled land like California, where almost everyone was related, families averaged ten children, and all were named after the same popular saints. *Patas Largas* was aptly descriptive but not unpleasantly so; other men were saddled for life with names such as *Pinacate* and *Stinkbug*.

Like his shipmates, Garner soon made up his mind to stay in California and "go no more a'whaling." Watson and McKinley became clerks, then storekeepers in Monterey, but William Garner had little interest in tending shop and keeping books. The free, careless life of the *ranchos* was a welcome change after his long confinement on malodorous whalers under tyrannical masters.

During these first halcyon years he probably rode lazily about California, eating beef and frijoles and drinking aguardiente, earning his way by doing odd jobs of carpentry or mechanics in a country where scarcely anyone "worked" and hard cash was rarely needed. With his educational background he was quick to learn Spanish and to write it correctly in an elegant hand. He may have contracted for hides and tallow on behalf of foreign firms or trading ships; he may have gone back to sea for a short interval as officer or supercargo on a coastal trader. He became

---

owing to the carelessness and drunkenness of the crew." Charles S. Stewart, *Journal of a Voyage to the Pacific and a Residence in the Sandwich Islands During the Years 1822, 1823, 1824 and 1825* (New York, 1828), p. 271; Andrew Bloxam, *Diary of Andrew Bloxam, Naturalist of the 'Blonde,' 1824–1825* (Honolulu: Special Publication No. 10, Bernice P. Bishop Museum, 1925), p. 9. Elisha Loomis, Journal: Hawaii, 1824–1826, University of Hawaii, Honolulu (on film in Bancroft Library, University of California, Berkeley), gives exact time and cargo data for the wreck on April 9, 1825.

15. *Patas Largas* is consistently and mistakenly translated as *Big Feet*. The word *pata* ordinarily refers to the foot and lower leg of an animal; it is applied teasingly or in "baby talk" to humans ("footsies" or "tootsies"). If Garner's feet had been notably big, he would have been nicknamed *Patas Grandes* or *Patagón*, not *Patas Largas*. *Larga* always means "long," not "large." Garner's physical description was given to me in 1957 by the late Maria Antonia Bach Thompson, who knew Garner's daughter, Doña Clotilda, well.

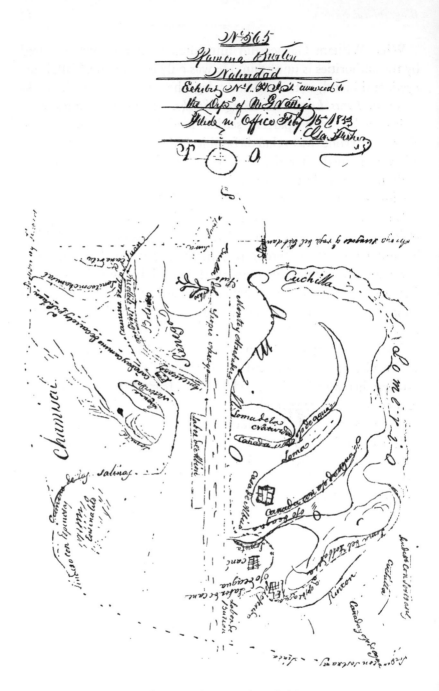

La Natividad. Places marked Cané probably mean Garner

well acquainted with southern California and spoke in the Letters with authority of the products, climate, and agricultural possibilities of the districts near the old Spanish missions of San Diego, San Juan Capistrano, and San Gabriel.

Early in November 1827 Jedediah Smith and his party of trappers appeared at Mission San José de Guadalupe and asked padres Narciso Durán and José Viader for time to gather fresh horses. The padres allowed the men to stay while Smith went on to Monterey to sign a bond for his party's good conduct and quick departure from California. Smith returned, and, as he wrote in his journal entry of November 27: "I went ahead of the company as far as the Pueblo [de San José] with Mr. Garnier, a man I had engaged to go to Monterey with two men and two horse loads of Merchandize to pay for some horses I had purchased at that place." On November 28, "I continued on my way to St. Jose, Mr. Garnier being with me for an interpreter." Garner was then sent south through the Santa Clara Valley to buy horses and mules from the rancheros. He succeeded in getting 180 animals. Smith settled with him; Garner then paid $25 to Smith for nineteen of the horses that had stampeded in the interim. On December 26 Smith's party resumed its way northward, and Garner fell back into the easy habits of the California frontier.[16]

By the end of 1828 Garner had decided to make his home in the Monterey area. Possibly invited by the Butrón family, he made his way across the grassy Salinas plains to the cattle ranchos on the low hills of the Gavilán range. Just over the crest in a fertile valley was the Mission San Juan Bautista, and here, on June 7, 1829, Padre Felipe Arroyo de la Cuesta gave him conditional baptism and received him into the Roman Catholic faith. The adoption of the faith marked Garner's definite decision to adopt the country. The Catholic religion was the only one rec-

---

16. Jedediah Strong Smith, *The Travels of Jedediah Smith: A Documentary Outline, including the Journal of the Great American Pathfinder*, edited by Maurice S. Sullivan (Santa Ana, California: The Fine Arts Press, 1934), pp. 45–50. Garner says that Smith paid an average price of about nine dollars for "the best kind that could be found in the country; and only one horse amongst them cost as high as fifteen dollars" (*North American*, April 26, 1847).

ognized by law in California, and its profession was an indispensable condition of citizenship, marriage, and landownership. He seems to have been a faithful if unenthusiastic convert: "An old Turk will never make a good Christian," he quotes in his letter of December 13, 1846, to the *North American*.[17]

Two years later, before the same altar, William Robert Garner married María Francisca Butrón, one of the heirs to the nearby Rancho La Natividad. They built their new adobe home on the rancho, just north of her father's house, where the land was suitable for wheat and corn and the hill springs never failed.[18]

By this time, too, he had found a vocation that was not only more lucrative than ranching but also more suited to his talents as mechanic and carpenter. Around Monterey grew forests of tall, straight, tough pines. A few miles away, along the brooks that descended from the Santa Lucía Mountains to feed the Carmel River, were stands of redwoods. Here the trees did not tower so high as those near Santa Cruz across the bay, nor were the groves of such great extent, but these nearer giants had the virtue of being close to the port of Monterey, and at hand were the Indians of the Mission San Carlos Borroméo to serve as laborers.

Lumbering in the 1830's and 1840's was an arduous, backbreaking business. Only shortly before the American occupation were more elaborate methods than elementary two-man whipsawing introduced in the Monterey Bay woods. The first water-

---

17. See Appendix I for the certificate of baptism and a biographical note on Padre Arroyo de la Cuesta. Garner's letter on converting to Catholicism was published in the April 26, 1847, supplement to the *North American*.

18. María Francisca Butrón was the granddaughter of Manuel Butrón, a Spanish soldier who came with the first settlers, married Margarita (a neophyte of the Mission San Carlos), and received the first California land grant (a plot near the mission in Carmel) in 1775. María Francisca's father, Manuel, corporal of the presidio of Monterey, had long been occupying the Rancho La Natividad when its two square leagues were granted to him and Nicolás Alviso on November 16, 1837.

Garner and María Francisca were married on November 25, 1831, by Padre Juan Moreno, who had replaced Padre Felipe Arroyo de la Cuesta. The witnesses were her mother, Ignacia Higuera de Butrón, and her sister Juana Butrón de Soto. The best man was José Eusebio Boronda. California, Mission San Juan Bautista Archives, *Libro de Casamientos*, I, 67.

Lumbering

power sawmill was built in the fall of 1842 in the Santa Cruz redwoods. Previously, oxen dragged the logs to a sawpit and for endless board feet, day after weary day, month after month, a man on top pulled the long steel blade up, and a man in the sweet-smelling sawdust pit below pulled it down. It was unadorned, mindless drudgery, and Garner, at his peak, had up to two hundred Indians sweating at it. From the stacks by the pits, bullock teams hauled the lumber down to the beaches of Monterey Bay. There it was either sold for local use or rafted out to the trading ships.[19]

By 1835 William Garner had started sawing in the Santa Cruz forests as well as in Carmel Valley. He had a five-year contract to cut timber on the land of José Amestí and ship it to Thomas O. Larkin, the principal American merchant in Monterey. At the same time the young Englishman was raising wheat, buying cattle, and selling hides and tallow from his home on the Natividad rancho.[20]

Garner had chosen the slow path to riches. Whole hides had a value of $1.50, or $2.00 in barter, and were commonly called "California banknotes"; tallow sold for $1.50 per arroba. There was very little hard cash in the country; practically all business

---

19. Henry J. Bee, "Recollections of the History of California," 1877, MS, Bancroft Library (Berkeley, Calif.); *San Jose Pioneer*, Jan. 13 and June 16, 1877. Lansford W. Hastings, *The Emigrants Guide, to Oregon and California, containing scenes and incidents of a Party of Oregon Emigrants; . . . and a description of California* (Cincinnati, 1845), says that a steam sawmill and gristmill were being put into operation at Bodega in the fall of 1843. This was the work of Capt. Stephen Smith, who had a Mexican grant extending from the Estero Americáno (Bodega Bay) to the Russian River in that year. Smith probably used the gristmill that the Russians had installed at their Bodega headquarters, Kuskov, before they abandoned the area in 1841. Smith lived at Kuskov thereafter. Later authors claim that Isaac Graham had a water-power sawmill going in the Santa Cruz timber two months before Smith completed his. See footnote 34, below.

Garner's letter of October 4, 1847, below, calls for steam sawmills, because of the lack of water power: "We have fine forest trees for lumber, and yet boards are fifty dollars a thousand and difficult to get at that; much of the sawing is done by hand. Send us out a dozen good saw mills and men to manage them" (*North American*, January 29, 1848). See also his letters of November 3, 25, and 26 for descriptions and prices of timber in the Monterey area.

20. Thomas O. Larkin, *The Larkin Papers: Personal, Business, and Official*

was done through barter, but at this game the native Californian was at the mercy of the merchants. They had a monopoly on manufactures, especially after the missions were effectively snuffed out by the implementation of the Mexican government's 1833 secularization decree, which released the Indian laborers and took the mission lands. All the California merchants cheerfully extended credit — at 2 percent per month on good collateral. The cattleman, farmer, lumberman, or laborer was caught in a tight circle that kept him forever in debt. It was probably one of the reasons that Garner filled his letters with fervent pleas inviting the emigration of manufacturers and capitalists to California.[21]

* * *

The petty and confused intrigues for power between the northern families of Castro, Vallejo, and Alvarado, and the southern Carrillos and Picos seldom engaged the active participation of the foreign residents for the first few years after the break with Spain in 1822. As businessmen, however, the foreign colony in the capital at Monterey much preferred a stable, though incompetent, government to anarchy. In January 1832, in a crisis, they formed a homeguard, the *Compañía Extranjera*, captained by William E. P. Hartnell, to hold the capital for Agustín Zamorano,

---

Correspondence of Thomas Oliver Larkin, Merchant and United States Consul in California, edited by George P. Hammond, 10 vols. (Berkeley: University of California Press, 1951–1964), I, 15–16, 21 (Garner to Larkin, July 7 and Aug. 6, 1839).

21. This was true even after the American troops arrived in 1846. On October 10, 1847, Garner wrote: "What signify the many thousands of dollars spent and circulated here by the United States army and navy; as fast as the money falls into the hands of the residents, it is shipped off again for wearing apparel, *pickles* and *sweetmeats*, and the mass of the people are as poor now as they were when no money circulated in the country. . . . What we now require are . . . machinery of all kinds, and persons who know how to make use of them. These once introduced, and this noble country, already rich in its own resources, must become one of the most flourishing States in the Union" (*North American*, Jan. 29, 1848). Garner gives current prices for common products, manufactured articles, and labor throughout the letters. See especially his letters of October and November 12, 1846, and October 10, 1847, in the *Journal of Commerce*. The comparable prices for labor in the Eastern cities are given in footnote 8, above. Hubert Howe Bancroft, *California Pastoral: 1769–1848* (San Francisco, 1888), p. 469, gives a good list of prices current for 1844–1846; Walter Colton, *Three Years in California* (New York, 1850), p. 22, gives a list for August 4, 1846.

the northern claimant for the governorship. William Garner was one of the fifty *extranjeros* who answered the call to arms.[22] The company drilled, patrolled the few muddy tracks called streets, and disbanded victorious in April, never having left Monterey or fired a shot. Innocuous and even comic as the *Compañía* was, it had a serious aftermath: the idea of a foreign legion had been introduced into California politics.[23]

Four short years and six governors later Juan Bautista Alvarado and José Antonio Castro, the northern leaders, rebelled against the new Mexican governor Nicolás Gutiérrez. This time the prominent merchants kept aloof. William Garner, however, was José Castro's friend and neighbor. With Isaac Graham, a newly arrived Rocky Mountain trapper, he formed a company of twenty-five to thirty English, Irish, and American adventurers to help the northern cause.

Graham was about three or four years older than Garner, a strongly built man with the hearty, open manner of the backwoodsman, illiterate but shrewd, generous to his friends, bold, reckless, loud-mouthed, overbearing, and unprincipled. He had successively left Tennessee and then Taos under a cloud before coming to southern California about 1833 or 1834. His favorite song might have been written solely for him:

> Oh, the great big bull come down from the mount'in,
> Rangle mi, rangle re,
> He tore up trees and pawed a saplin'
> Rangle mi, rangle re.

In this year of 1836 Graham and his partners, Henry Naile and Bill Dickey, signed a five-year lease for the site of a still with Garner's father-in-law, Manuel Butrón. Garner lived about two

---

22. David Douglas, the botanist-explorer for the Horticultural Society of London, was also an *extranjero* and may well have discussed the natural history of California with Garner, who must have found it a rare treat to talk to someone whose conversation was not bounded by the price of lumber, hides and tallow, lazy gossip, and local politics.

23. Hubert Howe Bancroft, *History of California*, 7 vols. (San Francisco, 1884–1890), III (1886), 221–222.

miles south of the place with his wife and three young children, and he soon became acquainted with the newcomers.[24]

The small band of English-speaking adventurers led by Graham and Garner included the knot of ship deserters and loafers who hung around Graham's new distillery and grogshop near Natividad. Castro and Alvarado also enrolled about seventy-five rancheros, and the little army advanced on Monterey.

The capture of Governor Gutiérrez's stronghold, the Presidio, took two days of negotiation and one cannonball. A single lucky shot sent crashing through the roof of the commander's house decided the issue. The garrison surrendered forthwith on November 5, 1836, the governor was put aboard a ship for Mexico, Alvarado became governor, and the jubilant rebels prepared to march south to quell the recalcitrant Carrillos and Picos.

"Lieutenant" Garner seems to have acted at first as a bilingual aide to Castro and Alvarado on behalf of the *Rifleros Americános*. After a week or two, either because he had already fallen out with the quarrelsome "Captain" Graham, or because he could not further neglect his family and business, Garner dropped out of the ranks. His place as second in command of the swaggering little company was taken by another British sailor, John Coppinger.

Thereafter Garner went on about his ranching and lumbering activities, but he still considered himself the liegeman of General Castro. On February 14, 1837, acting on the orders of Mariano Guadalupe Vallejo, Commandant of the Monterey district, he led Quintín Ortega, Mariano Castro, and a squad of militia to the rancho of Francisco Pérez Pacheco. There they arrested a number of persons and confiscated weapons to frustrate a counter-revolution.[25]

William Garner's support of the winning side brought handsome

---

24. James W. Weeks, "Reminiscences," 1877, MS, Bancroft Library, pp. 106–107.

25. Bee, "Recollections"; Mariano Guadalupe Vallejo, Documentos para la Historia de California, 36 vols., 1769–1850, MSS, Bancroft Library, vol. XXXII, pt. 2, no. 72; Antonio Francisco Coronel, "Cosas de California," 1877, MS, Bancroft Library, pp. 20–22; Hubert Howe Bancroft, Reference Notes: Gar-Gil, 1874–1890, MSS, Bancroft Library.

returns. He had applied for naturalization in 1829, immediately after his conversion to the required religion, but had been refused, probably because he had neither property nor link with a local clan. Now General Castro, José Amestí, and Joaquín Escamillo vouched for his good moral conduct, his religion, and his marriage. On August 30, 1839, his petition for citizenship was granted by Governor Alvarado. Within three years as a Mexican citizen he was able to buy the Rancho San Francisquito, spreading for some nine thousand acres over the hills above the Carmel Valley where he was logging.[26]

In 1840, however, Garner became enmeshed with the rest of the *rifleros*, who also wanted rewards for their support of Alvarado. Like many a politician, the new governor found that victory has its price; Graham and the disbanded mercenaries now clamored for their rewards in land and money. The first Alvarado could not give to noncitizens; the second he did not have.

Some of the *rifleros* talked too much and too loudly in the grogshops of Monterey of what they would do if satisfaction was not immediately forthcoming. They swaggered through Alvarado's chambers and addressed him familiarly, united in their contempt for all Mexicans. They toasted the new Republic of Texas with drunken cheers: "California next!" Governor Alvarado was first irritated, then apprehensive. It was imperative to act against the challenge, but on what grounds?

That problem soon solved itself. On April 3, 1840, the governor received a hasty letter from Padre José María Suárez del Real, pastor of the presidio chapel of San Carlos in Monterey. The padre had a most urgent message to relay. He had been called to

---

26. Archives of California, vols. XV–XX, Provincial State Papers and Departmental State Papers (Benicia) Military, 1767–1846, MSS, Bancroft Library, XVII, 38. The grant had been made originally to Doña Catalina Manzanelli de Munrás in 1835. On March 7, 1842, it was sold to Francisco Soto and resold to María Josefa Rodríguez de (Ricardo) Juan, a French sawyer. Two days later Garner borrowed $2,206.50 from Larkin and bought the property.

27. California, Mission Santa Barbara, Archivum Provinciae, Santa Barbara, doc. 1383. Padre Suárez del Real sent a copy of his letter to Alvarado to the president of the missions, Padre José González Rubio, April 28, 1840. Bancroft was unaware of the existence of this copy, which is particularly important because

hear the last confession of one of the *rifleros,* an old trapper friend of Graham's named Tomlinson, married to María de Jesús Bernal. In the course of it, Tomlinson laid bare a scheme concocted by Graham and his friends to seize Monterey and cast off Mexican sovereignty. The horrified priest pleaded for and received permission to warn Alvarado and then had hastened to do so for the uprising was scheduled for that month.[27]

The governor called a special meeting of his junta on April 4. Before the meeting started Teodoro González brought up the subject of the inflammatory talk commonly heard from idle foreigners in public places. Alvarado thereupon broke the news of the revolutionary plot. The council at once set about to quash it. For obvious reasons, secrecy was maintained.

General Castro was directed to arrest all foreigners who did not have permission to reside in California — all, that is, except those married to *hijas del país* (daughters of the country) or engaged in well-known and honorable occupations. Every alcalde up and down California, from Sonoma to San Diego, was given identical orders.[28]

Garner, a natural leader and often a drinker with the rest at Graham's moonshine still, was widely mentioned as one of those most implicated in the nebulous, whiskey-befogged intrigue. When approached confidentially by Castro, he was either trapped into admitting its existence, or, loyal to his benefactor and at odds with Graham, who was dunning him for his father-in-law's debts, he confirmed enough of the rumor to warrant speedy action by the suspicious general.

In the middle of the night of April 6–7, 1840, General Castro

---

it sets the date for the uprising in April and thus explains the haste with which Alvarado and Castro acted. (Courtesy of the Reverend Maynard Geiger, Ph.D., O.F.M.) See also Florencio Serrano, "Apuntes para la Historia de California," 1877, MS, Bancroft Library, p. 65; James Meadows, "Statement . . . Respecting the Graham Affair of 1840," 1877, MS, Bancroft Library, pp. 3, 7; Robinson, p. 225. Bancroft, *History of California,* vol. III, chap. 1, gathers and presents all the evidence known in 1886.

28. Archives of California, Provincial State Papers, 1767–1822, VIII, 139–140. Alvarado to Vallejo detailing plot and plan to arrest all illegal foreigners except married men and "honest workmen at honest jobs."

and posses from San Juan Bautista and Monterey seized Graham and several of his cronies at the distillery after a good deal of inaccurate shooting and the wounding of Henry Naile in the leg with a sword. Garner had already been arrested in San Juan Bautista, tied to his horse, and brought over the hills by General Castro. During the tumult, he was kept at Castro's side on a slope some distance away.[29]

Elsewhere, the wholesale arrests were carried out quickly and thoroughly. Foreigners loafing in the towns and working in the forests were rounded up by guile or force. By April 11, thirty-nine illegal aliens had been caught in the Monterey district. In the next few days still more were brought in and crowded into the inadequate old adobe *calabozo* or lodged in neighboring houses.

Some men were dismissed the morning after they were locked up, but the next ten days were occupied in interrogating the sixty-five or so remaining. No concrete evidence of a genuine plot could be discovered; all those questioned swore that there was no plot.

Garner was apparently held for a time in Alvarado's house in Monterey. Witnesses say he was threatened with death for refusing to give evidence.[30] He was never brought to testify against the accused, many of whom were set free within a few days and allowed to return to work.

Forty-five vagrants, troublemakers, and loud-mouths were sorted out from the press and shipped off in irons, April 23, 1840, on the schooner *Joven Guipuzcoana*, to Tepic, Mexico, to stand formal trial. William Garner did not share their misfortune; he got off scot-free. For this, the deportees, and especially Isaac Graham, convinced that Garner had saved himself at their expense, nursed the most bitter grudge.

It would not have made the slightest difference whether Garner had spoken for or against them. Governor Alvarado and his ad-

---

29. For more details on the raid and Garner's role in it, see Appendix II, pp. 213 and 223–232, below.

30. James Stokes, "Deposition in Case of Garner vs Farnham," Monterey County Archives, XIII, 179.

31. John Chamberlain, "Memoirs of California Since 1840," 1877, MS, Bancroft Library. Larkin later wrote several accounts of the affair that are much more pro-exiles and often inaccurate, e.g., "Naile & Graham were . . . stabbed in several

visors were determined to rid themselves of such a dangerous group, and they did so. That the act had general approval is evidenced by the absence of protest by any of the respectable foreign residents. John Chamberlain, the blacksmith who put the fetters on the exiles at Alvarado's orders, said that when he expressed the wish that the deportees would soon return, "Mr. Larkin said he hoped not," and "Mr. David Spence said also they all deserved what they got, for they were a pack of damned rascals."[31] But although they were frank, they were not callous. Spence gave the prisoners bullock hides to cover the damp sleeping places in the jail and persuaded the governor to allow periods of exercise. Larkin supplied those jailed with abundant tea, meat, bread, and beans three times a day for the first week and twice a day thereafter. When the exiles were in Tepic, he forwarded $600 to Isaac Graham for their necessities. As far as Larkin was concerned, this was strictly business; he submitted bills to the authorities.[32]

More than five months passed before the exiles were cleared of the charges against them, largely through the efforts of Eustace Barron, British consul in Tepic (about one-half the men expelled from California were deserters from British ships), and Thomas Jefferson Farnham, a fire-eating American journalist. Twenty were given permission to return to California to get documentary proof of their losses in order to present claims against the Mexican government; they landed in Monterey on July 15, 1841.[33] The rest of the deportees simply drifted away.

Graham, still nursing his resentment but hoping for a profitable return on the time he had spent in jail, did not re-establish the saloon at Natividad. The lease had run out and Graham was eager to enter the lumber business. His old friend of the Taos days, Joe Majors, had just acquired the Rancho Zayante in the

places, Naile being hamstrung to keep him from running away" (*Larkin Papers*, VII, 73 [Larkin to Buchanan]), which is not true.

32. *Larkin Papers*, I, 36–37, 63.

33. The story of the fantastic claims for damages by the righteous twenty and their long-sustained assaults on the red-tape bastions of both the United States and Mexico has been told best by Hubert Howe Bancroft in his *History of California*, vol. IV. Our concern with the claims will appear later.

heart of the Santa Cruz redwoods on April 22, 1841. When Graham and Naile appeared with the $250 Barron had advanced the exile in Tepic, plus the money dug up from its hiding place near the old still, Majors sold them the ranch at once. This was illegal, for neither of the new owners was a Mexican citizen. Majors, therefore, kept the title in his own name while Graham, Naile, and a William Ware went into partnership with Peter Lassen and Frederick Hoegel, who were already building a sawmill on Zayante Creek.[34]

William Garner had moved into Monterey or the Carmel Valley from La Natividad in the fall of 1840. He is recorded as being a resident carpenter giving instruction to Indian apprentices, but this was in addition to his work as a lumberman and rancher. He bought cows from Simeón Castro and paid in lumber; he complained to the justice of the peace at Monterey that Francisco Ventura and Agustín Hernández "borrowed" three of his horses and ruined them chasing wild cattle in the hills.[35]

The year 1841 opened with Garner buying saws, waist ribbon, needles, fish hooks, men's stockings, and other supplies from Larkin, and selling him lumber. Not all of it reached its destination. With sardonic humor Garner wrote:

---

34. Doyce Blackman Nunis, Jr., *The Trials of Isaac Graham* (Los Angeles: Dawson's Book Shop, 1967) is the indispensable reference on a number of hitherto mysterious details in the life of Graham: his birth, trapping days, land holdings, and legal and marital problems. The Rancho Zayante intrigue is fully documented on pp. 33-35, 45-47, 90 104.

Joaquín Buelna was the first grantee of Zayante, July 18, 1834. He sold it to Francisco Moss for $80 and Moss had the grant confirmed to him May 25, 1840. Majors must have bought Moss out at the suggestion of Naile, for his ownership antedates by but three months the return of Graham from Mexican exile in July 1841. Majors testified before the U.S. Land Commission in 1852 that he had acted "for Graham and others who not being citizens could not hold it in their own name."

Naile later became a Mexican citizen to protect his interest in the rancho and, just before his death, deeded it to Graham. In 1852 Graham and Ware paid Majors $1,000 to clear their title to the whole property. More legal trouble arose. It was not until August 18, 1870, that the 2,658 acres were patented to Graham's estate, but his lawyer got the land.

The place called Zayante is the present Mt. Hermon. Graham and Naile had their mill here, but Graham lived in a board shanty a short distance away at the

Sometime back several people complained of my boards. I saw some the other day at Rodríguez's farm that I am sure will not turn out over 500 ft. to the M on account of the rot. However, I suppose by the time they go in to Monterey they will get well for they are now turned into a large commodious sheep pen. There is no occasion to say that I mentioned this but you can inquire. By the bye they are not all turned into a sheep pen for some of them I believe are turned into a hog pen or some other pen.[36]

In October Garner had more trouble with the Hernández brothers. Moreover, he was out of favor with his wife, probably over an affair with another woman. His brother-in-law, Nicolás Butrón, taking his sister's side (or seeing a chance to turn it to his own profit), refused to pay Garner for wheat he had sold from Garner's portion of the Natividad ranch. It would be credited, he said, to María.[37]

In 1842 Garner continued traveling between his sawpits in Santa Cruz and the Carmel Valley and even extended his cutting in the valley still higher, into the Palo Escrito region. However, the year was not without problems. In August his Indian headman and the workers at the San Francisquito logging camp told him they were bewitched. Garner noted:

My work is going on like a mill that wants water. I have now my head man and part of the others with their wives under a spell. They neither eat drink

---

present village of Felton. Many other loggers lived in the vicinity. Mildred B. Hoover, H. E. and E. G. Rensch, *Historic Spots in California*, rev. ed. by Ruth Teiser (Stanford: Stanford University Press, 1948), p. 354; Leon Rowland, "Isaac Graham, Swashbuckling Soldier of Fortune," *Santa Cruz Evening News*, Aug. 1, 1936; Nicholas Dawson, "Reminiscences, California in 1841," n.d., MS, Bancroft Library; Robert Granniss Cowan, *Ranchos of California; a List of Spanish Concessions, 1775–1822, and Mexican Grants, 1822–1846* (Fresno, Calif.: Academy Library Guild, 1956).

35. Monterey County Archives, IX, 1174, and XIII, 627–642. The Hernández brothers preyed on the cattle between present-day Salinas and Santa Cruz. One, Domingo, was a highwayman and wanton murderer. He and the bandit Capistrano López were finally "sent to God on a rope" by vigilantes in Santa Cruz about 1851. See footnote 70, below.

Francisco Hernández was "a lazy, drunken gambler and cattlethief." He joined the Daniel gang of cutthroats and was said to have been killed in Los Angeles. Agustín, a third brother, was an accomplice of Tiburcio Vásquez, hanged at San Jose, 1875. See Bancroft, *California Pastoral*, pp. 684–687.

36. *Larkin Papers*, I, 71 (Garner to Larkin, Jan. 7, 1841).

37. Vallejo, I, no. 490.

nor work. They say for one month they are all laying night and day covered up within blankets without speaking to any person. Of course I know this is all a humbug but I am obliged to put up with it. Of course I cannot oblige them to work having nothing to pay them with.[38]

The domestic troubles of William and María Garner reached an open break that fall. On October 6, for scandalously wrecking the house of María Ignacia Amador, a single woman, Garner was fined ten dollars by Alcalde Teodoro González. This episode, added to family quarrels about the Rancho La Natividad, pushed María Francisca to a step rarely contemplated by a woman of her time and place: she sued for divorce on November 10, 1842.

As her spokesman (for there were no lawyers as such) she chose Rafael González; her husband had David Spence as his *hombre bueno*. The alcalde and the two representatives conferred. The alcalde then ordered a week's cooling-off space while the *hombres buenos* tried to effect a reconciliation. Apparently they were successful, because Alcalde González announced that both parties "having affirmed that they would forget all resentments occasioned by this demand, the reconciliation is now officially celebrated, both now being under the bonds of matrimony and trying to forget the *motivos* which may occasion new *disgustos*."[39]

The next year things went better. In November 1843 Garner went into debt $955.12½ to Larkin, probably for the hardware and furniture used in the fine new two-story, balconied adobe home he built on what is now Pacific Street at the head of Decatur in Monterey. The Viscaino-Serra Oak in the ravine where the ships came for water marked the northeast corner of his property.

Thomas O. Larkin's home, the showplace of Monterey in 1839, had set a new standard in luxury with its long balconies on the second floor, shining glass windows, and elegant fireplaces. Garner followed the budding fashion in architecture. His grandson,

---

38. *Larkin Papers*, I, 260–261 (Garner to Larkin, Aug. 5, 1842).
39. Monterey County Archives, VI, 461, 750. There was an epidemic of divorce proceedings in Monterey in 1842. On February 19 María Ana González Castañares sued her husband, José María Castañares, whose illicit love life had scandalized Monterey in 1836. The passing years had not cooled his ardor. Alcalde José Fernández sent María Ana home to her father, Rafael González, to think it over.

Peter Gonzalves, who was born in the house, said, "It had a fire-place in every room and a wall around the property. The furniture, I was told, was brought from England on an English battleship."[40]

Even discounting the "battleship," the house was one of the better ones in Monterey. William Rich Hutton and a party of government surveyors lodged there in 1847, and the young draughtsman put a very rough sketch of its facade in a drawing he made of the town. It was a spacious house. In May 1849 it held comfortably not only the six members of the Garner family but also Captain Elias Kane, army quartermaster, and his wife.

Although argument by lawyers, or *hombres buenos*, was rarely known in California before the American invasion, there was no dearth of litigation. Garner's lawsuits are typical. The sum he owed Larkin was, as usual, to be paid in lumber, but Garner's own debtors were harder to pin down. On January 30, 1844, old Simeón Castro died and Garner sued the heirs for $250 on a note signed by their father for the purchase of the Corral de Padilla land from Garner on January 27th. Manuel Castro, the principal heir, countered with a note for $110 signed by Garner on November 19, 1841, for twenty head of cattle. Garner declared that he had paid Simeón in lumber, but alas, he had no receipt. Florencio Serrano, the alcalde, and the contestants' *hombres buenos*, Francisco Araiza and Ignacio Ezquer, decided that since Castro had the land, his heirs would have to pay Garner the $250, but as Garner could not prove that he had ever paid their father the $110, this amount must be deducted from the Castros' debt. Therefore Don Manuel, as head of the family, had to pay $140 to William Garner.[41]

Garner had another claim against Simeón for lumber valued at $263.50, but there was no argument on this score; Don Manuel

---

Almost a year elapsed before she withdrew her complaint and rejoined her husband on December 7. On March 18 María Guadalupe Castillo asked for separation from Edward Watson on grounds of cruelty. Her plea was granted with twelve dollars a month alimony. Bancroft, *California Pastoral*, pp. 314–316.

40. In an interview by Mrs. Amelie Elkinton, 1940.

41. Monterey County Archives, VI, 966.

Sn. Francisquito Ferº 17 de 1844

Sor. D Manuel Castro

Muy Señor mio mandé a
su rancho por el ganado como haviamos
quedado y me entregaron conforme V me
prometió solo tengo que decirle que no les
pusieron la venta porque José María dijo
que la venta no estaba en el rancho y así
es que es muy indispensable que V me los
manda ventear aqui tanto por los cueros
que tengo que entregar como por algunas va-
cas que no tengo intenciones de matar.

Tres cueros de este ganado salen hoy para
Monterrey y van a la casa de D Salvador
Munras y le suplico a V que pase por la
casa del Señor marcador y le da cuenta
de estos tres cueros para que a mi no de siga
causan atrasos en mis negocios

Espero que no dejara V de venir o man-
dar a alguno que me vengan a ventear el
ganado que queda Soy de V su affmo Sr

M B

Guillermo R. Garner

Letter to Manuel Castro from Garner

appears to have exhausted his stock of retaliatory bills. However, he had apparently agreed to pay his $140 debt in cattle, and on February 17, 1895, Garner wrote him a polite note asking that the "venta" or "sale" brand be put on them. Don Manuel was smarting under the judgment, and Garner was putting him on record to avoid a later suit for cattle theft.[42]

In another typical case, in September, Garner was back in the alcalde's office with a claim against a certain Ricardo Juan for $72 worth of wheat, probably from La Natividad. Juan, unable to pay, offered a store he owned in Monterey, which Garner was unwilling to accept. As usual in cases of deadlock, the alcalde and two *hombres buenos* arbitrated: Juan was to pay forty arrobas of flour at $2 the arroba within a month and six days. (An *arroba* weighs about twenty-five pounds.) The judge acknowledged that this added up to $8 too much, but awarded it anyway because Juan had delayed so long in payment and because he had borrowed Garner's cart to haul the wheat in the first place.[43]

*　　　*　　　*

In the meantime Isaac Graham was having his own troubles. In August 1844 he and his partner Naile refused to pay the 5 percent tax on the lumber they were cutting in the Santa Cruz woods. They were ordered to pay up or cease operations, but the alcalde was afraid to serve the notice on them. It meant taking away their saws, and he did not think they would permit it. Graham, in particular, had been critical of the tax. Governor Micheltorena wrote to Manuel Jimeno, alcalde of Branciforte (Santa Cruz):

Tell Señor Graham that the fact that he is living in this country makes him subject to its laws without arguing whether they are right or not. Tell the sawyers to come to Monterey immediately to make their complaints, and if they don't come by September 12th, they will be brought in bonds.[44]

---

42. Manuel de Jesús Castro, Correspondence and Papers: 1830–1863, MSS, Bancroft Library.

43. Monterey County Archives, VI, 990. The alcalde in this case was Gregorio Castañares. Florencio Serrano appeared for Garner, and Vincente Gómez for Juan.

44. Vallejo, I, no. 475; Archives of California, Departmental State Papers, XVII (Juzgados), 77–78.

Graham did not hold these words particularly against the governor. He disliked all Mexicans, but he hated General José Castro and Juan Bautista Alvarado. Navy Surgeon Wood, talking to him in October 1844 noted, "He only bides his time to redress the wrongs and outrages heaped upon him by the Mexicans." In November 1844 when Castro, Alvarado, and the Picos rebelled against Micheltorena, he thought he saw his chance. Heedless of the bitter fruit reaped from past meddling in politics, he joined John Sutter in supporting the governor and officiously subscribed the services of his old *riflero* companions. But much of the former magic was gone from Graham's name. Many of the men, remembering 1840, disclaimed allegiance to him and stayed home.[45]

William Garner, according to some recollections, aligned himself as usual with General Castro, but he took small part. His former shipmate James McKinley, William Workman, and Bill Fallon were the most active in recruiting a counter "foreign legion" for the rebels. This, however, was the last appearance of the *rifleros* in such bickering — and with good reason. When the rival armies drew up in battle array at Cahuenga on February 21, 1845, the two mercenary companies looked each other over, decided that the point at issue was not worth dying for, and stood apart from the impending conflict. Upon this, Governor Micheltorena surrendered, Pío Pico took his turn as governor, and Sutter and Graham made their way ingloriously homeward.

Once back in the redwoods Isaac Graham soon succeeded in raising up a storm among the loggers. In September 1845 he seduced, apparently without much trouble, a young American, Catherine Bennett, and, despite her family's protests, married her by taking vows before another logger. The woodsmen would

---

45. Rowland; Bancroft, *History of California*, IV, 478–508.

46. Vallejo, I, no. 419. *Larkin Papers*, IV, 101–102 (Larkin to Bolcoff, Nov. 19, 1845) and 115–116 (Bolcoff to Larkin, Dec. 4, 1845).

47. Time did exactly that. Graham went off to the gold mines early and came home with well-filled pouches. Eliza Woodson Farnham says that in early 1850 the two sons he had abandoned in Tennessee arrived on his doorstep, and Catherine took her two young daughters and ran away to Honolulu with the help of her four brothers and some of Isaac's hoard of nuggets. In the quarrel that grew

probably not have objected to a native mistress, but an American girl was a *rara avis*, and either her abrupt tumble or Graham's good luck was hotly resented. Besides, as they were quick to notify Larkin, now the United States consul, Graham had already abandoned a wife and family in Tennessee. Larkin wrote to José Antonio Bolcoff, justice of the peace at Santa Cruz:

> Mr. Isaac Graham and Catherine Bennett both citizens of the United States of North America are living together as married people, without being legally married, and as this cannot be permitted according to the laws of this country . . . you will confer a favor on the undersigned by causing an immediate separation of these two people without any excuse from either party, and in case that Mr. Graham cannot on account of sickness, present himself with Catherine Bennett at this consulate, do me the favor to remove her from the house of Mr. Graham, and send her to her parents or place her in some respectable family for the present.

Bolcoff evidently saw Graham and reported back to Larkin:

> Graham said that they were well married and that he would not separate from the side of Bennett, that he would lose a thousand lives before he would give her up, and that Mr. Parrott [Panaud?] and other Gentlemen having approved of his Marriage, that nobody could force a separation from Bennett, and that he could not present himself before you account of his infirmities.
>
> You well know the character of Graham. He never likes to obey any authority; I leave it to your judgement. I would have taken from his side Bennett, but to avoid scandal, and I tell you that he talks much against whoever it may be.[46]

What seemed best to Larkin was to drop the matter and let time take care of it; his duties as consul gave him more to do than attempting the moral reformation of Isaac Graham.[47] For example,

---

out of this Graham's son Jesse went gunning for the Bennetts and killed one brother, wounded another, and put five buckshot in Mrs. Bennett, Catherine's mother. He then ran off to the San Joaquin and later to Texas. Isaac Graham was arrested as an accomplice but released for lack of evidence. Eliza Woodson Farnham, *California Indoors and Out: Or, How We Farm, Mine and Live Generally in the Golden State* (New York, 1856), pp. 89–90; Rowland. Nunis, *Isaac Graham*, p. 96, could find no documentary evidence of Graham's arrest and thinks that Mrs. Farnham may have confused this case with Graham's arrest and fine for

he had to succor American seamen and, as there was no regular hospital or hotel in Monterey, to provide lodging and care for indigent and sick sailors in private homes.[48] Larkin paid William Garner fifteen dollars a month per man for providing bed and meals during October, November, and December, 1844, for Harry Coffin, George Washington, and John Pillikin, who were Kanakas from the Sandwich Islands (Hawaii) put ashore sick with scurvy from the American whaler *Monmouth*.[49] In addition he paid Garner forty-one dollars and fifty cents for care of Thomas Jones Todd, left by the ship *Sterling*.[50]

In 1845 Larkin contracted with the government for construction of an adequate wharf for the Custom House in Monterey. Garner supplied the lumber, and Esteban de la Torre, 1,500 cartloads of stone. A newcomer named A. Barron was hired to do the carpentry with a discharged sailor, James Henry, as his helper. On July 22 the lumberman was paid $468.50 for local pine beams, mostly twenty feet long by twelve inches square, at $16 per thousand feet. These were to form the first two cribs which were to be filled solidly with stone. In October he received $241.62½ for more pine for the same purpose.[51]

As the year 1846 opened, William Robert Garner could look forward to a secure future. His lumbering business was prospering, he was a respected and responsible citizen, his friends were

---

assault and battery in another case in June 1850. It is possible, though, that Graham was held for questioning in the Bennett murder without a formal written charge.

By 1846 Graham's surly behavior and the woman scandal provoked his fellow lumbermen to such a pitch that after Naile, egged on by Graham, was killed by James Williams in a quarrel over a sawmill contract, they signed a petition to the governor to expel the truculent mountaineer again. A particularly revealing feature of this document is that at least five of the twenty signators had been arrested with Graham in 1840 and two had shared his deportation. Vallejo, II, nos. 192, 193. The name of Graham's old partner, Joe Majors, heads the list.

48. In the smallpox epidemic of April, May, and June, 1844, a rough temporary hospital for Indians and indigents had been established by community effort in Monterey, but it seems not to have been used for American sailors. See Archives of California, Departmental State Papers, XVIII (*Juzgados*), 128–130; *Larkin Papers*, II, 132–133.

49. Larkin evidently believed that the Kanakas were entitled to consular protection. However, a Treasury Department circular to consuls, dated September 20, 1844, specified that "Foreign seamen, although they may sail in our vessels, are

among the most influential in California, he owned great tracts of land and town lots in Monterey, his children were growing up strong and healthy, his wife and he were reconciled and happy. As a mark of civic trust, the new alcalde, Manuel Díaz, appointed Garner head constable for Monterey on January 27, 1846. Serving with him were Jesús Soto, Francisco Granados, and Adelbert Thomes.[52]

The day after being sworn in Garner was in court suing José Antonio Acedo for money owned him. After the customary settlement between the *hombres buenos* (Dolores Valenzuela for Garner and William Hartnell for Acedo), Judge Ignacio Ezquer ordered Acedo to pay $10 a month on a debt of $63.37½ until it was cleared. The debt was then four years old.[53] Garner's position as constable was responsible for his being reprimanded and fined by the alcalde on March 18 for not obeying orders to beat a drunken man whom he was taking to jail.[54]

The last appearance of William Garner's name on the Mexican records occurred on June 9, 1846, when he appeared before the alcalde to obtain action on an 1844 judgment against José Antonio Romero, who had been found guilty of robbing Garner's home of seven hundred dollars. According to the testimony of José Antonio Chávez, formerly clerk to the 1844 city council, Romero had sworn then that he would pay back the stolen money at fifty

not entitled to relief" (*Larkin Papers*, II, 238–240). Larkin's vouchers for repayment were rejected, although he had not received the order at the time that he arranged for the sailors' board (ibid., II, 350; III, 235).

50. Garner sent in two vouchers for Todd: one for $30 and one for $11.50, "for attendance" (possibly to cover additional medicines). Larkin submitted a bill to the Treasury for $41.50, but the Treasury disallowed the excess over the fifty-cents-per-day rate (ibid., II, 349–350, 353; IV, 83).

51. *San Jose Pioneer*, March 24, 1877; Bancroft, *California Pastoral*, p. 441. The wharf is shown in the frontispiece.

52. Monterey County Archives, XII, 305.

53. Ibid., VIII, 501. Poor Acedo! He was one of the first to fall afoul of American justice. On August 29, 1846, Alcalde Walter Colton sentenced him to a month at public labor for borrowing a yoke of oxen from an Indian and then selling the oxen to clear a debt of twelve dollars. Acedo's defense was ingenuous: he had not really sold the Indian's oxen, only pawned them (ibid., 656).

54. Vallejo, III, no. 144.

dollars per month. He had never paid a cent. Garner had no illusions about Romero. He asked that the sum be assessed in goods, "after making sure that the said goods belong to Romero."[55]

*   *   *

On July 7, 1846, Commodore Sloat sailed into Monterey in the *Cyane* and captured California without a shot fired, except in salute to the new American flag hoisted on the staff before the Custom House, and the slow wheels of Mexican government rolled to a halt.[56]

When Alcaldes Manuel Díaz and Ezquer declined to carry on under the invaders, Commodore Sloat delegated Surgeon Edward Gilchrist and Purser Rodman Price of the *Cyane* to act as first and second alcaldes. The rest of the Mexican officials, after debating their duty for almost a week, signed an oath of loyalty to Mexico on July 13 and resigned their posts. Because William E. P. Hartnell, the natural choice for interpreter, scribe and go-between, had signed the oath, Price, probably at the suggestion of Consul Larkin, selected William Garner as his secretary.

Gilchrist seems never to have acted as alcalde, and Price did not occupy his office for much more than four weeks. On July 28, 1846, the naval chaplain Walter Colton, a Congregationalist minister, was appointed to the alcaldeship.[57]

Mr. Colton spoke no Spanish and knew nothing of California life, customs, and politics. In compensation he was blessed with a generous sense of humor, patience, tact, and good, sound New England common sense. He and Garner seem to have taken an

---

55. Monterey County Archives, VIII, 643, 655.

56. "Under the influence of John C. Frémont the Americans set up (1846) a republic at Sonoma under the Bear Flag. The news of war between the United States and Mexico reached California soon afterward. On July 7, 1846, Commodore John D. Sloat captured Monterey, the capital, and claimed California for the United States" (*The Columbia Encyclopedia*, 3d ed. [New York: Columbia University Press, 1963], p. 318).

"Sloat's conquest ran so smoothly that the sole casualty was a woman who, kneeling in church, suffered a bruised leg in the rush for the door at the announcement of his landing. He made the rounds of the town, posting a proclamation ending the republic and announcing California's absorption into the Union" (Leonard Pitt, *The Decline of the Californios: A Social History of the Spanish-*

instant liking to each other. William Garner became not only his efficient clerk and skillful translator but his guide and mentor — showing him the country, accompanying him to Christmas mass at the presidio chapel, explaining the manner of thinking and living of the Californians.

Walter Colton was a naval chaplain primarily for the sake of his health. His vocation, aside from his devotion to his ministry, was writing, and now he was gathering material for his famous *Three Years in California*.[58] More important for Garner was the fact that his employer was thoroughly familiar with journalism. Colton had been editor of the Philadelphia *North American* in 1841 and 1842, and he had promised to find it a local correspondent in California. He also set about publishing, with Robert Semple, California's first newspaper, the *Californian*. In Garner, Colton found a willing reporter and an apt pupil.

Colton's favorite form of composition for his books was the journal. It was his habit to keep meticulous daily notes and later to work them up into books. Only occasionally now did he send articles directly to the newspapers, but his example of daily jottings and his eager interest in the California scene were not lost on the "local correspondent." Small wonder that Garner's style closely parallels Colton's, except, naturally, in the latter's artful humor and urbanity.

It was a fruitful arrangement for both men. Occasionally, the teacher paid the student that highest of all compliments: he copied his words verbatim into his own journal. For example, his entry for November 23, 1846, in *Three Years in California* is taken

Speaking Californians, 1846–1890 [Berkeley: University of California Press, 1966], p. 31).

57. Rodman M. Price, in *San Jose Pioneer*, July 6, 1878. Colton, *Three Years in California*, seems to limit Price's tenure to August 11, 1846, for he uses "we" and "our office" before that date and "my office" thereafter. See also Ignacio Ezquer, "Memoria de cosas pasados en California," 1878, MS, Bancroft Library, and Pablo de la Guerra, Letters and Papers, various dates, MS, Bancroft Library.

58. He had already published two popular travel books, *Ship and Shore* (1835) and *A Visit to Constantinople and Athens* (1836), based on his three-year cruise in the U.S. *Constellation*. *Deck and Port*, containing his impressions of the voyage around the Horn to Monterey, had just been roughed out.

almost in its entirety from Garner's letter of November 8, which also provided, sentence by sentence, Colton's comments for December 4. His item for December 9 is from Garner. His entry for December 11 copies entire sentences from Garner's letter of December 1 on the habits of grizzly bears. There was nothing reprehensible in this — Garner must have been proud that his writings on the customs and oddities of the country interested a professional author and glad to be of service to his new friend.

On September 17 Garner had the satisfaction of announcing in Spanish in the *Californian*, the results of the election for the *ayuntamiento* or city council. Walter Colton received a slim but effective plurality and took his place as elected, not appointed, alcalde of Monterey and judge of first instance for its enormous jurisdiction. Immediately and gracefully, Alcalde Colton named the unsuccessful contenders, Spence, Hartnell, Juan Malarín, and Manuel Díaz, as councilmen, Milton Little as vice-alcalde, and Esteban Munrás as treasurer.

In the same issue there is an article in Spanish advising the carefree Californians to stop "borrowing" horses and slaughtering other people's cattle, and to seek honest employment. "Two of your friends are now in jail at public labor; justice is no longer sold, nor sentences revoked." The style and local knowledge are William Garner's. Since Colton and Robert Semple were the publishers of the *Californian*, it is very natural to find the alcalde's secretary phrasing his warning in the vernacular.

Besides such semiofficial items, Garner wrote and signed two other articles in the *Californian* intended for the eyes of his Spanish readers during this critical time. The November 28, 1846, issue has a full column appeal, beginning "O, mis amados paisanos," an eloquent, well-reasoned plea for the California *guerrilleros* to lay down their arms and accept the amnesty of the United States. The Christmas number has an open letter to his fellow parishioners of the presidio chapel of San Carlos in Monterey, describing the poverty of the pastor, Padre Doroteo Ambrís, and urging everyone to subscribe a small monthly sum to maintain him. "We remember him when we are ill and forget him when well. We must join together and contribute some agreed-upon amount from each of us so that we can support a person we all need and thereby redeem our characters as Christians." To start the list Garner pledged $2 monthly.[59]

Possibly because he wished to poll public interest in such things, Garner first tried out the letters he wrote to the *North American* on November 1 and November 2 in an abbreviated form in the little weekly paper on November 7, 1846. On November 28, while Semple was in San Francisco, the third paragraph of Garner's November 23 letter was used to describe the psychology of war as waged in California. Colton's article on the eggshells in the *Californian* of January 9, 1847, has some very close echoes to Garner's letter of December 7, 1846. The similarity in wording may also be seen in his letter of December 16 and the article on Pacheco and the Indians in the *Californian* of December 25. Garner, too, is probably responsible for the *Pastores* item on January 2, 1847; his letter of December 29, 1846, has identical wording in part.

Garner's duties as secretary to the alcalde were satisfying financially as well as intellectually. He moved in the governing circle now, and in September 1846 Larkin paid him $155 for services as translator at the consulate. On September 4 Garner acted as clerk for the first jury trial in California, *Isaac Graham* v. *Henry Roussillon*, in which, as Colton put it, "One [Graham] got back his property, which had been taken from him by mistake, the other his character, which had been slandered by design." [60]

Garner's fortunes continued to rise. He sold a house and lot for $60 cash to Pedro (Pierre) Artellán on November 1, 1846. In January 1847 Romero's debt of $700, which had seemed impossible to collect, was squeezed out of him, not in cash or dubious goods but in land. Romero and his wife Tiburcia Acedo de Romero gave Garner in compensation one square league north of the

---

59. Susanna Bryant Dakin, *The Lives of William Hartnell* (Stanford: Stanford University Press, 1949), pp. 272–274, makes Hartnell the Spanish-language editor. Hartnell's responsibility, according to this new evidence, seems to have covered only translations of official documents. In addition to the articles signed by Garner, other squibs are in his style, and after Hartnell left for Honolulu in December 1846, Garner apparently took over the Spanish editorship in toto.

60. *Larkin Papers*, VI, 305. Monterey County Archives, VIII, 798–836; Colton, *Three Years in California*, p. 48.

Carmel River between the Cañada de la Segunda and the Corral de Padilla granted them by Governor Alvarado on January 27, 1840. Garner recorded the transaction on January 30, 1847, and within thirty days he sold the land to Larkin for $500.[61]

In his position as secretary to the alcalde of a seaport Garner was brought back to the element he had avoided since the 1820's. To adjudicate the case of the small British-owned Mexican schooner *William*, which had been taken as a prize in Mexican waters by the United States navy, Military Governor Stephen W. Kearny appointed Alcalde Colton judge of an admiralty court. Garner served as clerk. James Alexander Forbes, the British consul, appeared for the owners, but Colton found against them. On April 7, 1847, the vessel and her cargo of Mexican sugar were sold at public auction by Jonas Dibble. The successful bidder was James A. Forbes. Two days later, Garner and James Scott were appointed port wardens to pass survey on the cargo of the American ship *Mt. Vernon*. This was the first of several such surveys and auctions for Garner. He did not mind the responsibility; there was a 5 percent commission attached.[62]

On the day that the *William* was auctioned off Colton named Garner sheriff and special constable to serve writs and warrants in the jurisdiction of Monterey.[63] He needed a courageous and experienced man, for the times were troublesome. Even the alcalde with his tasseled staff of office was not always respected, as the following scene shows.

Colonel Frémont had been ordered in March to bring his irregular troop of unruly Bear Flaggers, trappers, recently-arrived immigrants, and Indians back to the capital to be discharged. On

---

61. Monterey County Archives, XIII, 1011. A more famous land deal bears William Garner's signature. On February 10, 1847, Colonel John C. Frémont paid $3,000 through Consul Larkin to Juan B. Alvarado and his wife, Martina Castro de Alvarado, for the Mariposa grant of ten square leagues in the Sierra Nevada foothills that Gov. Micheltorena had assigned them in 1844. Alcalde Colton presided at the sale, and Garner and Hartnell signed as bilingual witnesses (Charles G. Crampton, "The Opening of the Mariposa Mining Region, 1849–1859," Ph.D. dissertation, University of California, Berkeley, 1941, p. 30).

62. Bancroft, Reference Notes, Gar-Gil.

63. Monterey County Archives, XIII, 699.

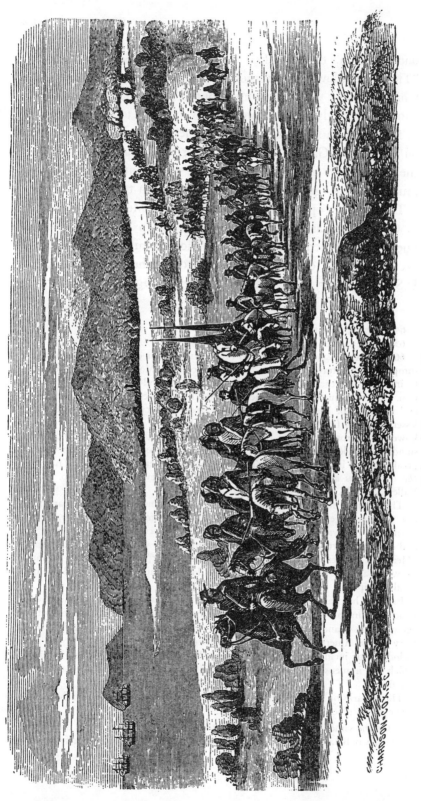

Frémont's Entrance to Monterey

one occasion, the horrified Don Florencio Serrano recorded, "Those men, low and common in character and excited by drink, what they did was to throng about [Alcalde Colton], begin to dance mockingly around him, and even dared to throw handsful of flour upon his clothing and stick pieces of spittle-wetted paper on his back!" Garner and some other Americans had to rescue the nonplussed little Yankee, for the ex-volunteers would have murdered any "greaser" who dared call them to order.[64]

The summer opened quietly enough. The Mexican War, as far as California was concerned, was over when the Treaty of Cahuenga was signed by Frémont and Pico on January 13, 1847. The excitement was over in Monterey, too, although Company F, U.S. 3d Artillery, had come with the *Lexington* on January 28

---

64. Serrano, "Apuntes," pp. 117–119.

65. Monterey County Archives, XIII, 699.

66. The whole story went back to the Graham affair of 1840. Farnham, a consumptive lawyer traveling for his health, had come to Monterey on April 18, 1840, to interview Hartnell on the work of the missions and the effects of secularization. He arrived just as the American and British prisoners were being questioned, and the sight of Mexicans presuming to arrest and try Anglo-Saxons drove all lesser thoughts from his mind. He appointed himself defense attorney. Unable, however, to pronounce more than a few words of "kitchen Spanish" and understanding even less, his efforts were of no avail. As a last resort he planned a jailbreak and an insurrection a la Texas. (Thomas Jefferson Farnham, *Travels in the Californias and Scenes in the Pacific Ocean* [New York, 1844], p. 54, 98; Vallejo, XXXIII, pt. 1, p. 66; Bee, p. 25.)

This bizarre interference in a case of which he knew neither the particulars nor the language astonished and alarmed the Californians. However, despite Farnham's extravagant threat to wrap one of the accused in an American flag and defy the court to shoot him through it, his clients were embarked for Mexico (Meadows, "Statement Respecting the Graham Affair," p. 4). Nothing daunted, he wrote a hasty note excusing himself to Hartnell and soon followed them in another ship.

In Tepic he drank in the lurid tales the prisoners had to tell — especially what Isaac Graham had to say about William Garner, the supposed government witness against them — and accepted their version as gospel. He sent this highly colored story to the American newspapers, and then, at white heat, made it the most melodramatic incident in his new book on Western travel, *Travels in California*, which was immensely popular in the United States as tension rose over the Texas question.

The remarks on Garner occur in Farnham's transcription of Isaac Graham's tale of the events preceding his arrest (p. 78):

On the same day, however, Jose Castro, Bicenta Contrine, Ankel Castro, and a runaway Botany Bay English convict by the name of Garner, a vile fellow and

and was engaged in building barracks up on the hill across the ravine from Garner's house. Values were rising in real estate: on July 3, 1847, he sold a lot about one hundred yards square in the heart of town to James B. McClurg for $250.[65]

Then, on July 17, William Garner strode into Alcalde Colton's chambers livid with anger. He had just read the spiteful vilification of himself in Thomas Jefferson Farnham's *Travels in the Californias and Scenes in the Pacific Ocean* (New York, 1844). Everyone in town had already heard about the scurrilous epithets applied to Garner in the book for his role in the 1840 Graham affair, in which Farnham had come to the defense of the exiles. Shortly after, the outraged Garner filed suit for libel against the author.[66]

---

an enemy of mine, because the foreigners would not elect him their captain, passed and repassed my house several times, and conversed together in low tones of voice. . . . A little later in the day . . . the vagabond Garner called at my house, and having drunk freely of whisky became rather boisterous, and said significantly, that the time of some people would be short.

There is no suggestion that Farnham ever saw, knew, or spoke to Garner during the ten-day period he described. He had little acquaintance with the California authorities, yet he painted them in words of hatred and contempt. The art of vituperation on short acquaintance, as these passages from his book show (pp. 59, 96, 97, 147, 148), has sadly declined since Farnham's day.

We . . . entered the presence of governor Juan Baptiste Alvarado; a well-formed, full-blooded, Californian Spaniard, five feet eleven inches in height, with coal-black curly hair, deep black eyes, fiercely black eyebrows, high cheek bones, an aquiline nose, fine white teeth, brown complexion, and the clearly marked mein of a pompous coward, clad in the broadcloth and whiskers of a gentleman. . . . He rose as we entered, and received us with the characteristic urbanity of a Spanish body without a soul; waved us to chairs, when he would have seen us tumbling from the balcony; smiled graciously at us with one corner of his mouth, while he cursed us with the other.

A man of good reputation, Corporal Rafael Pinto, drew a special spurt of venom because he happened to be in charge of the prisoners.

This Pinto was a small pattern even of a coward, but what there was of him one could not doubt was the genuine article. He had a small narrow head, very black stiff hair, a long thin nose with a sharp pendant point; small snakish eyes, very near neighbors, and always peering out at the corners of the sockets; a very slender sharp chin, with a villainous tuft of bristles on the under lip; a dark swarthy complexion burnished with the grin of an idiotic hyena.

General Castro, as might be expected, fared little better.

This man was his [Pinto's] monster superior. With the general outlines of the human frame, he united every lineament of a thoroughbred orang-outang; as, very long arms, very large brawny hands, a very heavy body, and a very con-

Farnham, who had returned overland to California by June, 1847, was probably at that moment in Santa Cruz. There he met Isaac Graham again, and the mountaineer, remembering the way Farnham had stood up for him in 1840, either gave or sold him a piece of ground on the Zayante rancho near his own place. Farnham may already have started building the redwood board shanty that his wife found when she arrived in 1850. He had not yet officially settled down but was in continual travel between Monterey, Santa Cruz, and San Jose searching out material for a new book.[67]

Farnham did not respond to Garner's challenge for almost two weeks. Part of that time he undoubtedly spent with Isaac Graham going over the grounds for his allegations against Garner, for his book merely repeated what Graham had told him. Graham surely supplied him with the names of men who would testify in his behalf; Farnham was a stranger and some of the witnesses suggested were totally unknown to him. The writer's fiery nature, too, was probably fanned by his friend's violent urging to make Garner suffer for what he considered his treachery in 1840. On July 29, 1847, Farnham appeared before Alcalde Colton, accepted the suit and declared that his words: "that the plaintiff was a 'runaway Botany Bay English convict by name of Garner, a vile fellow' and 'the vagabond Garner', were true and he prays that this may be inquired of by the country."

During August, September, and October, 1847, the contestants in the libel suit gathered depositions from their witnesses. Farnham's harvest was scanty and slow in coming in; he was a sickly man and complained that riding around the country tired him.

---

temptible face, wrinkled and drawn into a broad concentrated scowl of unsatisfied selfishness.

As a grand finale, here is his considered estimation of a people who had treated him kindly, entertained him and humored him:

Indeed, there never was a doubt among Californians, that they were at the head of the human race. In cowardice, ignorance, pretension, and dastardly tyranny, the reader has learned that this pretension is well founded. . . . In a word, the Californians are an imbecile, pusillanimous, race of men, and unfit to control the destinies of this beautiful country.

The ladies, dear creatures, I wish they were whiter.

Garner continued his duties as scribe to Colton and sheriff in Monterey.

On September 16, as clerk of the court, he wrote out and certified the decision of the nine arbiters in the dispute over the boundary between José Amestí's Corralitos grant and Joaquín Castro's Rancho de San Andrés.[68] Garner was selected on October 4 to auction off the brig *Primavera* to satisfy debts against her owners. The sale took place on November 9, and two days later Garner paid over to Larkin, the creditor, the $1,050 received for the vessel.

On October 6 two Indians, Domingo el Artillero and Manuel Castro, from the Bolsa de Ratones farm of Trinidad Espinosa were brought before a grim-faced Monterey jury. They had murdered a young American named Coe near the Pueblo del Refugio (the present day Castroville). The Indians had shot Coe in the back for his striped shirt and pistols when he stopped at their huts on the edge of the marshes. When Garner, acting as sheriff, induced Manuel to guide him and his deputies to where the body had been thrown in the tules, it was so rotten that it could not be moved. The two Indians blamed each other for the actual shooting, but they had shared the loot.

Juan Malarín, as foreman of the jury, delivered the verdict of guilty, and the two Indians were condemned to death. Alcalde Colton submitted the sentence to Governor Mason for review on October 11, who signed his approval, "There being no provision for a substitute penalty either by the laws of Mexico or the United States."[69]

The hanging of Domingo and Manuel provided a legend in

---

67. The *Californian* (Oct. 17, 1846) says Farnham was leaving Arkansas for California in April 1846. He may have gone to Oregon or been delayed by the opening of the war; the first mention of him in California is at a meeting in San Francisco in June 1847.

68. Alcalde Colton had named Alvarado as president of the board. Military Governor Richard B. Mason (who replaced General Kearny on May 31, 1847) brushed aside some quibbling over the use of the word "jury" instead of "arbitrators" in the document and approved the verdict on January 22, 1848. Monterey County Archives, XIII, 1390.

69. Ibid., pp. 1395–1419.

Monterey history. Hanging was a novel and distasteful method of execution to the Californians. For that reason, this first public demonstration of American civil justice was made as solemn and impressive as possible. Sheriff Garner officiated and, according to one version, a squad of soldiers with muffled drum marched the prisoners to the new gallows in the old cemetery on October 15, 1847.

The execution, however, was grotesquely bungled. As a result of inexperience, mistake, or forethought, the ropes were ill tied. When the trap was sprung, the two criminals landed on their feet. Padre Ambrís raced to Governor Mason with the happy news and asked for the culprits' release: they had been hanged, and by God's grace, saved from death.

Governor Mason was not impressed. They had been sentenced to be hanged by the neck until dead; the sentence had not been carried out. He ordered it to be completed. This time Sheriff Garner personally adjusted the nooses and the second attempt at hanging was legally effective.[70]

The next day Garner was appointed by Larkin, who was acting as U.S. naval storekeeper at Monterey, to auction some condemned naval provisions and clothing. It is only of distant interest now to know why Albert Trescony, an Italian innkeeper, James Watson, William Lumsden, A. Townsend, William Risley, James Gleason, Albert Toomes, William Chard, C. B. Sterling and E. Hyatt, many of them shopkeepers, paid $265.44 for the presumably unfit barrels of flour, salt pork and beef, bottles of mustard, and casks of hardtack. The $9.97 paid for old peajackets and a uniform coat does not arouse such apprehension.[71]

---

70. Harry A. Wise, *Los Gringos, or an Inside View of Mexico and California* (London, 1849), p. 132; Colton, *Three Years in California*, p. 132. Colton adds, "Had the accident or strategem in question rescued the criminals, not a noose in California would have held" (ibid., pp. 232–233). William Rich Hutton tells a similar story and places it in 1847, but since only one culprit figures in his tale he is referring to the case of Domingo Hernández, hanged as a horsethief in 1849 by order of Alcalde Florencio Serrano, who succeeded Colton. Serrano says that a well rope was used and that it broke. Hernández was returned to jail and pardoned — to be properly hanged a couple of murders later in Santa Cruz. The

By the middle of October Thomas Jefferson Farnham, a trained lawyer, had had time to evaluate the evidence with which he intended to prove his charges against William Garner. The outlook was not encouraging.

Isaac Graham, his star witness, had shown a positive talent for making enemies since 1840. Within the last two years he had been disowned by his neighbors as a dissolute mischiefmaker and adulterer. In California's first jury trial, in September 1846, he had been proven a liar.[72] The others on whom the loose-tongued author tried to lean turned out to be weak reeds indeed. The testimony Farnham got from Mariano Macario Castro was almost worthless, and his method of getting it showed his desperation. Instead of bringing Castro before the proper alcalde at San Juan Bautista to be sworn, Farnham had interviewed him himself. Tipsy old John Gilroy had gone along as interpreter and Bill Anderson, his own defense witness, and John Tierney served as witnesses.[73]

The trick did Farnham little good. When Castro and Gilroy were called by Garner for cross-examination before Alcalde Colton, Gilroy swore that Farnham had tried to persuade him to play the part of an alcalde, and when he refused, asked him to interpret. Castro, with Hartnell as interpreter, vehemently denied much of his previous testimony and that imputed to him by Romana Sánchez, his mother-in-law (the old lady had given Farnham a rambling tale of Garner's actions before and after the arrest of Graham, but when asked to swear to it by Farnham, she developed religious scruples and would not take the oath).[74]

Henry Wood and John Burton, arrested in 1840 but released, contributed nothing but hearsay about skulduggery alleged by

---

Hutton story is told in "Two Letters on Post-Conquest Monterey," *Monterey Historical and Art Association Quarterly Noticias* . . . 5 (June 1961); Serrano, "Recuerdos historico de Don Florencio Serrano," 1874, MS, Bancroft Library; Monterey County Archives, XIV, 627–642.

71. Larkin Accounts, U.S. Navy Agent, 1847–1849, MS, Bancroft Library.
72. See above, p. 41.
73. Monterey County Archives, XIII, 737–739 (Castro for Farnham).
74. Ibid., pp. 755–759 (Sánchez for Farnham), 783 (Castro before Colton). See Appendix II, below, for the strange story told by Romana Sánchez and its relevance to Garner's actions in the Graham affair.

Graham when Garner had been a member of the *Compañía
Extranjera* in 1836. Bill Anderson, a deportee of 1840 and pres-
ently a neighbor of Graham at Zayante, limited himself to testifying that Albert Morris, Graham's former handyman at the distillery and the only confirming witness, was not really insane and
that children as young as thirteen were sent as convicts to Botany
Bay.[75]

On the other hand, in Alcalde Colton's presence Farnham
examined Garner's old shipmates James McKinley and James
Watson. He could not shake their testimony that Garner had
been an experienced apprentice aboard the *Royal George* when
they sailed from England in 1824. They declared that his "character was the best a man could have on board a ship; he was cor-
rect and upright and highly esteemed by his officers." José Ábrego
told Farnham flatly that he "would not believe Graham under
oath." Captain Charles Wolter, asked the same question, begged
to be excused from answering it. James Stokes testified to Garner's
good reputation and his refusal to incriminate the men arrested
in 1840. Job Dye testified to Graham's grudge against Garner and
the latter's honorable conduct.[76]

In the end Farnham saw that his whole case rested on Isaac
Graham and on his own ability to sway a jury. It must have been
clear to Farnham that he could not hope to sustain the charges
he had so recklessly published against Garner at Graham's instiga-
tion from his own witnesses. (The complete deposition of Graham
is an interesting one and merits a full transcription: it is given
below, as Appendix II, with additional depositions and a discussion of their claims and historical relevance.)

Farnham had to prove Garner "a runaway Botany Bay English convict," and against the eyewitness evidence of Watson and

---

75. Ibid., pp. 741–743 (Wood), 745–747 (Burton), 749–750 (Anderson). Morris
wrote at least three versions of the affair of 1840. In his first, "The Journal of a
Crazy Man" (1853[?], MS, Bancroft Library), he said that W. E. P. Hartnell
and Thomas O. Larkin testified before Colton that he was of unsound mind and
blamed them for the fact that "now; wherever I go, people point me out as The
Crazy Man." Morris was not insane but so extravagant in speech and gesture
that he certainly was a curiosity.

McKinley that was impossible. The "vile fellow" and "vagabond" charges were equally futile when confronted with Garner's good local record. Dragging in a vague rumor of skulduggery in 1836 and Garner's unheroic position in the 1840 roundup would be of little avail before a jury in Monterey. The solid, long-time residents were dominant there. They knew the background of the affairs of 1836 and 1840 better than did Farnham; they knew Isaac Graham and his clique too well.

To make his style of frontier, spread-eagle oratory effective, Farnham needed a district full of recently-arrived, anti-Mexican immigrants, men to whom Graham was unknown except by legend as the brave mountain man who had been cruelly mistreated by the Californians. Farnham was a clever lawyer. If his defense, based on the feeblest of evidence and the most suspect of witnesses, would not stand scrutiny in Monterey, he would seek another and more propitious place for the trial.

Sometime around October 18, 1847, Thomas Jefferson Farnham made his first attempt to remove the case from the Monterey jurisdiction. He climbed the stairs of the big adobe *cuartel* that was California's temporary capitol and petitioned Governor Mason to change the venue on the ground that Alcalde Colton was prejudiced in favor of his secretary. Governor Mason, however, took no action but handed the paper back to Farnham to carry to Colton for an initial decision.[77]

Farnham walked out of the governor's office, threw the petition into the fire, and tried another tack. Around the corner in the old *calabozo* was the alcalde's office. He strolled in and proposed to Colton and Garner that, in view of the circumstances, a disinterested judge should be appointed by the governor. This seemed reasonable and fair. (Farnham did not mention his first idea that

---

76. Monterey County Archives, XIII, 711–712 (McKinley), 707–708 (Watson), 713–714 (Ábrego), 725–726 (Wolter), 719 (Stokes), 717 (Dye). Dye was the last witness called to give a deposition. Not that Garner had exhausted his slate of people willing to vouch for him: he still could call Salvador Munrás, Gabriel de la Torre, Juan Malarín, and Hartnell. Farnham had statements from all his witnesses except James Alexander Forbes, whose testimony was apparently of little moment for Farnham made no attempt to get it.

77. Ibid., XII, 246–248.

the trial be held elsewhere.) Garner agreed at once to the request and Colton, as magistrate, notified the governor that another jurist should be selected to try the case. Governor Mason scanned the short list of available lawyers and within a day or two asked John Ricord to preside as a special judge for the occasion.[78]

Ricord seemed heaven-sent to Governor Mason for this duty. Ricord had just arrived in Monterey from the Hawaiian Islands on September 24, 1847. From 1844 to 1846 he had been attorney general to King Kamehameha III and had compiled the laws of his realm. In Hawaii he had gotten into difficulties with Reverend Judd, the king's prime minister, and had left posthaste. Commodore Biddle, during his stay at Honolulu, had gained a low opinion of Ricord and relayed a cryptic warning about him to Commodores Stockton and Shubrick. Apparently, however, the Army was blissfully unaware of Ricord's flaws.[79]

On October 22 John Ricord took the special judgeship and asked both parties to the suit to acknowledge his jurisdiction, the loser of the case to pay $500 for court costs. There was no need to mail the notice in the 1847; Judge Ricord simply handed his notes to Farnham and Garner as he strolled through town. As soon as Farnham received his notice, he played the card he had been holding since the day the governor turned down his petition: he put in the judge's hand a request that the venue be changed to the Pueblo de San José de Guadalupe, alleging that Monterey was so

---

78. Ibid.

79. William Tecumseh Sherman, *Memoirs of General W. T. Sherman*, 2 vols. (New York, 1875), I, 69; Bancroft, *History of California*, V, 695. Sherman despised Ricord for being a shameless liar, sycophant, and shyster. The only complete record of Ricord is found in Gerrit Parmele Judd, IV, *Dr. Judd, Hawaii's Friend: A Biography of Gerrit Parmele Judd (1803–1873)* (Honolulu: University of Hawaii Press, 1960), pp. 127–154.

Ricord, born in Massachusetts in 1812, was called to the bar in Buffalo, New York, and went to Louisiana, Texas, Florida, and Oregon before arriving in Hawaii in February 1844. A tall, handsome man, he soon ingratiated himself with the Reverend Dr. Gerrit P. Judd, Secretary of State for Foreign Affairs to King Kamehameha III. On March 9, 1848, Ricord was appointed attorney general and did good work in reorganizing the legal structure of the kingdom. Dr. Judd had great confidence in him, and Ricord gained a preeminent position, but the tug-of-war between the favor-seeking American and British merchants tore

prejudiced against him that he could not get a fair trial, that his witnesses lived nearer to San José, and that his domicile was there.[80]

The next day, October 23, when William Garner brought in his formal acceptance of Ricord's jurisdiction, the judge let him read Farnham's request for a change of location. Garner scoffed at it and immediately sat down and wrote out his objections to Farnham's maneuver (perhaps with the advice of his new legal counsel, Lewis Dent, who had agreed to prosecute the case).

First, Farnham's witnesses — Mariano Macario Castro, John Gilroy, and probably Romana Sánchez — all lived within the San Juan Bautista jurisdiction and were nearer to Monterey than San José. The depositions of Romana Sánchez, John Burton, and Albert Morris had been taken already and had been examined by the magistrate in San José. They had not been cross-examined by the plaintiff yet, but that was his business, not Farnham's. Alexander Forbes, the only witness for Farnham whose deposition had not been taken, was coming to Monterey and would be there for the trial.

Second, Farnham claimed he had other witnesses still to examine in San José.

It is his own fault if there are any. He has had three months to take depositions with the perfect acquiescence of the plaintiff. Besides, if these witnesses were so important, one would think the defendant might know

---

Ricord's character apart. As land commissioner and judge to quit titles, he could please neither faction. "A designing if not unprincipled man," said George Brown, the disgruntled American commissioner to Hawaii. "Mr. Ricord often pains his best friends by his eccentricities and impulsive temper," said Mrs. Judd. He spent money lavishly, and Dr. Judd refused to honor his drafts on the royal treasury. He fell madly in love with the Judd's fifteen-year-old daughter, who was more frightened than flattered by his passion. She refused him, he tried "to enforce his demand, and not succeeding, poured forth a torrent of abuse." He formally resigned office on May 17, 1847, and left for California on August 21, 1847. Previously a teetotaler, he now began to drink heavily. After the muddle he made of Garner's case, he went to the mines leaving his bills unpaid. He did not dig for gold but made a good sum selling watered whiskey (Ben Kooser, *San Andreas Independent*, January 10, 1857). He then wandered to Tahiti, Siam, and Algeria. He died in 1861, still unwed, in Paris.

80. Monterey County Archives, XII, 389.

enough of them, at least, to favor the court with their names, but they are probably phantoms. Shadows, even in man's hope, do not justify a change of venue.

Third, Farnham's claim of domicile at San José was false.

The defendant has no "domicile." Santa Cruz has perhaps the best claim on him, but even there he can only be regarded as an unsettled resident. Something more than these transient stoppings in a man's peregrinations are requisite. The bird in its autumnal migration might almost as well claim the tree on which it chances to light for the night as its home.

Fourth, excitement at Monterey would be prejudicial to the trial.

What do the people of Monterey know or care about the calendar of Botany Bay twenty-five or thirty years ago? It would be difficult to excite the Botany Bay people themselves about the escape of one of their inhabitants thirty years ago. This would be true of a *fact* where it occurs. What then shall we say of a fiction, out of its sphere? Could such a fiction, of such a date, even if half, or quite believed, excite men so prodigiously as to put the cause of Justice in peril? The supposition is answered in its own absurdity.[81]

Farnham replied by finding three men — George L. Barnes, James Lowe, and Richard M. Harmer — to back his petition to move the court to San José. On October 26 Judge Ricord gave his opinion. He agreed with Garner that Farnham's reasons were not valid and disposed of a few more that Farnham had evidently made orally: that Garner was an enemy alien and not eligible to sue a citizen of the United States, and that the court did not sue him in his proper domicile, San José, and thus was out of order and had no jurisdiction over him. "The defendant has admitted his authorship," wrote Ricord, "and has not protested court at the proper stage of proceedings, so his points are no longer useful as a defense against the bringings of action. He has chosen to justify,

81. Ibid., pp. 353, 389–392.
82. Ibid., pp. 395–399, 415. George L. Barnes, bartender of the Bola de Oro saloon in the Alvarado Building, signed on October 24. James Lowe signed on October 25. He was a quartermaster sergeant of the First New York Volunteer Regiment who had arrived in Monterey in April and was already invalided out of the service. Finally, on October 27 (the day after Ricord handed down his

and thus not only waived all advantage under them, but has admitted the plaintiff's right of action against him in the courts of the country." [82]

However, while Ricord gave with one hand, he took away with the other. Looking at the paper signed by Barnes and Lowe, he conceded that Monterey might not be the best place for the trial. He granted the change of venue; in fact, he had just read aloud, "San José, the first Monday in November," when Garner protested.[83]

Garner evidently had not dreamed that Ricord would change the venue to San José, and only now, when Ricord did so, did he hasten to save something from the wreckage. It is odd that Colton, who was surely told of developments by his clerk, did not inform Ricord that he was exceeding his instructions. Apparently the judge, as an ex-attorney general, saw no need to consult with a minister on legal matters. He may have had an aversion to the cloth, considering his flight from the Islands; Colton never mentions him in his diary.

Judge Ricord was completely confused in his decision because he had not read his commission carefully. Neither had he regarded Lewis Dent's advice in the rebuttal to Farnham's plea for a change of venue: "Where the court is prejudiced, another judge is appointed, but the case is never permitted to wander about in quest of a neutral position. Its locality is always with the court in whose jurisdiction it originated. There it commences and there it terminates." [84]

Ricord had proudly assumed that he was a sort of special superior judge with all California for his circuit and that he might set up court where he pleased. He did not realize that he was merely a stand-in for Alcalde Colton and competent only in

---

decision), Richard M. Harmer, a bricklayer, swore to Farnham's claim that "great excitement exists in Monterey in reference to the issue pending and in his opinion it will be impossible to obtain a jury of six good and lawful men in the said town and vicinage who have not already formed or expressed their opinion on the merits of this cause."

83. Ibid.   84. Ibid.

Monterey. By changing the venue to San José, he had, in effect, abandoned the case and put it into the hands of the alcalde there, James W. Weeks, who was hardly a friend of Garner.[85]

That Farnham understood Ricord was handing him the case on a silver platter may be doubted. He knew even less about the powers of an alcalde than did Ricord. Probably Garner had not realized the full implications of the change of venue either. It was enough for him to know that unless he acted quickly, the tables would be completely turned and he would have little chance to win the case with a jury from San Jose.

San Jose was quite a different town from Monterey. It was in an area full of Americans squatting on the pueblo lands and loafing in the town, resentful that they were not allowed to take what land they pleased from the enemy "Mex." They had already tried to grab the property of the two nearby missions of Santa Clara and San José, despite the protests of Padre Suárez del Real.[86] The picture of Farnham, Isaac Graham, and John Burton haranging a jury of those hard-jawed, tobacco-chewing farmers from the border states of Missouri, Arkansas, Iowa, and Illinois with a tale of Mexican outrage abetted by a renegade Englishman must have made Garner's blood run cold — and Farnham's run hot with anticipation. It would have made scant difference to a jury of emigrants that Farnham and Graham could not prove the points at issue and that their highly colored, irrelevant stories of piracy and betrayal in 1836 and 1840 were a farrago of exaggerations, lies, and misrepresentations.

Faced with this grim prospect, Garner demanded the right to

---

85. San Jose Alcalde John Burton, Farnham's witness and collaborator, had resigned in mid-September, and James W. Weeks, his sheriff, had replaced him. Weeks was not so anti-Garner as Burton, but he was Burton's friend and had been arrested with him in, as he sarcastically described it, "the Garner et als Revolution." Neither he nor Burton had been deported, but they had lost property. On the other hand, Weeks was no admirer of Isaac Graham. Of the deportees, he said, "There was a few which was the cause of the difficulty. Captain Graham was the worst; he was the cause of several deaths and a deal of humbug by his filibustering spirit that he attained. This old fellow thought he could play Hell and turn up jack." Weeks had also signed the 1846 petition to expel Graham from

show that San José was unfit for the trial scene, too. Farnham, pleading (as well he might) urgent business in Graham's Santa Cruz and Burton's San Jose, borrowed the judge's pen and dashed off a note asking for a postponement until late November. Ricord's refusal is dated 4:00 P.M. the same afternoon. Then, telling both men that he would give his final decision on the change of venue the next morning at 9:00 A.M. in his office, he adjourned court. Farnham, eager to be off, wrote a note to William H. H. Wheeler, a recently arrived New York Volunteer, asking him to act for him in court the next day, pleading that his health was so bad that twenty miles a day on horseback was all he could stand and that he had to leave immediately.[87]

Although Garner had had only a few hours to complete his task, promptly at 9:00 A.M. he delivered to Ricord the affidavits of Moses Schallenberger, Talbot Green, and James Stokes "that the excitement at the Pueblo de San José is of such a character as to render it unsafe for the plaintiff in the case to be tried there. Also, it would be impossible to obtain a jury that had not expressed an opinion or entertained a prejudice in favor of either one or the other of the parties litigant." It was witnessed by Walter Colton, alcalde. With the affidavit, Garner added his petition asking that the trial be held at "another place." [88]

Farnham's hasty departure now told against him. Judge Ricord veered like a weathercock on sight of the latest affidavit. Striking his pen through the words "San José, the first Monday in November," he wrote in over them, "San Luís Obispo, the first Monday in January." Wheeler, Farnham's substitute, made no objection; he had been too short a time in California to see any differ-

---

the Santa Cruz area. Weeks, "Reminiscences," pp. 106–107.

86. It was only when Governor Mason warned the squatters in June, and then sent an army detachment under Captain Henry M. Naglee on July 10, 1847, that the newcomers sullenly made arrangements to acknowledge the land as private property and pay the priest rent for it. United States, President, *Message . . . on the Subject of California and New Mexico*, House Executive Document No. 17, 31st Cong., 1st sess. (Washington, D.C., 1850), pp. 334, 340–341; Weeks, pp. 119–120.

87. Monterey County Archives, XIII, 803.

88. Ibid., p. 789.

ence between the two towns.[89] Why the date was postponed to
January is unknown. The rains generally began in November and
lasted until April, the worst storms coming in the winter months.
A worse time for the consumptive Farnham could not have been
chosen.

The next day, October 28, Ricord spoke of his decision on
changing the venue to Governor Mason. The governor was furi-
ous. Without mincing words, he let the judge know that he had
botched the job. Ricord, conscious at last of his error, strained to
get the case back into his hands, but he had gone too far. The
governor officially took it from him.[90]

Wheeler, innocent of his faux pas in approving of San Luís
Obispo, rode up to San Jose to bring Farnham the news. On November 5, 1847, the lawyer, his plans thwarted, fired off an irate
letter to Ricord. "I confess myself most profoundly astonished at
the course of the court," he fumed. "It is farther away for my
aged witnesses, it is impossible to obtain a jury there that can
speak English, and the season for the appointment of the trial!!
The decision is most remarkable. By its natural operation the ends
of justice are utterly destroyed. I shall send the court affidavits
showing the *falseness* of the said counter-affidavits. I ask the court
to open the said motion anew for argument. I am confident that
the court will see the best reasons for reversing its decision." [91]

But Ricord was no longer in charge of the case. The hot potato
now lay in the unwilling hands of José Mariano Bonilla, alcalde

---

89. Ibid., p. 412. In none of the correspondence is there any mention of
changing the venue to Santa Cruz or San Juan Bautista. They were probably
suggested orally by either Garner or Ricord, but if Farnham objected to Monterey, he would surely have raised the same objection to the other two towns.
They were really within the Monterey zone of legal jurisdiction. Graham certainly would not have been received with credulity in Santa Cruz, and San Juan
Bautista, except for the Breens of Donner Party fame, had scarcely another English-speaking person. The judge therefore chose a spot well outside the area of
"excitement," even though it was inconvenient.

90. To Ricord's humiliation, the letter of dismissal was published in the *Californian* (San Francisco), December 15, 1847. See Appendix II for the complete text.

91. Monterey County Archives, XII, 1601.

92. Ibid., XIII, 727–730. The governor was well aware of the problem, but at
least Bonilla did not have to worry long about his responsibilities. His term ended

of San Luis Obispo. Alcalde Colton sent all the pertinent documents to Bonilla on December 1, and on December 20 they came winging back accompanied by an almost illegible letter in Spanish. The alcalde of San Luís Obispo regretted that the United States had substituted its laws for the Mexican code so early in the war, for he was ignorant of them and could not in fairness try the case. According to Mexican law, Bonilla went on, the accused should be tried in his local court, not in that of a distant town like San Luís Obispo where there was neither translator nor a jury of five qualified persons. "Please let the Governor know of this; I don't want to disobey superior orders, but I wanted to let you know the Mexican law in such cases." [92]

Farnham seems either to have refused to go to San Luís Obispo or to have gained a postponement until the weather improved because he was too sick to travel. His next residence was San Francisco, where he opened a law office in early 1848. Garner apparently expected the trial to begin in San Luís Obispo in the spring and made no objection but continued his work as Colton's secretary. His witness, Francis Job Dye, dated his deposition in favor of Garner December 21, 1847.

No more documents in the case are to be found. [93] In all probability, it fell between several stools: Ricord had withdrawn with his ears burning, Alcalde Bonilla had begged off for very good reasons, the case had been taken out of Alcalde Colton's hands, neither party would agree to the other's preference for court loca-

---

with the year, and on January 25, 1848, Governor Mason appointed as alcalde John Manuel Price, another of the ubiquitous deserters from English whalers and a deportee of 1840. The documents, however, stayed in Monterey awaiting the governor's pleasure. Richard Barnes Mason, Correspondence and Papers, 1847–1849, MSS, Bancroft Library.

93. The Garner–Farnham case, although the most important of its type, was not unique in California at the time. The Yount–Chiles slander suit came up in Sonoma on June 25, 1847, and was settled by Chiles' apology. All this was reported in the *Californian* (which had moved to San Francisco with Semple after Colton dropped out as co-publisher with the April 17th issue). Although a good deal of the official correspondence of Ricord and Gov. Mason concerning the Garner–Farnham case appeared in the newspaper, not a single editorial comment is made about it.

tion once Ricord had muddied the legal waters, Farnham was ill
and getting worse, Governor Mason had bigger fish to fry — and
mining fever was in the air.

*   *   *

On December 3, 1847, William Garner, Felipe Castro of San
Juan Bautista, Vicente Castro, and James Watson laid claim to a
silver mine on the rancho that had been granted to Joaquín Solís
but then belonged to Mariano Macario Castro. (Little was done
to develop it, and it was abandoned after the Gold Rush began
four months later.)[94]

A more famous mining company was formed in Alcalde Colton's office on February 1, 1848. Abrego, Larkin, Ricord, Blackburn, and Grove C. Cook organized the Santa Clara Mining Company to develop a quicksilver lode discovered by Abrego on
Cook's Los Capitancillos Rancho on December 10, 1847. Garner
and Hartnell served as witnesses.[95]

Both the Garner and Ábrego claims had been made under the
Mexican mining laws. To check this, Governor Mason proclaimed
on February 12 that the Mexican practice was abolished and that
all claims for subsequent finds would be held for determination
of their legality after the signing of a peace treaty with Mexico.

Toward the end of February, by order of Colton's Court of
Admiralty, the prize ship *Admittance*, of 420 tons, was ordered
sold at public auction by William Garner on March 16, 1848. The
cargo consisted of 2,707 bales of cotton, 174 bales of foolscap
paper, and 89,384 pounds of Swedish bar iron.

As Garner had predicted in his letter of February 13, 1847, the

---

94. Monterey County Archives, XIII, 531.

95. *Californian*, Feb. 12, 1848; *Larkin Papers*, VII, 263–264.
The site was about two miles from the famous New Almaden workings. However, the Santa Clara Mining Company did not prosper. The vein was inferior,
was lost in May, and when the gold strike drew attention from it, the mine was
deserted.

96. *Californian* (San Francisco), Feb. 9, 16, 1848, March 22, 1848; Jacques
Antoine Moerenhaut, *Jacques A. Moerenhaut: The Inside Story of the Gold Rush*,
trans. and ed. Abraham P. Nasatir (San Francisco: Special Publication No. 8,
California Historical Society, 1935); Sherman, pp. 71–72; Chester A. Lyman,
Around the Horn to the Sandwich Islands and California, 1845–1850, edited by

rancheros were beginning to feel the pinch of changing times and cultures. The foreign merchants began to call their debtors to account. On January 24, 1848, the Rancho Los Verjeles, lying on the western slope of the Gavilan hills where the old road ran to San Juan Bautista, was advertised for sale to clear debts. José Joaquín Gómez, to whom it had been granted in 1834, had kept open house for all travelers, but his generosity and improvidence had ruined him. There were no bidders at the first call. On March 2 Garner again announced that it would be put up for auction, this time on May 1. Early in March, however, news came to Monterey of the gold found in Captain John Sutter's millrace.

Captain Sutter was not eager to spread the word, but he wanted the land upon which his mill stood (and where the gold was found) granted to him legally. To carry his application to Governor Mason, he chose as messenger Charles Bennett and cautioned him to secrecy. He might as well have published the news in the *Californian*. Bennett showed samples of gold everywhere he stopped along the way. At Monterey, the governor had to refuse Sutter's request, for the land as California was technically still a Mexican province. Bennett let the governor test his gold and displayed it freely in the town.[96] Many disparaged the importance of the find, but by mid-May there was no denying the fact: the Gold Rush had started.[97]

The Rancho Los Verjeles again went begging while the fever spread. The auctioneer, William Garner, however, was not one of the first to throw down his pen and start for Eldorado. He had a responsible position; he had also been on wild goose chases for

---

Frederick J. Teggert (New Haven: Yale University Press, 1924), pp. 247–248.

97. *San Jose Pioneer*, April 27, 1878; Colton, *Three Years in California*, p. 242; James H. Carson, *Early Recollections of the Mines, and a Description of the Great Tulare Valley* (Stockton, 1852), p. 10. Colton says that the news of gold came to him on May 29, 1848, which is curious: he must have heard of Bennett's errand. Carson says he left Monterey on May 10 after seeing the riches of a returning friend. Larkin, in his letter to Secretary of State James Buchanan, June 1, writes: "Ten days back the excitement had not reached Monterey" (*Larkin Papers*, VII, 287). Moses Schallenberger, in a letter to Larkin on June 8 says that many had already left Monterey (ibid., p. 296). Colton dates the real exodus from the return of his messenger on June 20.

The Site of the Discovery of Gold, 1848. Engraving of detail from the
painting by Charles Nahl

treasure before, as he tells in his letter of November 9, 1846. Like many other old residents, he knew there was gold in the hills. Late in 1846 he had shown Colton a crude golden bow-clasp he had just obtained from a wild Indian of the Sierra. It signified little to him except that his claims for mineral wealth in California were valid. At present, he was reluctant to believe current rumors as to the extent of the deposits.[98]

Garner watched Colton send off a trusty man on June 6 to verify the tales of gold and tried again to sell the Verjeles property. This time he was more successful. On June 7 Colton signed his approval of the sale to James Stokes for $3,000, and Garner, as his clerk, set the alcalde's seal to the document.[99]

The investigator that Colton had sent to the gold fields galloped into Monterey on a jaded horse on June 20, 1848. Leaping down from the saddle, he pulled from his pocket proof that nuggets of yellow gold lay free for the taking. Within a week, Monterey was practically emptied of able-bodied men. Garner, his son José, Captain Joseph Aram, John M. Montgomery, and probably James McKenzie and the new vice-alcalde William Longley made up a party and rode away for the "dry diggings" on the south fork of the American River.[100]

Garner was back in Colton's office by the middle of August with tales of riches and a bag of gold to prove it. He and his son may have been part of the group of "four citizens" mentioned by

---

98. Colton, p. 368; Bancroft, *History of California*, VI, 53–54, cites many instances of disbelief in the value of the discoveries in the first months. The knowing ones joked about it: Semple said, "I would give more for a good coal mine than for all the gold mines in the universe." Governor Mason questioned Bradley, a visitor from San Francisco in Monterey on May 1. "I have heard of it," Bradley told him. "A few fools have hurried to the place, but you may be sure there is nothing in it."

99. Monterey County Archives, XIV, 441, 449.

100. José Garner remembered them leaving April or May and staying a month in the mines (*San Jose Pioneer*, April 27, 1878), but Lyman was running a survey line in San Jose with William Garner on May 17, 1848, and on June 7 Garner signed the Verjeles sale in Monterey. W. R. Longley left Monterey on June 28 (Thomas Larkin letter in Edwin Bryant, *What I Saw in California: Being the Journal of a Tour by the Emigrant Route . . . in the Years, 1846, 1847* [New York and Philadelphia], 1848), appendix, p. 126.

Colton as having come back to Monterey on August 16 with $67,844 to share between them for the journey of seven weeks, three days of it spent in the placers.

Young José Garner says that his father carried thirty-six pounds of gold dust when he returned to Monterey, having purchased it in the diggings at $3 an ounce in Mexican pesos. Since gold was then selling for $16 an ounce in Monterey, on that one trip Garner would have realized a tremendous profit.

Extraordinary as this may seem, it appears to be true. To buy that quantity of gold at $3 an ounce, Garner would have had to carry $1,718 in silver to the diggings, a considerable sum in those days. Many of the gold seekers in the first few months were Indians, and he could easily have purchased the nuggets for very little in the hard cash that they recognized. The $3 price is even generous by comparison with Bancroft's records of $1 to whites and 50¢ to Indians for each ounce of gold in October and November of 1848. Nicholas Carriger comments that gold was bringing as low as $6 an ounce when he bought his farm in Sonoma early in 1849. He considered himself lucky to get $8. Many miners cited $4 to $6 prices in 1848 and early 1849. James Carson was bitterly resentful of the victimization of the miners. The gold was worth $18 an ounce at the United States mint in Philadelphia, but the local traders and merchants would only give $6 in 1848 and $10 in 1849, and raised their prices for merchandise scandalously high. If a miner tried to evade their clutches by sending the gold east in bullion to get the mint price, the dealers charged him 5 percent to 10 percent for shipment.[101]

The defrauding of the miners, however, was not the prime reason why Governor Mason and Alcalde Colton called a citizen's meeting on July 26, 1848, to discuss the establishment of a United States mint in California. As they saw it, "if this course be not adopted, gold to the amount of many millions will pass yearly to other countries to enrich their merchants and capitalists."[102]

101. Nicholas Carriger, Autobiography, 1874, MS, Bancroft Library; Carson, passim; Bancroft, *History of California*, VI, 91–92.

102. Monterey County Archives, XII, 235; Mason, Correspondence, to Adj. Gen. R. Jones, Aug. 17, 1848.

An Alcalde at the mines examining a lump of gold—catches the fever—drops his staff of office, and tells his sheriff to go home and hang the prisoner whom he left at the bar, and he will sentence him afterwards. From Walter Colton's *Three Years in California*. At the time of the Gold Rush Colton was alcalde for Monterey and Garner was his sheriff

After his spectacular success in the goldfields, Garner could not sit quietly in Monterey. At the end of August he loaded some mules with trade goods and was off for the new diggings on the Stanislaus River — a journey of four or five days. Garner had seen on his first trip that trading was not only less laborious but a surer road to fortune than standing in a wet hole searching for flakes of gold. Indians were doing most of the work on the Stanislaus then. Serapes brought $60 to $100 each from natives who collected the yellow dust which was useless to them but so prized by the traders. All colored calico was eagerly bought for $20 a yard, while white miners gladly paid $100 for a pick, a miner's pan, or a gallon of whiskey.[103]

Garner sold out his stock within three weeks. On the road back to Monterey, he was passing through San Jose when he met Captain William Marcy and John Wilkinson repacking their balky mules. They told him that Walter Colton had fallen to the lure of gold and was going with them to the mines. With Lieutenant Simmons and William Stewart he was waiting their return only a few miles beyond Mission San José.

Garner, delighted at the prospect of seeing his friend, rode back and caught up with the alcalde in Niles Canyon about noon on September 26. They traveled along side by side, Garner telling of the new goldfields and of the wonders he had seen, Colton enlivening the miles with anecdotes of his life in a deserted Monte-

---

103. Coronel, "Cosas de California," pp. 142–143; *Larkin Papers*, VII, 339; Bancroft, *History of California*, VI, 92; U.S. President Message on *California and New Mexico*, p. 528; Mason, Correspondence, Aug. 17, 1848. Lyman, *Around the Horn*, says that the Stanislaus Camp area opened in July 1848.

104. Colton, pp. 257–266. Colton left Monterey with Charles T. Botts, naval storekeeper, John Wilkinson, son of the U.S. minister to Russia, and William Marcy, son of the late secretary of war, on September 21, 1848. At San Jose Botts received orders to return to Monterey, but the two naval officers joined the party in his stead.

105. *Larkin Papers*, VII, 367.

106. "Intermittent fever" would probably be malaria. It was very common in the Sacramento Valley at this period. John S. Williams' letters to Larkin tell a common story:

Sonoma May 2nd 1847 . . . When you send the goods I would like for you to send me a small assortment of medicines laybilled in case of sicness which is very common on the Sacramento. . . .

rey. After spending the night around a bonfire at Livermore's ranch, Garner turned back to San Jose and his waiting son.[104]

Home in Monterey at the end of September,[105] Garner went back to work in the alcalde's office. He planned no further ventures in the mining camps for that year. The rains fell heavily in the Sierra in October 1848, and two-thirds of the miners came down to the coast to spend the winter and enjoy their new wealth. Colton stayed on, however, watching the continuing scramble for gold in the creeks and hillsides and occasionally picking up a few nuggets for his wife in the east.

William Garner found disheartening news awaiting him in Monterey. His adversary, Farnham, had gone to the goldfields too, but the exertion had been too much for him. He died of intermittent fever in San Francisco on September 13, 1848.[106] The obituary in the *Californian* of September 16 gave Farnham's age as about forty-two and his residence as New York State. He left a wife (the redoubtable fighter for woman's rights, Eliza Woodson) and three children. His interposition in favor of the exiles of 1840 was eulogized, but there was no mention of the libel suit that he had so persistently prevented from coming to trial.

Garner's effort to clear his name of Farnham's irresponsible reporting was completely frustrated, for he had only sued the author — not the publisher nor Farnham's informants. In the eyes of his friends and the responsible element in the community

---

Sacramento July 28th 1847 . . . Wee are very sickly here just now, my wife has been verry sick but has got some better. Mr. Chase has had the fever verry bad but is getting about again. I wish you to send up a good supply of medicene as soon as possible. Wee have rode down all of our best horses going about for medicene. It is getting quite sickly all over the vally. The indians are dying off here verry fast. . . .

Sacramento River, Sept. 13th 1848 . . . You are aware that we have had much sickness at our camp. For this reason I have resolved to go home with my wife; and also Jim and his wife. (*Larkin Papers*, VI, 142, 241, VII, 357).

Colton, on the other hand, was quite happy with his trip to the goldfields:

The southern mines are in elevations which exempt them from the maladies incident to the low lands which fringe the streams farther north. There are no stagnant waters, no decomposition of vegetable matter, no miasma drifting about in the fog, to shake and burn you with alternate chill and fever. I never enjoyed better health and spirits (Colton, p. 342).

he had morally vindicated himself; his enemies, whose slurs had escaped public rebuke, considered their accusations unrefuted. Farnham's book continued in circulation and, in the twenty years after its first publication, went through several more editions. Whatever idea Garner might have had of pursuing the case further was made impossible when the gold fever scattered judges, jurymen, and witnesses into the hopeless jumble of a thousand ephemeral tent-cities along the creeks.[107]

Garner and Wolter, acting for the creditors in the sale of the Rancho Los Verjeles to James Stokes, still had problems with the estate. On October 4, 1848, Stokes paid Garner the $3,000 agreed upon, but in less than a week Garner and Wolter preferred charges of fraud against him. Stokes was accused of trying an old trick in such bankruptcy cases.

We have good reason to believe Stokes has worked in bad faith and falsehood regarding the bill of $605 that he presents to the group against the said Don Jose Joaquin Gomez, the latter having subsequently declared that such a debt was not legal but that it was an agreement between the two of them, Gomez and Stokes, to defraud the rest of the creditors, as was done. We request the alcalde to make the strictest investigation and that Gomez be made to make declaration of Stokes' guilt under the strictest formality of law.[108]

---

107. Professor Nunis, *The Trials of Isaac Graham*, quoting Paul Parker's article in the *Salinas Independent*, November 1, 1935, states that "Garner won the case" (p. 57), but neither he nor I, working on parallel subjects, have been able to find documentary proof of a trial in the state archives or the county archives of Monterey, San Luis Obispo, or Santa Cruz, or in the city of San Jose.

Because all the pertinent material, depositions and their copies are collected in the Monterey archives, it appears that no trial was held away from Monterey. Of course, Farnham may have refused to appear and the verdict rendered by default in favor of Garner. In that case, there should be evidence of a summons, some word from Farnham, a petition for a verdict by Garner, a publication of the decision by the court, or a contemporary comment on the verdict. I have been unable to find anything of this nature, although I have had the National Archives searched. There is no record in the General Accounting Office (Record Group 217, 1847–1849) of payment of the $500 court costs to Governor Mason nor any mention of a decision to be found in the Old Military Records Division. California Federal Court records begin only with 1851.

The strangest thing about the whole affair is that not a single contemporary makes any reference to the outcome in letters or the memoirs collected by Bancroft. Paul Parker, now almost ninety, may have based his comment on some local in-

Stokes must have made good the disputed bill or withdrawn it; he retained the land. In 1875 he received the patent of the United States Land Commission to the Rancho Los Verjeles, a tract of 8,760 acres.

Colton's term as magistrate and alcalde expired at the end of September; Florencio Serrano became his successor. Garner continued as secretary for a short time, but he had done so well on gold-buying and trading forays that nothing could keep him long in sleepy Monterey. He gave up the clerkship at the new year, and William R. Longley was reappointed vice-alcalde to help Serrano in his dealings with English-speaking citizens.

By February 10, 1849, Garner's letters to the eastern newspapers had come full circle. On that date the *San Francisco Star*, not attempting to guess the authorship — or knowing it well — noted with approbation his letter in the *Journal of Commerce* about the deposits of quicksilver, silver, lead, and iron in California. However, it pronounced these eclipsed now: "The news of gold will produce a great revolution in the United States."

*   *   *

Garner knew that the miners, having begun to move south into the Stanislaus area, would continue in that direction when the

---

formant, but he wrote me that "I haven't the slightest idea where I got the information that Garner won the libel suit." The members of the Garner family whom I have contacted have no information.

Garner does not seem to have been a vindictive person. The evidence was all in his favor and his triumph assured. Farnham knew this, and he was a sick man. He may have written a personal letter of apology to Garner which induced him to let the suit lapse and spare Farnham the $500 court costs. All Garner wanted was to clear his name, and a display of Farnham's letter in Monterey would have been sufficient to accomplish that. The precious letter would then have been placed among his papers and later burned with the rest in the housecleaning of the 1930's. Had the *Californian* remained in Monterey, the news would probably have appeared in it, but the newspaper was then in San Francisco and occupied with other affairs.

But no matter how we rationalize it, the fact remains that not a scrap of contemporary evidence has been found to show that the case of *Garner* v. *Farnham* was ever decided legally.

108. Monterey County Archives, XIV, 441–444, 449, 575, Mortgages, Book A, p. 61.

winter rains ceased and the snow melted. Farther south yet, lay the untouched gorges of the Tuolumne, the Merced, the Chowchilla, the Fresno, and the Kings rivers, each with its scores of feeder creeks. To the first trader in this virgin territory the profit would be enormous.

Garner intended to be that first trader. From past expeditions chasing horse-stealing Indians, he knew the country east of the Tulare swamps. As his son José ingenuously phrased it, Garner determined "to make a trip south of the Tuolumne River to conquer the wild Indians and see if they had any gold." [109]

William Garner may have had specific information about gold in the Kings River region. James Carson said that Garner invited him to be one of the party and that Tulare Indians from Mission San Miguel, acquaintances of Garner's, "had brought into Monterey large specimens of gold and reported it to have come from King's River and vicinity" and shown them to him. Carson, however, had already made the big strike at Carson's Creek in the "dry diggings." He intended to go back there, and it seemed to him that Garner's expedition was not strong enough to repulse a determined attack by Indians. All the tribes in the region where Garner intended to travel were part of the Yokut. They had learned to distrust and hate the Californians who had harried them for over forty years, killed their fighting men, and carried off their women and children to the pueblos and the missions. As Garner wrote in his letter of July 21, 1847, the Californians refused to work as servants, and Indian children were captured for this semislavery. The Yokut had become as aggressive as they were suspicious. For these reasons Carson declined the offer. Colton, too, was urged to go along and come back a rich man, but he was longing for his home and family, his passage was booked, and he did not accept. [110]

José Garner, then seventeen years old and a member of the party, gave his account of what happened on the journey when he was interviewed in 1878 (*San José Pioneer*, April 27). Carson gave some information in 1852 when it was fresh in his mind.

---

109. José Garner, "Obituary of William R. Garner — A Pioneer of 1826 — Sketch of his Life," *San José Pioneer*, April 27, 1878.

José's story is more complete, but Carson appears to have had access to at least part of the now lost journal that Garner kept.

It was Garner's plan to cross over to the Tulare Lake swamps from the upper Salinas Valley pass of San Miguel. He consequently made his base at San Luís Obispo; where he had friends — the two Scotch seamen John Wilson and James Scott. Captain Wilson had married the widow of Romualdo Pacheco and with Scott, owned the Rancho Cañada de los Osos and several others. His stepson, Romualdo Pacheco, the future governor of California, was a boy about José's age.

Garner was in San Luís Obispo in December 1848 to enlist friends from Indian-chasing days and to gather supplies. There is an item from Monterey, dated January 13, in the January 25, 1849, *Californian*, that he and Captain Wilson had returned to San Luís Obispo from Santa Barbara bringing news of the execution of the American toughs who had barbarously murdered the Reed family at San Miguel mission.

The people at San Luís Obispo were almost exclusively Californians. Their ranches took the brunt of the Indian thievery, but the American military government was not prepared to station a garrison in so isolated a place to shield them from attack. The Indian raids could not be ignored, however, and the authorities compromised by sending munitions for home defense. On March 21, 1848, Governor Mason forwarded twenty-five or thirty pounds of powder and the same weight of lead to Alcalde Price, telling him to form a posse of twenty-five or thirty good men to act in emergencies. When William Garner wrote to him on March 15, 1849, from San Luís Obispo asking for powder and shot to be used against marauders, the governor evidently suspected that he was stockpiling for his private expedition. In his reply on March 22 he told Garner that he had directed Captain Henry Burton to send him twenty-five pounds of powder and fifty pounds of lead, but he cautioned: "Distribute it to *farmers* and

110. James H. Carson, *Recollections of the California Mines*, p. 9; Colton, *Three Years in California*, p. 369.

such other persons who will use it *in a proper manner* for the protection and defense of the settlement." [111]

Garner had been in Monterey in February to make final preparations. Carson wrote that Garner "left Monterey the 1st of March with five or six ox wagons, with Indian drivers, and four Spaniards as companions." From the letters between Garner and Governor Mason, it is clear that Garner went to his staging area near San Luís Obispo, not immediately to the Kings River as Carson had believed. [112]

José's account has his father gathering a group of fifty Californians, including Romualdo and Mariano Pacheco, and starting for the gold regions in April. He does not mention the ox wagons. However, later he says that although the road gave out beyond the Salinas Valley, "Mr. Garner knew how to make his own road." There would have been no need to do this if only pack animals were involved, but José may simply have meant that his father knew the way and guided the rest. A year later, Lieutenant George Derby, on a reconnaisance around the Tulares, had very little trouble taking mule-drawn wagons over the same route. [113]

The cavalcade set out from San Luís Obispo and followed the well-used *camino real* up the long grade to Santa Margarita and then to the Rancho Atascadero. Eleven miles farther on, at Paso (de los) Robles, it turned east to the place called Estrella, then

---

111. Mason Correspondence (Mason to Price, March 21, 1848); U.S., President, *Message on California and New Mexico*, p. 896; Richard Barnes Mason, "Correspondence with United States Adj.-General Jones . . . on the Gold Discovery (1848)," House Executive Document No. 1, vol. I, 30th Cong., 2nd sess., 1848–1849, described the problems caused by the desertion of soldiers: "August 28, 1848 . . . I will find myself compelled to issue to the inhabitants arms and ammunition to defend their lives and property against the Indians."

112. Carson, p. 9.

113. George Derby, *Report of the Secretary of War Communicating, in Compliance with a Resolution of the Senate, a Report of the Tulare Valley, Made by Lieutenant Derby*, Senate Executive Document No. 110, 32d Cong., 1st sess. (Washington, D.C., 1852), pp. 5–9 with map. William Rich Hutton, *Glances at California, 1847–1853; Diaries and Letters* (San Marino: The Huntington Library, 1942), gives road from San Luis Obispo to Monterey; Victor Eugene August Janssens, *The Life and Adventures in California of Don Agustín Janssens, 1834–1856*, ed. William H. Ellison and Francis Price (San Marino: The Huntington Library, 1953), p. 146, gives the composition of Garner's party.

Yokuts Tule Lodges

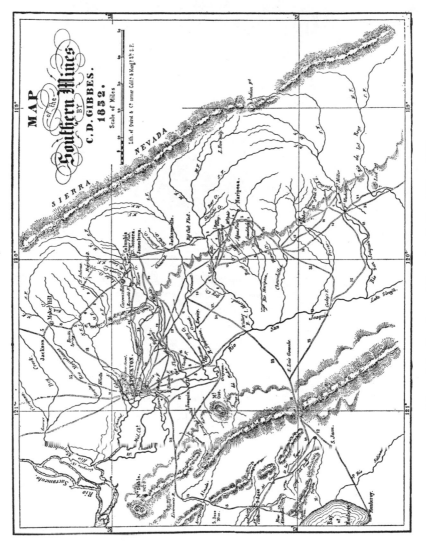

Map of the Southern Mines by C. D. Gibbs, 1852

up that stream and over the gentle San Miguel Pass to the great valley. Garner's party rode eastward along Cottonwood Creek and probably made camp at the sink of Avenal Creek on the edge of the barren ground between the low Kettleman Hills and the tule marshes.

From there it was a thirty-seven mile ride across the desert to the Arroyo San Cayetano (probably the present Deer Creek) on the other side of Tulare Lake and its swamps. The small party had crossed this morass on the hundred-yard wide ridge of sand that raised itself like a dike some ten feet high between the upper and lower lakes. The water was much lower than it had been ten years before, the receding levels marked by ledges of decaying tules and stinking mud.

It had taken them about five or six days to get to the eastern side of the Tulares. They now rode up the south bank of the Kings River until they came to some Indian settlements. Here Garner pitched camp for several days while the animals rested and he tried to find clues to new goldfields. The Indians offered no opposition to Garner's well-armed company, but they professed ignorance of the yellow metal. They suggested he question the villagers upstream and provided him with an interpreter. Leaving the bulk of his party in camp, Garner took five men and the interpreter into the mountains to a rancheria called Goshowu.

The Goshowu would not provide any information. Garner withdrew, but in a couple of days he returned with twenty men to break their resistance. When Garner's party arrived at the rancheria, the Indians fled. José said that the huts were burned, but he does not make it clear whether it was done by the fleeing Indians or by the Californians. No gold could be found in the smoking ruins, and the Indians could not be coaxed back. The expedition returned to camp empty-handed.

In such a hostile atmosphere it was useless to try to trade. Abandoning their camp, the party crossed the Kings River and traveled northward through the foothills. They forded two or three creeks tumbling with snow-water and finally reached the San Joaquin River where it emerged from the mountains. Wading and swimming their horses, the gold hunters crossed the icy stream and again rode north. On the night of May 14, 1849, the weary company made camp on the Fresno River at the foot of the hills.

Carson, Garner's last journal in hand, writes that the party was met here the next morning by "Indians in large numbers from the mountains, who displayed large quantities of gold; they refused to trade with him unless he came to their settlements; they having every mark, apparently, of friendship for him."[114] Garner did a brave but foolish thing. He took only seven men and some pack animals laden with merchandise and followed the well-marked trail upstream toward the village of the Chowchilla.

This tribe was not unknown to history. In April 1828 Sebastian Rodríguez, hunting them down with a troop of rancheros from San Juan Bautista, sent Simeón Castro and thirty-three men to attack their village and carry off the women and children. Castro exhausted his horses in the chase, but he caught not one person. Forewarned, the Indians had fled deeper into the Sierras out of reach of the slavers. In the twenty-odd years since, the Chowchilla had continued to eat horses, and from their rugged hills, they raided the California ranchos with ever-increasing boldness.[115]

According to José, his father went one day's journey into the canyons; Carson says two days and quotes the last entries from Garner's journal:

We have travelled about twenty miles today, the number of Indians around us have increased every hour for the last three days, and now number over a thousand — most of them have gold which is generally coarse, and to my enquiries of them where they obtained it, they pointed to the Eastward. There is a great stir among the Indians, and their squaws and children have left. I have now the greatest fears for my safety.[116]

At this point José takes up the story's thread:

This was on the 15th of May, 1849. They arrived at the settlement that day; the Indians showed some hostility, and as the men were passing by their

114. Carson, p. 9.
115. Sherbourne F. Cook, ed., *Expeditions to the Interior of California, Central Valley, 1820–1840*, University of California Anthropological Records, 20 (1962), 5. See also below, Garner's letter of Dec. 9, 1846, note 1.
116. Carson, p. 9.

The Attack

huts, one of them spoke to Mr. Garner, calling him by name. It was an
Indian named Ventura, that he had raised at Monterey.

While in conversation with this Indian, Mr. Garner was shot in the fore-
head, and upon turning to go to his companions, he was shot several times
more. A general war followed, which resulted in the killing of Mr. Garner
and six of his men.

The survivor stumbled into camp the next day with news of the
disaster, and there was a scramble to get out of the mountains
and down to the open plains to the west. That night, José remembers, Colonel John Frémont and fifty or sixty men encamped
within a hundred yards of the demoralized rancheros. Actually,
Colonel Frémont was in Monterey at that moment, but the newcomers were his men. The colonel had decided to work his Mariposa land grant before the tide of prospectors descending from
the Stanislaus diggings should preempt his claim to it. He had
contracted with a large group of experienced Mexican *gambusinos*, or prospectors, from the mines of Sonora to take out on a

fifty-fifty basis what gold might be found on his property. Alexis Godey, his dashing guide on the famous explorations, had been sent ahead to the Mariposa to manage the first fifty Sonorans to arrive. It was Godey and this crew José saw.[117]

The orphaned boy took his friend Romualdo as interpreter (for José could not speak English then) and hastened to Godey to beg assistance. Godey refused, saying that he himself had been up there before and had had to retreat. "He said that the best thing they could do was to leave the place, which they did." Godey's rebuff seems cold-blooded. But he had an errand to fulfill and the less attention he aroused the better.[118] At that moment, he and the *gambusinos* were heading straight into those hills to make good Frémont's claim to his enormous and ill-defined land grant. An invasion of the territory by revenge-seeking Californians might have caused an Indian war and disrupted Godey's mission. It also might have led to a gold strike, and Frémont would then have had to whistle for his legal mineral rights against a horde of heedless gold panners. As it was, although Frémont did develop his mines first, he had to defend them with arms and lawsuits when his property was overrun the following year.

José returned sadly to Monterey. Walter Colton notes the news of Garner's death in his diary on May 22;[119] José probably reached home on that day or the previous one, and Colton would have been among the first to be informed. It was not until June 2, however, that Major Edward R. S. Canby, Assistant Adjutant General at the capital, sent orders to Lieutenant Clarendon J. L. Wilson of the 1st Dragoons to ferret out the murderers of Mr. Garner and his companions. On June 11 General Bennett Riley, who had relieved Colonel Mason as military governor of Califor-

---

117. Crampton, "Mariposa Mining Region," pp. 37–38.

118. Godey was referring to the series of fights Frémont's party had with the Yokut Indians in the same foothills during the explorations of December 14, 1845, to January 14, 1846. See John C. Frémont, *Memoirs of My Life, Including in the Narrative Five Journals of Western Exploration, during the Years 1842, 1843–4, 1845–6–7, 1848–9, 1853–4*, vol. I (Chicago, 1887), p. 447.

119. "Mr. Garner is now dead: it was his melancholy fate to fall with five others

nia, reported the tragedy to Washington and made the interesting comment that the slaying was done "as is stated by the Indians, to revenge themselves for the aggressions committed by Americans upon the Indians of the Sacramento; indicating an evident understanding between different tribes speaking different languages and separated by a distance of two hundred and fifty miles." [120]

The "evident understanding between tribes" to resist the devastating flood of gold hunters may be largely discounted. News of the brutal slaughter to the north may have alarmed and angered the Chowchilla, but they needed no extra incentive to revenge themselves on the hated rancheros. Once peaceful hunters and seed gatherers, these Yokut had been forced to become cunning warriors and hard-riding raiders. It was probably the weakness of Garner's little group far from the main body, the lure of the goods spread out for barter, and the unparalleled opportunity to take him by surprise that tipped the scales toward the attack.

It has never been determined with certainty who Garner's killers were. There is no record of execution of anyone. Some time after Major Canby had ordered pursuit of the Indians, José met Lieutenant John Hamilton. This officer told him that he had been to the spot where José's father was killed. He, too, had clashed with the Indians and lost some men, but he had held his ground and given decent burial to William Garner and the other slain Californians.

Carson blames the "Chowchillas, Chowochicimnes & Kaweeahs — the most thieving, treacherous and blood-thirsty tribes of the Tulares." [121] Lieutenant George Derby, on a mapping expedition to the Tulare area in May 1849, wrote:

---

by the wild Indians on the river Reys. To that party I should have been attached had I remained in California another month. How narrow those escapes which run their mystic thread between two worlds! On the grave of my friend, gratitude for important services, and a remembrance of many sterling virtues, might well erect a memorial." Colton, *Three Years in California*, p. 369.

120. U.S., President, *Message on California and New Mexico*, pp. 913, 915–917.
121. Carson, p. 13.

I was informed by Col. Hampton at the upper ferry (on the Kings *River*) that the Cho-e-minee rancheria, situated in his vicinity and numbering about ninety warriors, had been quite troublesome of late, using his horses without permission and on one occasion attempting to take his boat. . . . On my return to camp I found a party of Indians armed with bows and arrows . . . had stopped at the ferryman's hut and told the occupants they must leave that part of the country in four days. . . . It was this band that murdered Garner and his companions in 1849.[122]

It is difficult today to locate the site of the rancheria of Chowchilla, but the upper reaches of the Fresno River, probably saw the last act in the eventful life of William Robert Garner. His graves lies lost there still.

The husband and father gone, the Garner family lost the land and the position he had toiled so long to achieve. James McKinley, Garner's oldest friend, was named administrator and guardian for the minor children: Guadalupe, born 1834, Ignacio, born 1839, and Clotilda, born 1846. In December 1850 McKinley withdrew, and the court appointed a prominent Monterey merchant, Milton Little, in his stead.

Soon Little had to sell a town lot at the angle of Alvarado and Calle Principal to maintain the widow and her family. Another lot of forty-four yards frontage on Larkin Street went next, then one of fifty-one feet on Van Buren Street, then another on the same street, and finally one near the Custom House. The Rancho San Francisquito, 8,813 acres, went under the auctioneer's hammer for $12,000 in 1853 to Louis Belcher, a speculating lawyer called The Big Eagle of Monterey. Not all the money went to the heirs; the two oldest boys, José and Manuel Garner, had already sold their portions to José Ábrego, and he received 32/50ths of the proceeds.[123]

The Garner adobe and the spacious lot on which it stood were set aside from the general unloading as a home for Mrs. Garner and her children. In the early 1850's she married Manuel "Chanate" Castro and started a new family, the older children scattered,

---

122. George Derby, *Report*, pp. 5–9.
123. Probate of estate of William Robert Garner, Monterey Courthouse.

and the memory of tall, blond William Robert Garner, sailor turned ranchero, lumberman, sheriff, writer, and Argonaut faded into legend.

Even the historic old adobe homestead is now gone. The only things that endure of William Garner are the letters he wrote so hopefully in 1846–1847. They alone survive.

William Robert Garner

etters from
California
1846-1847

"But westward look, the land is bright!"

OCTOBER 1846

October, 1846[1] — Just as I was finishing my last letter to you, a Mexican gentleman, who is one of the most prominent persons in favor of the American cause, stepped into my house, and seeing a number of papers on the table, asked to whom I was writing. I told him I was giving my American friends some information on the state and prospects of California. His first words were, "For God's sake, let our American friends know that we want some person here who knows how to make blankets; the winters here are chilly and raw, and I cannot find where to buy a blanket."

This may appear to you and your numerous readers as something incredible, in a country like this, where sheep are so plentiful, and where it costs nothing to breed them and keep them, but a boy and a dog; but I can assure you that there is not, neither has there ever been, a man in this country who knew how to weave a blanket.[2] It is true that they make here a sort of rug; but even of these there are not sufficient made to supply one-twelfth part of the population. The blankets chiefly used in this country

---

NOTE: Garner's letters have been transcribed verbatim from the original newspapers, except for obvious typographical errors caused by line breaks. See Table of Contents for publication dates.

1. The *Journal of Commerce* prefaced Garner's letter with this statement: "We have received from an old resident in California a voluminous correspondence extending from October to the 23 of January. Being chiefly occupied with the events of the California revolution, or conquest, as the case may be, most of the details have lost their interest by delay. Such as have not, we proceed to lay before our readers."

2. Garner is talking about a close-woven, fine-combed blanket — not a coarse *serape* or the weaving of cloth by Indians at the missions — and the refusal of the non-Indian Californians (*gente de razon*) to engage in the industry.

come from Tepic, in Mexico, and are sold at from ten to ninety
dollars each. What enhances the price of these blankets, is their
color; a few red or blue spots, with a border, will make one of
these blankets sell for almost any price.

Common to second-best cloth has always been worth from
twelve to fourteen dollars a yard, and the tailors charge eighteen
dollars for making a coat and furnishing the plainest trimmings.
Common wool hats are worth here, among the natives, who
prefer them to all other kinds, eight dollars apiece. Wool stockings of the coarsest kind are one dollar and twenty-five cents per
pair.

It has been fairly proved that the sheep of this country need
nothing but a little care and attention to produce wool of the
finest quality. Another great advantage is, there is no sickness
amongst them ever known of any kind whatever.[3]

Should any of your readers be weavers who wish to make an
independent fortune, I would advise them to fly to California,
where there is little doubt of their soon accumulating one to their
satisfaction.

Having employed some men to quarry stone a few days ago, I
went to see how the work went on. They had quarried about
eight feet deep; in going into the quarry, I perceived a sort of

3. Some sheep were always raised: Mission-made cloth had to be used at the
presidios by government decree, and Governor Borica ordered each settler at
San Jose in 1797 to keep three sheep for each head of larger livestock. However,
sheep raising was never popular on the ranchos. Reliable herders were hard to
find, sheep needed too much care — especially at lambing and shearing times —
and were easy prey. After secularization of the missions took full effect in 1835,
when the Indian laborers left, the wool industry declined rapidly. Production
dropped so low that blankets became one of the main articles of trade brought by
the New Mexican horse buyers in the 1830's and 1840's.

The usual breed was the *churro*, a hardy but small, long-legged and rangy sheep
with rarely more than two or two and one-half pounds of long, coarse, straight
wool. After 1800 some efforts were made to improve the breed by introducing
the merino, a sheep with superior wool, but the churro remained dominant until
long after the American conquest. See Levi Turner Burcham, *California Range
Land*, Sacramento: State Printing Division, 1957.

4. There were two main quarries from which old Monterey drew its rock.
The granite quarry from which the stone was taken to fill the cribs that Garner
furnished for Larkin's wharf in 1845 can still be seen. Local potters have experi-

Fuller's earth. I ordered one of the men to dig a little deeper, and to my great satisfaction discovered a stratum of potter's clay, of the finest kind. There is not a particle of grit in it. In rubbing it between my hands, it felt like soap.[4]

Like all other manufactured articles, all the crockery ware used in California has come from the States; and the family which can boast of a full set of good crockery is to be considered almost a prodigy. This scarcity of all sorts of manufactures, we hope will in a short time be remedied. Should the United States retain California (which is not to be doubted), here is room and opportunity for thousands of mechanics and artisans to enrich themselves.

About a fortnight ago a new coal mine was discovered, situated in or near the mission of San Luis Obispo. This article was sold here last year for five dollars a bushel by an American whaler. There are no less than three coal mines within a distance of three hundred miles or less, but such business as this, like many other branches in California, requires a capital to put it in operation, and there are no capitalists in California. If there were, they would not risk their money in this branch of business, because there are no persons here that understand it, or anything else that requires practical knowledge.[5]

---

mented with a clay found there and assure me that it bears out Garner's contention, but the deposit does not seem large enough for commercial purposes.

The other quarry, about two miles southeast of town at the base of the hills, provided the soft, yellowish-white sedimentary rock called "chalk rock" or "Carmel stone." Josiah D. Whitney, *Geology: Report of Progress and Synopsis of the Field-Work from 1860 to 1864*, Geological Survey of California, vol. I (Philadelphia, 1865), pp. 160–166. Colton Hall (built 1847–1849), is made of this rock, as are the foundations of most of the substantial adobe homes and garden walls in the Monterey area.

5. Low-grade bituminous or lignite coal is not uncommon in the Coast Ranges. Near Monterey, coal has been found not far from Point Lobos. "I am informed by Don Jose Rafael Gonzales that on his Rancho sixty or eighty miles south of Monterey there are coal mines. At San Pablo there are others" wrote Larkin on May 2, 1846 (*Larkin Papers*, IV, 356).

The veins in Slack Canyon, Stonewall Creek, Garapata Creek, and Mal Paso Creek were first worked seriously in 1873–1875. The coal was hauled to Monterey by wagon and shipped to Santa Cruz and San Jose. By 1890 commercial mining at these sites had closed.

Even shoes are obliged to be brought from the States before we can go out-of-doors. Norwithstanding that ox-hides are sold here for a dollar and fifty cents each for cash, or two dollars in barter, you cannot buy, one-half the time, in any part of California, as much leather as will sole a pair of shoes; and when, at some singular time they can be bought, shoes cost from three to four dollars a pair. Still, ox-hides can be taken from California to America, and the same hides there tanned and dressed, and made into shoes, and then brought out again around Cape Horn, a distance of ten thousand miles, and an importation duty paid on them of at least one dollar per pair, and after all this trouble and expense, they are sold here at the same price as those manufactured in the country, and very frequently, from twenty-five to fifty per cent less.

Any person not acquainted with California, or the manners and customs of the inhabitants, will naturally inquire the cause of this. I answer, the want of industry on the part of the people, and the want of encouragement on the part of the government. Whoever lives to see California in the hands of the Americans for the space of ten years, will be able to more than prove whatever I have advanced in its favor.

We now entertain the most sanguine hopes that a conclusion will speedily be put to the war now existing between Mexico and the United States, and that the government of the latter will be firmly established in this country.

Should this be the case, what an amazing field for enterprise will California hold out! At present there is not a yard of tape, a pin, or a piece of domestic cotton or even thread, that does not come from the United States of North America; and this in a country where everything connected with their manufacture can

---

From San Luis Obispo southward there were large asphaltum or petroleum seeps. The coal mine referred to by Garner was probably one of these bituminous shales on the rancho of his friend Captain John Wilson, very near San Luis Obispo; see Whitney, *Geology*, p. 142.

6. Thomas Larkin, the American Consul, wrote in his 1846 report: "The climate of California is surpassed by no other. The lowest rate of the Thermometer in the shade in Monterey in 1845 was 44, the highest 86. From 60 to 70 is the com-

be procured with less trouble and expense, on account of the superiority of the climate, than in any other part of the American continent.

What in California is called winter, would in most parts of the United States be termed the middle of spring. Here are no snows, that is to say, none which lie twenty-four hours on the ground, unless it be on the summits of the mountains. In twenty-two years' residence in California, I have never seen on the plains or lowlands the snow last long enough for the boys to gather a snowball. What little snow does fall melts immediately on its reaching the earth. As another proof of the mildness of the winters in this country, I must inform you that such a thing as a chimney or a fireplace in houses, was never known until within a few years. They were introduced by foreigners, and not so much from necessity as luxury.[6] The rains in the winter are heavy, and generally last from the middle of December to the end of February or the middle of March, during which time the earth imbibes sufficient moisture to promote the growth of all vegetable matter. When the weather has been what is here called severe, the travelling is very bad. On account of the country being so thinly populated, the roads are nothing more than beaten tracks, and in most parts of the country, the traveler must be very careful not to let his horse leave those tracks, or he will immediately sink into the ground above his knees, and often in such a manner as to make it difficult to extricate him.

Here are no bridges. In the rainy season, that which in the summertime is nothing but a small creek or rivulet, will increase with the freshets to an inconceivable degree; so much so, that they become quite impassible for a few days; but the country being somewhat mountainous, these rivers soon subside, though the

---

mon rates throughout the year" (*Larkin Papers*, IV, 310). Larkin's house, built between 1835 and 1838, was the first to have an indoor fireplace. Garner's last letter, also to the *Journal of Commerce*, a year later repeats many of the subjects covered in this first and closes: "now every house that is built has one or more fire-places in it. . . . Although the winters are not so severe here as they are in the United States by many degrees, still a fire is as requisite here as there. At all events the late comers find it so." See below, October 10, 1847.

passage still remains difficult on account of the mud which remains on each side of the stream.

The French Consul, Mr. Moerenhout, has been ordered by Col. Fremont to leave the town, for having attempted to uphold a false claim, made by one of the countrymen on the American government.

It appears that a Frenchman residing in Monterey, by the name of Clement Panaud, had by some means obtained a passport to go to the town of San José, where he had some property, which he was going to bring into Monterey, and an order had been issued by the Military Commandant of this place, prohibiting any person whatever from carrying arms, unless he was in the service of the United States. As Panaud was seen by a party of Americans, with a pair of pistols, he was arrested, his pistols taken from him, and his horses and saddles were likewise taken possession of by the American party. Panaud came into Monterey and made his complaint to the French Consul, and, as is supposed, was persuaded by that gentleman to bring in a claim against the American government to an extraordinary amount; it appears, however, that the French Consul made no inquiry into the justice or injustice of Panaud's claim, but immediately wrote an official letter to Capt. W. A. T. Maddox, Commandant of the middle department of California, demanding immediate satisfaction. At eleven o'clock this morning, Panaud was called before the civil Magistrate, Walter Colton, Esq.,[7] and on the claim which had been handed in by the French Consul being shown him, and his being asked if that was his claim against the American government, he said yes, it was. He was desired to swear to the truth of the statement of the property lost. He asked leave to go out of

---

7. The American alcalde, for whom Garner was secretary.

8. The other side of the Panaud affair is presented in the correspondence of French Consul Jacques Antoine Moerenhaut with the French minister of foreign affairs: "The French Consulate in California: 1843–1856: The Moerenhaut Documents," ed. Abraham P. Nasatir, *California Historical Society Quarterly*, XII (1933), 170–171. Maddox had given Panaud the pass. The Americans were from Frémont's volunteer forces, who were searching the country for horses and saddles. After Consul Moerenhaut's protest to Maddox the pistols were returned, but Frémont would not give back the horses or even a receipt for them. When Moeren-

the court for a quarter of an hour, that he might compare the account with his book. He was told that he might send for his book, or any thing else that he might require to make good his claim, and prove the legality of it. After vacillating a few moments, he said he would abandon the whole claim made by the French Consul in his behalf. On being asked if he wished to do so voluntarily, he said he did. He accordingly gave a certificate to the magistrate to that effect.

The truth is, he found himself unexpectedly in a bad scrape, and saw at once the impossibility of making his claim good. He had put down in his account, 300 arrobas of tallow, at $5 per arroba, when it was not worth more than $1.50 all over California; and everything else in proportion. The amount of his claim was nearly $7,000.[8]

This country is now opening a field for all sorts of enterprise; not only for male persons, but for females also. In the first place, there is not such a thing, all over California, as a hired female servant. The only female servants which the supervisory classes of the people have been able to procure are Indians, which have been brought wild from the mountains in their infancy. These remain in some houses until they arrive at the age of twelve or fourteen years, when they are almost sure to run away; and as none have been brought into the settlement for some time past, there are very few families now, who have any servants at all. A California woman, though she may be naked and cold, will not enter into regular service. They think it a degradation, and many of them will rather sacrifice their virtue, than enter into any kind of regular servitude.

Neither are there any tradeswomen in California of any class

---

haut persisted, Frémont threatened to send him to San Francisco; Panaud was sent to Alcalde Colton to lodge his complaint. There, says Moerenhaut, "because of a slight error in his accounts, he [Colton] intimidated him and made him sign a statement renouncing all claims for indemnity. On this condition, he was given a permit to go to San José . . . and a receipt for the horses taken from him." Moerenhaut's mention of the "slight error" throws his case away. Panaud, however, fared better than many victims of Frémont's scroungers; he, at least, got a legal receipt for his animals.

whatever. Most of them are pretty good seamstresses, but charge most unreasonable prices for their labor. They will not make a shirt of the coarsest kind under one dollar; and then they must be found in needles and thread. For washing they charge a shilling for each piece, and some of them make considerable money by this occupation, but they are very extravagant. The washer woman must have as many and as rich dress as the person she washes for, or she would feel debased in her own eyes. However, economy is contrary to all the ideas and customs of a Californian, whether male or female. The latter, as the former, would rather have two dollars to spend today, than ten dollars to lay by tomorrow.

The females, as well as the males, are very healthy and robust people, and mostly live to a great age. Their fecundity is extraordinary. Those instances are very rare, where a female does not have a birth within each two years after her marriage, and many of them have a birth every year. There are now no less than three women in this town who have had a birth every year since their marriage; and they have all been married twenty years or more each. I have no doubt, on the whole, that all women who have been married within the last twenty years in California would average each the birth of a child every fifteen months.[9]

The same cannot be said with regard to idleness of the females, as may with much truth be said of the men. The women are always occupied in some useful employment, either in their houses or out of them, and do a great deal more service in their families than the men; and there are many women in all parts of this country, who actually maintain their husbands and their children by their own personal labor; the husband acting as a mere cypher in the family, when he does not, by all the dis-

---

9. Bancroft (*California Pastoral*, pp. 312, 613–615), after checking the records, calculates that a California family had an average of ten children. As Garner says, not a few had twenty to twenty-five. Births outran deaths three to one, except among the Indians. Juana Cota left five hundred descendants. Secundino Robles' wife had twenty-nine children; José Antonio Castro's wife had twenty-six. Mrs. W. E. P. Hartnell (born María Teresa de la Guerra) bore twenty-five children and was an accomplished hostess and *grande dame*.

honorable means in his power, try to deprive his wife of her hard-earned dollars, to carry it to the gambling table, or the tavern. This, in a great measure, is the reason, and has been for years, that many women have sacrificed the connubial bond, which is very rarely the case where the husband behaves to his wife as all husbands ought to behave.[10]

---

10. See the biography above, and footnote 39 for the rash of divorce actions — including one brought by Mrs. Garner.

NOVEMBER, 1846

November 1, 1846

To the Editors of the North American:

Gentlemen: — In wishing to give you all the true information in my power respecting California, I cannot avoid mentioning its productions of many various kinds of exquisite fruits. In fact, California from one end to the other, is capable of being metamorphosed into a perfect orchard.

There are twenty-one Missions in Upper California, and each of them have one or two large orchards, consisting of from four to ten acres of land. All of these orchards are full of fruit trees, of different kinds and classes, and not withstanding they have had no care taken of them for the last six or eight years, (many of them are not so much as fenced in) still they yield fruit in abundance, and to my certain knowledge, not one of these fruit trees have been pruned, or attended to in any manner whatever (unless to strip them of their fruit) for the space of ten years.

Besides the orchards, which contain apples and pears of various kinds, peaches, pomegranates, plums, nectarines, and in the more southern part of the Territory, oranges in abundance. They have each, with the exception of two missions, one or two large vineyards, which produce both the blue grape and the Muscatel in the highest perfection; the vines some individuals take the trouble to prune every year, and in the month of September gather the rich clusters, which very amply rewards them for their trouble.

Santa Barbara, though the soil is not so fertile as the more northern parts, is a complete garden, almost every house having its orchard, and most of them a vineyard; the town of the Angels surpasses Santa Barbara in its productions of fruits, on account of the facility with which it can be watered. The same may be said of the *Puebla de* San Jose, except where vineyards have been spoken of.

Gooseberries and currents can scarcely be said to have been introduced into this country, there being as yet but a very few vines, which are in the possession of one or two private gentlemen, who are cultivating them with great care; perhaps they do not amount to thirty bushes or vines in all California. Like most other things, with a little industry, intelligence and care, California would be one of the first fruit countries in the world.

Here are likewise sylvan fruits in abundance, such as raspberries, strawberries, whortleberries, blackberries and various others, which in many parts are highly flavored. In short, I verily believe that from the general fertility of the soil, and the difference of climate, that almost every kind of fruit may be produced and brought to perfection in this country; because what one part of it will not produce, another part will.

November 2, 1846 — The Californians are acting most destructively on the farms; there is not at present a single farm between Santa Barbara and Monterey, that has one horse left to look after their stock. The depredators stop all carts and persons they find on the road, and plunder them; there are about thirty or thirty-five of them scouring within ten leagues of this town, but as yet there are no means of going after them, for want of horses. Col. Fremont has about three hundred horses here, but they are in such poor condition that not twenty would travel thirty miles, and his own horses are not yet arrived from the Sacramento.[1]

---

1. The French consul wrote in a Nov. 22, 1846, dispatch:

From the day after receiving the news that M. Fremont was aboard the *Sterling*, the Americans began to take horses and saddles from the people of the country and even from foreign residents at Monterey and environs. The same orders have since been given at San Francisco and surrounding towns with the

Yesterday, having sent his horses out to graze, one of the men remained some distance behind the party and fell in with two Californians, who kept him in conversation until they got some distance from the town, and then asked him to allow them to look at his rifle; the man at first refused, when one of them took hold of the rifle and dragged the man off his horse, and whilst he was in the act of remounting, the man who held the rifle deliberately shot him. The ball went through the thigh and the man fell; he remained on the spot about two hours, when some of his companions fell in with him, one of whom came into town to report what had happened, and take an escort to bring in the wounded man, the rest of the men remaining by him in the mean time.

This action has exasperated Colonel Fremont's riflemen to an almost uncontrollable degree. How many innocent men will eventually suffer for it, it is hard to say, but we already daily see some innocent persons suffer considerably in the loss of his property, for the actions of some foolhardy villians. Should this insurrection last two months longer at this time of year, it will injure the prosperity of California to an incalculable degree.[2]

The rains have set in, emigrants without provisions are daily arriving, troops are on shore in each town, and the inhabitants are getting pretty numerous, and there are no provisions in the

---

object of forming a mounted force with the riflemen of M. Fremont. By this means they assembled in a few days two to three hundred horses, and on October twenty-eighth about sixty riflemen, fairly well mounted, left Monterey to go to the nearby farms to raise the remaining horses and saddles. . . . Already the rebels, seeing that the Americans took horses even from the people who had remained with them, seem to wish to forestall them [by seizing] the horses which still remain. (Moerenhaut, "The French Consulate," p. 167)

2. Colton, *Three Years in California*, gives a less detailed story of the wounding of Frémont's horse guard (p. 83).

1. The kinds of manufactures ordered from the Sandwich Islands (Hawaii) and the markup are shown by an order from merchant Larkin (*Larkin Papers*, I, 207) of April 22, 1842: "I wish you would purchase in Oahu for me the following articles and I will pay you the cost and fifty pr cent on the same, I paying here also all duties you may pay. Zinc fifty to Eighty dollars worth with nails to suit; Round Iron for bars of Six windows; Flat Iron for the cross pces; 1 keg of spikes for 2 inch plank . . . nails . . . S. I. Moss for a bed or a large bed ready made; A bed for my son if he comes with you; 4 or 5 very large locks for the custom

country excepting beef. The Californians see this, and are aware that they now can get sale for their crops, and be paid in cash, and still they are so infatuated or so ignorant as to be running all over the country, without knowing for what, or with whom, at the very time when they might be sowing their grain, with every expectation of raising extraordinary crops, as the season appears to set in for plenty of rain, which is all that this country requires for its agricultural productions.

November 3, 1846 — An extensive commerce between this country and the Sandwich Islands has been opened within the preceding two or three years, but like every thing else here, it has not been carried on to one-fiftieth part of the extent it might be were the inhabitants inclined to industry.[1] Lumber is now annually shipped from this place to the Sandwich Islands; inch boards are sold here at fifty dollars per thousand feet, and all sorts of lumber from one inch thick upwards, at forty dollars per thousand, cubic measure; methinks I hear you say, what an enormous price! yet still, before timber began to be sawed here, which was in 1829, Boston ships used to sell the most ordinary kind of inch lumber from eighty to one hundred dollars per thousand feet.[2]

Now, sir, here is a country (the northern part of it) which produces a kind of timber, the easiest in the known world to

---

house. 3 do pad locks; 2 or 3 boxes sperm candles . . . 1 or 2 chains for hauling logs . . . 5 or 6 reflecting Candle Sticks; Set of Signs (handsome) for ball room; 50 or 60 dollars worth of sash, match, and moulding planes; 2 canton trunks, middle size, colour red or chocolate; Paper (handsome) for 1 room 6 feet high." (Punctuation added.)

2. Larkin's official report (*Larkin Papers*, IV, 305, dated April 20, 1846) states that in 1822:

An American Ship arrived from Boston, and prepared the way for the future trade which since that day has been carried on almost exclusively by New Englanders.

The present export of 1846 amounts to about eighty five thousand Hides, sixty thousand arrobas of Tallow, ten thousand Fanages of Wheat, one million feet of Lumber, some staves and shingles, ten thousand dollars worth of Soap, twenty thousand dollars worth of Beaver, land and Sea Otter Skins, one thousand barrels wine and aguadente, two hundred ounces of Gold worth seventeen dollars per ounce.

work, and in immense quantities. I mean what is here called red wood; it is a species of the pine, and grows at an average of two hundred feet high. This wood is not subject to the worms, perhaps on account of its bitterness, as I have heard some naturalists say; neither does it speedily rot. I have seen some of it taken out of the old buildings in the mission of San Carlos, which was built about 1775, and it appears in every respect as sound as the day it was hewn out of the tree. It makes most excellent shingles, perhaps the best in the world. The first houses that were shingled in California were shingled in the year 1831, and the shingles do not appear to be injured by time or the weather, even in the slightest imaginable degree; for house building it is invaluable.[3]

The other branch of commerce I mentioned in the beginning of this letter is soap; the ease with which it is manufactured in this country, and the execrable quality of it: its consumption and exportation are sufficient proofs of what the extension of this branch of commerce would be in the hands of industrious and intelligent persons. It is generally sold here at about fifteen dollars per cwt., and I have known a man with the help of two Indians, after having the lime ready, make one thousand dollars worth in twelve days. The cost of this would be about two hundred and fifty dollars — what an enormous profit! Still, this profit will not excite a Californian to constant labor. If he makes a thousand dollars in one month, or in one day, he will not go to work again until that thousand dollars is spent, and perhaps not until he has run himself one or two thousand dollars in debt. After this he goes to work, if at all with a bad heart, and it is ten thousand chances to one if ever he works that debt out. Rare is the instance in which the above remarks will not hold good.

November 4, 1846 — In searching among some documents in the Mission of San Carlos a few days ago, I found one relative to the

3. Garner gives a more detailed account in his letter of Nov. 25, 1846, below.

1. The cotton of which Garner speaks was probably introduced from Mexico by Franciscan missionaries as an experiment. In 1795–1796 the manufacture of cotton blankets and sheets was a principal industry at the missions of San Luis Obispo, San Gabriel, and San Juan Capistrano, but the cotton was imported from San Blas, Mexico. In 1842 José de Jesús Pico reported what were probably im-

productions of California. There are five articles mentioned in it, but neither of them have been brought to a conclusion; like almost every thing else, where the benefit and advancement of the country were concerned, they have been thrown aside after one or two hour's attention.

The first concerns the growth and manufacture of cotton. There is not the least doubt, that in San Diego, San Juan Capistram, San Luis Rey, San Gabriel and the town of the Angels, cotton might be cultivated with success, as I have seen it growing in an uncultivated state in or near each of these places. I have likewise seen this wild cotton gathered by the Indians, and taken to the Missions, where it was wove into a sort of coarse blankets. This circumstance alone, is a proof that the climate and soil in those parts above mentioned, are adapted to the growth of this article; what I have seen of it grows very thick, and the bushes close together; they run about eight or nine feet high, though generally speaking, not more than six feet, and the boll they produce is about the size of a small horse chesnut, which opens in the month of August or the beginning of September. Since the missions have been secularized, there has been no notice taken whatever of these wild cotton trees, and as lands have been granted, and cattle spread all over the parts of the country herein mentioned, there are very few traces of them left.[1]

The next article is on wool, for which this country and climate are particularly adapted, but having mentioned this article in a former letter to you, I shall not enlarge on it here, more than to state that with one-tenth part of the care, trouble, and expense with which this article is attended in almost any other country in the world, California would produce this commodity in an extraordinary degree, and I think I may affirm, that ten thousand dollars laid out in procuring a suitable tract of land, (of which there are many in this country) say two square leagues, and stock-

---

ported bales of cotton at San Luis Obispo. E. Philpott Mumford, "Early History of Cotton Cultivation in California: Researches Among the Old Spanish Manuscripts," California Historical Society *Quarterly*, 6 (1927), 159–166. Robinson (*Life in California*, p. 266) mentions that cotton as well as flax and hemp were grown to advantage.

ing it with three thousand sheep, would in the course of five years repay the cost ten fold. Mulberry trees a few years since were not known, some two or three were brought from Sonora and planted here, about twelve years ago; they bear well, but no person has taken pride in the cultivation of them, though from the experiment, there is not the least doubt of this country and climate being entirely adapted to the growth of this useful tree.

Of the silk worm I can say nothing, this animalculae not having come within the sphere of my observation.[2]

Bees have never been brought to this country, but I cannot but suppose both the country and the climate perfectly adapted to this insect, from the numberless classes of honey flowers with which the northern part of this country abounds.[3]

November 5, 1846 — The whole coast of California abounds in most exquisite fish, of many kinds, but although a small codfish, of which there are plenty all over the coast, sells for a dollar, still a meal of fish is very rare on shore; for no other reason but because no person will take the trouble to catch them; and I have known in time of lent, a small boat to go out fishing, and one hour after its return the owner of it has sold from twenty to thirty dollars worth of fish, and this after about seven hours' fishing.[1]

In the winter season, every rivulet that leads into the sea abounds in salmon, and salmon trout. Many of these are taken in nets, and they certainly are of the very finest kind. Here are

---

2. Silk was not destined to be a successful product of California, although valiant efforts were made on its behalf. Louis Prevost introduced mulberry trees in 1854 at San Jose to feed the worms from imported Chinese eggs. The eggs did not hatch. In 1860 some French eggs did hatch, and in 1863 the state legislature offered $100,000 to encourage new industries. In 1868 it gave $250 for every plantation of 5,000 two-year-old mulberry trees and $300 for every 100,000 usable cocoons. In 1870 there were 1,800,000 mulberry trees, and the Franco-Prussian War, hard times, and disease in the European industry augered well for California silk.

However, little silk came from California cocoons; mulberry trees and eggs were the main sources of income. The recovery of the French silk industry ended serious sericulture in California. By 1890 the local industry was dead. Nelson Klose, "Louis Prevost and the Silk Industry at San Jose," ibid., 43 (1964), 309–317.

3. The first domesticated honey bees were brought to San Francisco from New York via Panama in March 1853, by Thomas Shelton. His twelve hives dwindled

Hauling in the Seine. Salmon fishing on the Sacramento River

likewise numerous kinds of shellfish all along the coast, besides
hair seals, and the valuable sea otter;[2] and in the months of
September and October, a person may sit in the balcony of his
house in Monterey, and see the great whale killed, with all the
manoeuvres of the people employed in killing it, from the
moment of lowering the boats into the water, to their return to
the vessel, with the huge leviathan in tow.[3]

---

to one but recovered when he moved to San Jose. Shelton was killed in the explo-
sion of the steamer *Jenny Lind* in 1854, and two of the hives were sold for $215
to settle his debts. *Hutchings' California Illustrated Magazine*, April 1859, pp. 388–
392; *San Jose Pioneer*, January 27, 1877.

1. There are forty-nine species of "codfish" in Monterey Bay. Garner is probably referring to the ubiquitous rock-cod (genus *Sebastodes*).

2. The sea otter (*Enhydra lutris pereis*) was hunted so persistently in the
nineteenth century that it was driven to the verge of extinction. By 1925 the California sea otter was listed as extinct, but in March 1938 a small herd of the animals
was sighted near Monterey. Now a protected species, they are increasing in number.

3. Whaling and the supplying of whaleships was an industry of some importance to Monterey from 1822 to 1846, because the California coast was the winter
migration route of whales heading for the spawning grounds in the warmer
waters off Mexico. The return to the Arctic is made farther off shore. By the

Flax grows to an extraordinary length in this country. I have sown it several times in small quantities in a garden, and being well aware that the tilling and the ordering of it would be very profitable to any person who would undertake to cultivate it in a proper manner, I cannot but hope that some of the many emigrants who are daily arriving will place their particular attention on this branch of agriculture. The best time for sowing it, from San Luis Obispo to the northward, is in April; and in the middle of September the flax will be fit to pull. And the best manner of sowing it is in rows, about fourteen inches apart, and never dropping more than two seeds together; otherwise, when it gets an inch higher, it is necessary to thin it, by pulling up some of the stalks, which may be transplanted, and by these means produce flax equal, if not superior, to that of any other part of the world.[4]

California likewise abounds in game. Deer of different descriptions are plentiful in all parts of the territory. Elk, in the San Joaquin valley, are very numerous. The natives go out in the months of March, April and May, and lasso vast numbers of them. They are then very fat. As soon as the elk is caught and killed, they take off the hide and tallow. The former is tanned for shoe leather, and the latter is brought into the settlement, and used for making soap.[5]

Between the months of October and March, geese, ducks, curlew, &c., are to be seen in immense flocks, feeding on the plains, or darkening the air with their numbers.[6]

1850's the valuable sperm and right whales had almost disappeared from the area, and shore-based whaling for the more numerous gray, finback, humpback and sulphur-bottom whales was instituted in 1854 by Captain John Pope Davenport. By the 1870's the industry was failing, although whales were occasionally brought in. (Jack Swan, "Monterey in 1843 — By a Pioneer," *Monterey Weekly Herald*, August 1, 1874.)

4. Some Californians cultivated small patches of flax for making linen. Robinson, *Life in California*, p. 266, mentions it as a crop in the 1830's. Flax grew wild and untilled in the 1840's, and it was generally found in northern California. When mills for the extraction of linseed oil were established in the 1860's, flax raising came to have a modest importance, especially in the coastal areas of San Mateo and Santa Cruz counties. *Sacramento Reporter*, Aug. 16, 1870; John E. Baur, "California Crops That Failed," California Historical Society *Quarterly*, 45 (1966), 41–68.

The grisly bear is here to be found in all places where there is not much passing and repassing of human beings. They are not so dangerous as they have been represented. I have been a great deal among them, and I never saw a single instance of a bear having attacked a man, unless it had previously been molested, or it had been surprised on a sudden.[7]

November 6, 1846 — In the year 1825 California was overstocked with horses, and horned cattle, and sheep; and the natives considering horses of less value than sheep or horned cattle, killed off many thousands of the former that room might be left, and pasture for the other kinds. They would make large pens near some wood, and then twenty or thirty men would muster, and drive in horses and mares by hundreds, and after picking out such of them as they considered to be of the best quality, they lassoed and strangled the remainder.

In the year 1827, Captain Jedediah Smith came into this country overland from St Louis, and bought three hundred and ninety seven head of horses and mules, of the best kind that could be found in the country; and only one horse amongst them cost as high as fifteen dollars — the average price he paid for them was about nine dollars.[1]

In 1829 some New Mexicans came here, and bought many hundreds of mares, at the low price of fifty cents each, and among them were some very splendid animals; the following year the wild Indians began to steal horses from the settlements,

---

5. About three thousand elk and deer hides were exported annually at a price of fifty cents to one dollar each. Charles Wilkes, *Narrative of the United States Exploring Expedition During the Years 1838, 1839, 1840, 1841 and 1842,* V (Philadelphia, 1845), 158.

6. The flocks of wild fowl in the Salinas marshes were so vast that boys brought them down by throwing a cord weighted at both ends among them as they rose in flight. They were so common that an American officer who shot and presented wild geese to his hostess was considered stingy: domestic turkeys were much more costly. Hutton, "Two Letters on Monterey."

7. Garner's most famous letters are on the grizzly; see below, letters of Nov. 29, Dec. 1, Dec. 2, 1846.

1. Garner purchased many of the horses for Smith. See above, p. 17.

and between these, and the New Mexican traders, the settlements have been left literally without a horse to saddle.

But still, California, rich in all her productions, has a resource, which with some attention from government, may be made inexhaustible.

On the Tulares plains are numbers of wild horses and mares, I think I may say, without the least exaggeration, that I have seen on this plain in the course of two days' travel, forty thousand wild horses and mares, and amongst them are some as noble looking animals as ever I saw in my life. These for the last fifteen years have formed a complete nursery of horses for California.[2]

But the natives who have no forethought whatever, and have no feeling for dumb animals; if they are allowed by the authorities to act as they have been doing for the last ten or fifteen years, will soon destroy this whole race of useful animals. The people here form in parties of eight or ten men, and go and catch as many of these horses as they can; they are generally gone ten or fifteen days, and should they through mistake catch a mare, they immediately slaughter her from mere wantonness. And in the months of April and May, which is the time the mares are breeding, they very often start a band of from two hundred to a thousand head, and as they run them hard, the young colts are either trampled down, or left behind; and all those so left are killed in the night, by wolves or foxes; consequently it may easily be conceived how many hundreds of each year's breed are lost and destroyed in this manner.[3]

---

2. Garner's remarks on the teeming horse herds of the Tulares Plains, or San Joaquin Valley, are echoed by all contemporary travelers, as are his comments on the unpopularity of mares and on California horsemanship, below.

3. Although the best growing year California had between 1770 and 1864 was 1824–1825, the years from 1820 to 1832 were notable for drought. Along the coast, from San Francisco south, no rain fell for twenty-two months during 1828–1830. During this period forty thousand horses and cattle are said to have died, and to save pasture and water for the cattle and sheep, hundreds of mares were slaughtered by driving them over cliffs or by corraling them in box canyons. Bancroft, *California Pastoral*, p. 338; *Larkin Papers*, IV, 304.

Native Californians Throwing the Lasso

November 7, 1846 — In my last, I gave you some account of the manner in which the settlements in California are and have been for some time past supplied with horses, and knowing as I do, from experience, the value of this noble animal, and the usefulness of them, in this country in particular, I cannot dispatch this article without giving you some information of the reason why there is such a particular necessity for a great number of horses in this country.

In the first place, the whole territory is but very thinly settled; the grants of land which have been given by Mexico are very large, and it is often the case, that a man who lives on a farm will have to travel one or two hundred miles to purchase the actual necessitous clothing, or to sell his produce, which has all, or for the most part to be carried to market on horseback, on account of the badness of the roads; add to this, that all travelling has to be done on horseback, and as no provender of any kind is laid up by farmers here for winter food, the horses from September forward begin to lose their flesh, and by the latter end of November they are scarcely fit to travel at all; consequently, as things now stand, a man who lives a hundred miles from town, will need at least ten horses to carry him the journey.

A Californian will never ride a mare, unless he is actually drove to it by necessity; he thinks it a disgrace, and some years back, if a Californian had arrived at any farm with a tired horse, and his friend or countryman had offered him a fresh mare, that his own horse might be relieved and he pursue his journey, he would have looked upon the act as the greatest affront that could be put upon him, and I have many times known a man to defer his journey one or two days rather than ride a mare.

There were originally two distinct breeds of horses in this country, but for want of care, and curiosity, they have got so crossed and mixed up together, that they are not now distinguishable; though I have particularly observed that the best and the fleetest, as well as the handsomest horses in this territory, are those which have been caught wild after having come to their growth in the Tulare valley. I believe the reason of this to be, that those horses which are caught wild, have not been injured when very young, as those are which are bred in the settlements and on farms; these are greatly injured when young, by boys, who take every opportunity of driving them into pens to torment them with their lassoes, lassing their legs to throw them. &c. &c., and this is the reason that there are so very few horses of the age of six or seven years that can be found enterely sound.

Then their method of breaking them in likewise tends to break the spirit of the animals, and injure them in their joints. They will take a wild colt and put the saddle on it, and mount it, and ride it down; and when it is tired they take the saddle off it, and make it fast to a post, without any thing to eat, and keep it there for four or five days on nothing but water — saddling it two or three hours each day, at the end of which time they let it go. They are generally two years taming a horse.

November 8, 1846 — Perhaps there is no country in the world, generally speaking, where the inhabitants are so much on horseback, as in California, or where there are better riders — and it may almost literally be said that many of them are born on horseback, as I shall show in the sequel.

We may likewise almost say that they are married on horseback, for the day the marriage contract is agreed on between the parties, the bridegroom's first care is to beg, buy, or borrow, and sometimes steal, the best horse that can be found in his district; at the same time, by some of these means, he has to get a sac'dle, with silver mountings about the bridle, and the overleathers of the saddle must be embroidered. It matters not how poor the parties may be, the articles above mentioned are indispensible to the wedding.

The saddle the woman rides has a kind of leathern apron which hangs over the horse's rump, and completely covers his hinder parts as far as half way down the legs; this likewise, to be complete, must be embroidered with silks of different colors and gold and silver thread; from the lower part, upwards, it opens in six or eight parts, and each of these parts is furnished with a number of small pieces of iron or copper, so as to make a jingling noise

A California Party on a Picnic Excursion

like so many small cracked bells. I have seen one of these aprons with three hundred and sixty of these small jingles hanging to it.

The bridegroom must also furnish the bride with at least six articles of each kind of woman's clothing, and also buy up every thing necessary to feast his friends for one, two or three days, as the inclinations of the attendants invited or uninvited, may dictate.

The day being named for the celebration of the wedding, the two fine horses are saddled, and the bridegroom takes up before him on the same horse he rides, the godmother that is to be — and the future godfather takes before him on his horse the bride, and away they gallop to church.

As soon as the ceremony is over, the new married couple mount one horse, and the godfather and godmother the other horse, and they return to the house of the parents of the bride, where they are received with squibs, musketry, etc., and two persons station themselves at some convenient place near the house, and before the bridegroom has time to dismount these two persons seize him and take off his spurs, which they hold possession of until the owner redeems them with a bottle of brandy or a dollar.

The married couple then enter the house, where the near relations are waiting in tears to receive them; they kneel down before the parents and ask a blessing, which is by the parents immediately bestowed: all persons at this moment are excluded from the presence of the parties, and the moment the blessing is bestowed, the bridegroom makes a sign or speaks to some person near him, and the guitar and violins are struck up, and dancing and drinking is the order of the day.

The moment a child is born on a farm in California and the midwife has had time to clothe it, it is given to a man on horseback, who rides post haste to some Mission with the new born infant in his arms, and in company with the future godfather and godmother, who present it to a priest for baptism; this sacrament having been administered, the party return and the child may rest sometimes a whole month without taking an excursion on horseback, but after the lapse of this time it hardly escapes one day without being on horseback until the day of sickness or death.

Thus by the time a boy is ten or twelve years of age he becomes a good horseman, and it is difficult to get him to do any kind of work on foot, and almost any Californian would think less hard of riding one hundred miles than he would of working four hours on foot; add to this that most of the labor in California has necessarily been effected by means of men on horseback. The taking care of cattle and horses, lasting them, and going such long journeys as they are constantly obliged to travel, has made them expert horsemen to an extraordinary degree.

The horses themselves are of a hardy nature, as may be seen by the inhuman manner in which they are generally treated by the natives. If a man wants to travel from thirty to forty miles from his place of residence, he saddles his horse and mounts him; on his arrival at the town or place of destination, he ties him to a post; he may in some cases give him a drink of water, and should he remain away from home four or five days his horse gets nothing but water, without food all that time, and if he is a horse of the middling class of Californian horses, he will travel those thirty or forty miles back again with the same free gait at which he started on a full belly and good condition; of course this is only in the summer season when the grass has good substance and the horse is in good order.

I suppose this will hardly be credited by some of the farmers and horse jockeys in the United States, but it is nothing beyond the truth, and besides, a horse which completely equipped for a journey in this country generally carries besides his rider a weight of from fifty-five to sixty pounds of saddle gear, and should the weather be rainy and the saddle get wet, the weight is doubled. It requires two large tanned ox hides to fit out a Californian saddle, add to this the wooden stirrups three inches thick, the saddle tree, stout iron rings and buckles, with a pair of spurs weighing from four to six pounds, a pair of goat skins laid across the pummel of the saddle, with large pockets in them, and which reach below the stirrup, and a pair of heavy holsters with the largest kind of horse pistols, and I think it will be found I have

Vaqueros Lassoing Cattle by Charles Nahl

rather fell short than exaggerated in my statement of the weight which a horse in this country has to carry on a journey, notwithstanding they travel very freely and are active in their motions.[1]

November 9, 1846—The Californians here, to distinguish themselves from the Indians, style themselves *people of reason* (gente de razon) but a strict and impartial observer, would place both parties in many respects on an equality. I will state one or two instances that have happened, and of which I have been an eye witness in some of the circumstances.

Some few years ago an Indian blacksmith belonging to the mission of San Carlos, in company with about twenty more Indians, went to a farm which then belonged to the mission, and which farm I have since purchased, to gather acorns for a winter stock; the blacksmith, as he has since told me himself, was gathering acorns in a deep ravine, and in strolling from tree to tree he observed something rising out of the earth; he tried to gather some of it in his hand, but could not on account of its adhesion in all parts, and its being very hard. He then took an axe which he had with him, and by chopping and pounding got a piece of the substance separated from the mass. As it pleased his eye on account of its brightness, he carried it into the mission to shew it to the Priest; who on seeing it, asked the Indian where he had found it. The Indian pointed to the mountains that formed one side of the ravine, and the Priest told him he must never go there again, much less tell any person where the spot was; at the same

---

1. This letter is copied in whole sections by Colton in *Three Years in California* in his entries for Nov. 23, Dec. 4, and Dec. 9, 1846, pp. 102–104, 111–112, 116–117.

1. This may be the first mention of the legendary "Lost Mine of the Padres," which has kept prospectors burrowing into the rugged Santa Lucia Mountains; see Donald M. Craig, "Ghosts and Gold in Old Monterey," Monterey History and Art Association Quarterly *Noticias*, 9, 10 (Dec. 1965–Sept. 1966).

Gold has been found in small quantities in the Los Burros region southwest of Mission San Antonio since at least 1849, and there were mild flurries in 1854–1855. The Los Burros Mining District was organized in 1876, and Chinese were imported to work the gravels near Jolon for about two years. In 1887 gold was found in the same area, on Alder and Salmon creeks. The Manchester, Mars, King, and Grizzly mines produced ore valued at under twelve dollars a ton. The mines kept going in a desultory fashion, but activity has almost ceased. *San Francisco Alta*

time ordering him as he was a blacksmith, to make up the piece which he had procured into crosses, saying that as soon as they were made he would bless them and distribute them among the christians. The Indian did as he was ordered and the priest as he had promised.

This circumstance was told to me after I had bought the farm, and as soon as I had an opportunity, I sent for the Indian and inquired of him strictly where the spot was, but he never would tell, saying that the priest had told him that if he ever shewed the spot to any person his death would immediately follow. He held to this about a year. At last by threats and promises, and gifts, he agreed to go with me and shew me the spot, having previously pointed it out to me at a distance. We accordingly went, but when we arrived within two leagues of the spot he had pointed out, I took notice that he was all of a tremble. Judging from previous conversation with him the reason of this, I did all I could to inspire him with confidence, but in vain; he told me if he shewed me the spot he was sure of going to hell without ever reaching home again, that the priest had told him so, and he believed it; and neither threats, entreaties, or payment, had any effect on him. Consequently I and those who accompanied me, had a thirty mile ride for nothing.[1] There is another Indian living in Monterey who knows of a lead mine, and has twice brought me some ore, but nothing can make him tell where he gets it from.[2]

The people of reason are about as ignorant as the Indian above mentioned. Yesterday they went to church and had a raffle to find

---

California, Sept. 13, 1849; U.S. War Department, *Reports of Explorations and Surveys to Ascertain the Most Practicable and Economical Route for a Railroad from the Mississippi River to the Pacific Ocean*, 12 vols. (Washington, D.C., 1855–1860), VII, 48; Hoover, Rensch, and Rensch, *Historic Spots*, p. 279.

2. Silver was first found in northern California on the Alisal Rancho at the foot of the Gavilan hills about 1824, but the ore was mostly lead. The Arroyo Seco, or Tassajara Hot Springs, deposit was probably the object of Garner's quest and may be the one that Mariano Romero found and kept secret (Bancroft, *History of California*, II, 667). Whitney, *Geology*, p. 158, mentions that "small quantities of silver and silver-lead have been found at Arroyo Seco, but not in workable veins." As the *Monterey Weekly Herald* commented, "Rich silver mines are often talked of and expeditions fitted out to search for them, but they have never resulted in success" (Aug. 29, 1874).

out what man's soul should be prayed out of purgatory, of course
the fortune fell to a near relation of the man who wrote the bal-
lots and held the ballot box.

November 12, 1846 — Tradesmen of all kinds are very much
wanted in this country, and I would strongly recommend a large
number of them to emigrate here, for here there are next to none;
and those who are here, are mostly given to drunkenness, — or if
not, they invariably, after having been a short time in the country,
desert their trade and go to farming or speculating.

A tailor will charge twenty-four dollars for making a plain
frock coat, and finding trimmings; five dollars for the plainest
kind of pants, and every thing else in proportion. A blacksmith
(or a substitute for a blacksmith) will not work here unless he can
make from six to ten dollars per day, and even then, it often happens that the person who wants a job done, has to wait either
till some man who fairly knows how to strike a blow with a hammer, has time to get sober, or be in the humor to go to work.
There was a wharf partly built in Monterey last year, and a
crane put on it for hoisting bales, boxes, &c. An iron band was
required to go round the cap, in which the crane swung.[1] There
were then four blacksmiths in Monterey, and he who was considered the best workman, was engaged to weld this iron band,
which consisted of a piece of flat bar iron six feet long, four
inches and a half wide, and three quarters of an inch thick. On
asking the blacksmith what he charged to weld that band and
put it on the cap, he said six dollars per day; which was agreed
on. The job took the man six days to finish it. I mention these
incidents that your readers may plainly see the lack there is in
this country, of people who understand their trades, and the
opportunity it offers for their pecuniary advancement. There are
some few carpenters in the country, but they will not work day's
work. I have known some of them to make twelve dollars each
day when they thought proper to work, and *that* at the most ordi-

---

1. The crane with the cap in question may be seen on the wharf in the Hutton
sketch of Monterey used as the frontispiece.

nary kind of work. For instance, they charge eighteen dollars for making a panel door of the most ordinary kind, and of red wood, which is remarkably easily worked, and the same price for a pair of common shutters, made of the same wood. For making window sashes fifty cents for each pane the sash contains, and four dollars per square for laying a floor, if of red wood, and six dollars if of pine.

I could mention hundreds of instances of the same kind in all the various branches of trades; but let it suffice to say, that any tradesman, particularly one who is master of his business, who has a wish to emigrate to California, ought to do it without the least hesitation. There is no use in any man asking if such and such a trade will be advantageous to him in California; because no trade can be mentioned that is required in a civilized country, which is not requisite in California.

If a watch-chain should happen to be broken, the watch must be sent to the Sandwich Islands to be repaired, and the owner must wait six or nine months for his watch, and more than likely, when he gets it, it will be spoiled for ever.

November 13, 1846 — Having obtained a piece of quicksilver ore, I send it to you, as a specimen of the quicksilver mine now in operation in the Northern part of upper California. This mine is very rich, as you will perceive by the piece of ore I send you, which is by no means a selected piece, as it was the first I took hold of from a box full. All the stone contains quicksilver, but the richest parts are the red streaks which the stone contains. The experiment may be tried in the following manner. Take a piece of the stone, and beat it up very fine. Then take a piece of iron that is flat, the blade of a shovel for instance, and make it red hot. Then put the pounded ore on the shovel, and cover it over with a tea cup. The vapor will adhere to the cup, and with the finger this vapor may be gathered, when the quicksilver will be found by putting a piece of silver coin in the cup, or with the finger scraping the soot out of the cup upon a piece of silver.

But the best method is, take a gun barrel, and fill it with the ore beaten into pieces about the size of a small pea; keep the breech end of the gun barrel in the fire, and let the other end be immersed in a tub of water, — keeping a plate or basin in the water for the quicksilver to fall into, and likewise for the purpose of keeping it clean.

The quicksilver ore from this mine is procured with the greatest imaginable facility. You will perceive that the stone is easily broken, and from this you will form a pretty just calculation of the quantity of ore that may be procured in a day, either by one man or a hundred.

Notwithstanding the facility with which this mine may be worked, the owners of it have not as yet procured above two thousand dollars worth of the metal, owing to their slothfulness, and ignorance of every thing like labor. As this mine has never yet been properly explored, it is not known how far it may extend.[1]

Nature has been bountiful to this country in many wonderful ways, but her goodness has been disregarded by those who have held possession of it for so long a time. The reproductiveness of animals in this country is extraordinary; but indolence, carelessness, and the love of luxury, have within the last twelve years brought it almost into a state of desolation.

A farmer in California who may have for instance three thousand cows, considers that he ought to brand and mark during the season one thousand calves, allowing two thirds of the number he ought to brand, to be eaten by the wolves and foxes, which

---

1. The ore was probably from the New Almadén quicksilver mine. Long used by Indians as a source of paint, mercury was first mined there in 1824. Garner's description of the crude methods of extraction of the mercury reminds us that only in 1846 was this successfully accomplished.

The mine was owned by the British firm of Eustace Barron and Alexander Forbes & Company of Tepic, Mexico. When the quartz goldfields were discovered in 1849, mercury found a ready market as an aid in gold recovery. From 1850 to the present, 88 percent of all the mercury in the United States has come from California mines.

Many rival mines were attempted on neighboring properties, and the inevitable lawsuits followed, especially when the Land Commission to settle Mexican grant titles and boundaries met in 1852. The New Almaden Case is one of the most famous land cases in California and was not finally settled until 1874 before the Joint British and American Claims Commission in Geneva.

Fandango at the Village, Above the New Almaden Quicksilver Mines, Near San José

are constantly preying upon them. They lie about, watching for a cow to calve, when they immediately destroy the offspring. All the farmers are aware of this; still they take no steps to prevent it; except that about once in two or three years, some of them will procure poison, and mix it with the flesh of a dead horse or bullock, and scatter it about the farm. — They generally fix it in such a manner that it is certain death to any animal that eats of it.[2]

What I have said above, concerning a farmer's branding only one third as many calves as he has cows, is a general and established rule amongst all farmers in this country, and many of them do not reach that number.

November 15, 1846 — Mr. George Hastings arrived here at 4 o'clock this afternoon from the Pueblo of San Jose with a company of seventy-three men, to join Colonel Fremont in his expedition to the South; he likewise brought about 200 horses, and in pretty good condition.

The U.S. Frigate Savannah landed thirty men this morning, to remain here as a reinforcement to the commandant of this town. Col. Fremont has now about three hundred and forty or fifty men, and about eight hundred horses — but these are in a sorry condition, some of them die daily, being literally starved to death. The whole territory is now in a most pitiable state, both Americans and Californians having gathered into their possession all the horses they could find in the country. There is not a farm in the whole country at this present moment, that can boast of a horse or a saddle, unless they have secreted them in some place which has escaped the strictest searches of both parties.

The losses which the owners of some of these farms will suffer, is incalculable, for the want of horses to drive the cattle together, which ought to be done at least once in each week; otherwise the cattle being left unattended, will, in the course of three or four

---

2. The wolf was not ordinarily found in California west of the Sierra Nevada or south of Siskiyou County, although Bidwell, *Journey to California*, mentions seeing a very large wolf, place unspecified. The principal predators of lambs and calves were the coyotes. Many travelers remarked on their cunning, boldness, and

weeks, take to the mountains; and if left by themselves five or six months will become wild, and cost a great deal of money and labor for each owner to separate his cattle and induce it to remain on its respective land.

Still these people are so ignorant or headstrong that they cannot or will not see this; it appears they do not take into consideration that it is not an enemy's country and property that they are ruining, but it is their own and themselves are the only persons who suffer the injuries which they inflict. It is impossible not to pity many of the natives of California who are now suffering in their property from the evil dispositions of their countrymen. They are not well informed enough to know that in peculiar circumstances, such as the present, the property found in the enemy's country is liable to be seized to supply the necessities of the opposite party. When anything is taken from them, after a fair price has been offered for it, and they have not been disposed to sell it, they look upon the act as wanton plunder and oppression, without ever once taking into consideration that their nearest relations are the very persons who have created that necessity. Besides, money has not been spared by the United States whenever anything was required for any of the United States forces or their operations; a liberal price has been offered and paid for it; but many people hold back even their superfluities, when they were offered a higher price for them than they would formerly have thought of asking, and not being contented with cent per cent. profit, in many cases they have demanded from two to four hundred per cent, more for their property, whether this consisted in horses, saddles, provisions, or whatever else it might be, than the current prices, and by thus holding on to the last moment, they have at last been obliged to let it go without even knowing whether they would get anything or not, and then their complaints and invectives would be beyond all bounds. Still it is distressing to the feelings, particularly to a person who is acquainted with them,

---

unearthly howling at night.

It is difficult to determine what Garner means by "foxes." He knew a fox from a coyote, but he may have substituted terms for his eastern audience.

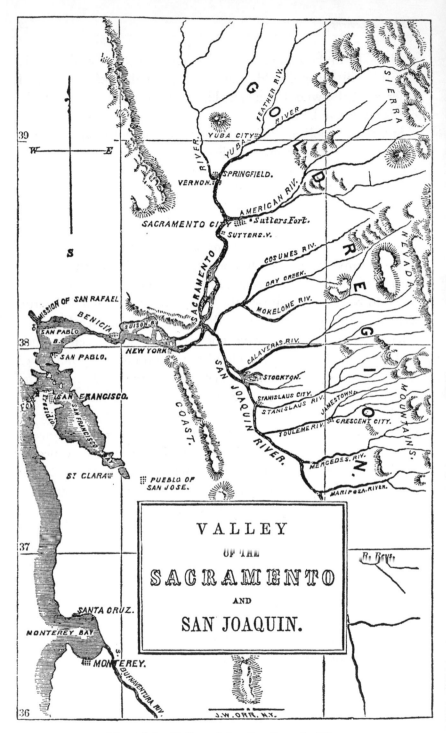

Map of the Valley of the San Joaquin River

to hear those complaints which many times are uttered by poor innocent and simple men, who really cannot understand the motives which actuate such proceedings.[1]

November 16, 1846 — The most beautiful part of California is still occupied by wild Indians. There are no parts in the settlements, nor in the Sacramento valley, equal to those situated on the western side of the snowy mountains. From the head of the river San Joaquin down to the elbow, or as it is called in Spanish, the *junta*, and on each side of the river *Merced* and the river *Reyes* lies the most valuable land in California.

From each of these rivers, two of which empty themselves into a lake, produce may be brought into the bay of San Francisco by going to the expense of removing some few impediments, which at present exist in the San Joaquin. The lake has an outlet which is a natural canal of about one hundred miles long and about one hundred miles wide, with a constant depth of from twenty-five to thirty feet. It is uniform in all these dimensions from one end to the other, and the current is so trifling that it is almost imperceptible. The reason of this is that where it enters the San Joaquin which is at the elbow above mentioned, the bed of the river is very high, consequently the water cannot run out of the canal so fast as it runs into the lake from three considerable rivers of which it is formed; and as the high bed of the river prevents the discharge of water from the lake through the canal. In the

---

1. Moerenhaut (the French consul), and most of the Californians interviewed by Bancroft's secretaries in the 1870's, gave the opinion that the indiscriminate and inconsiderate seizure of horses and gear by Frémont's rag-tag army aroused bitter resentment and caused adherence to the rebel cause by many rancheros who were, on the whole, indifferent to the American occupation.

The French consul wrote in a November 22, 1846, dispatch:

This severe measure, which left the country people, those who had remained peaceful, absolutely without resources, and exposes them to the loss of their crops and cattle, has occasioned general discontent, and the reaction will only become stronger wherever the Californians have the upper hand. . . . The people blame and are discontented only with the Americans; for they consider them the cause of all these violences and of all these misfortunes which they are suffering. (Moerenhaut, "The French Consulate," p. 167.)

See also above, Garner's letter of Nov. 2 and Moerenhaut's comment in note 1 to that letter.

months of May, June, July and August, the level ground all
around the lake to the distance of eight or ten miles is all over-
flown; and then the water is good as the overflow is occasioned
by the melting of the snow in the snowy mountain, but in the
other months the water of this lake is very brackish and very
unwholesome.[1]

On the dryer parts of this immense plain, where the waters
which overflow from the lake do not reach, the soil is generally
barren, and in some places for miles and miles the ground is so
soft and light, that though perfectly dry, a horse will sink up to
his knees almost every step; wherever this is the case the ground
is completely barren, bearing neither shrub, bush, tree, nor grass
or herbs of any kind. The whole of this valley is pestered with
rattle-snakes, so much so that it is dangerous to be down in the
camp on it, without taking the precaution to search well to see if
there are any holes, and if none are to be seen, it is necessary to
drag some bush which may be found on many parts of the plain,
where the ground is harder, and with it make a large circular fire,
and get into the circle where a person may lie with more safety
from these deadly venomous animals. I have been travelling over
this plain in hot weather, and for the space of ten miles have seen
rattle-snakes as thick as we commonly see ground squirrels where
they are considered plentiful.[2]

---

1. The California rancheros periodically made raids into the San Joaquin Valley
to punish Indian horsethieves, to retrieve runaway mission neophytes, and to
capture women and children for virtual slave labor. See Cook, "Expeditions."
Garner had evidently taken part in a number of these forays and knew the ground
well not only through the San Juan Bautista-Pacheco Pass trail but also through
the more southerly San Miguel Pass-Salinas Valley area. His account of the Tulare
Lake and the land surrounding it is one of the earliest in English.

2. As Garner says, the southern San Joaquin Valley was famous for its ground
squirrels and rattlesnakes. Arnold Rojas, *California Vaquero* (Fresno, California:
Academy Library Guild, 1953), p. 54, tells of four cowboys who killed twenty-two
rattlers "in the space of about one mile" by whipping them with their *reatas*
(whips). As to sleeping out in less congested snake country, the ordinary way was
to encircle the bed area with the prickly horsehair *mecate* or tie rope (and trust
in God).

1. Manuel de Jesús Castro (1821–?) was a prominent figure in Monterey.
Consul Larkin in his 1846 report describes him as, "Of little property, some information, insidious, ambitious, but shuns observation. Great influence among the

This vast plain extends about five hundred miles, running nearly north and south, and may on average be about sixty miles wide; and divides what is called the great mountain from the lower range of mountains which run up and down the coast. This lower range of mountains formerly was claimed by the missions in California, and to prevent individuals from obtaining grants of land from the Government, about the foot of them every mission established one or more sheep farms, and certainly the climate and the pasture were much adapted to this class of animals for they increase to an incredible degree.

November 17, 1846 — Troubles, disasters and difficulties are fast increasing in this country. A party of Californians, from one hundred and fifty to two hundred in number, with Manuel Castro, the former Prefect of the second district [Monterey], for their commander-in-chief,[1] and Joaquin de la Torre as second,[2] arrived within five leagues of this town on the 15th inst., on the evening of which day they took by force every man they could find and made him join their party.

Thomas O. Larkin, Esq., formerly United States Consul for California, was taken prisoner by them at the farm of Don Joaquin Gomez, distant about nine leagues from this town. This gentleman had some urgent business at San Francisco, which

---

Farmers and Youths of his own age and class. For two years actively engaged in Revolutionizing the country against Mexico. No known affection for Foreigners. Has hopes of his party continuing the command of the country by some fortuitous circumstances" (*Larkin Papers*, IV, 327). Castro was commander of the northern California troops against the Americans in 1847 and at the Battle of Natividad. After the revolt failed he fled to Mexico, and returned to California in 1852. A large collection of his corespondence and papers is in the Bancroft Library.

2. Joaquín de la Torre (1812?–1855) played a supporting role in the 1840 arrests and escorted the exiles to Mexico. Larkin, reporting on the incidents in the Bear Flag Rebellion, wrote that a few days after "thirty-four foreigners, some of them Americans, took possession of the town of Sonoma," de la Torre with a party of sixty to seventy men went to attack and oust the foreigners. Surprised "at the sight of so many men of whose vecinity the Foreigners were not aware [they] entered a stock corral close by, to defend themselves. De la Torre immediately retreated with his whole party excepting two or three killed or wounded, and did not stop until he reached Sauzalito a distance of twenty to twenty five miles, where taking a launch he reached Yerba Buena and proceeded to Santa Clara, a distance of eighteen leagues" (*Larkin Papers*, IV, 140–141).

obliged him to leave Monterey in great haste on the 14th inst., about 3 o'clock in the afternoon. On the same evening about 7 o'clock he fell into the hands of the enemies. His fate is at this moment very doubtful.[3]

From the information we have received here it appears that the natives were apprised of a number of horses which were coming from the Sacramento valley for the use of Col. Fremont, and they formed a determination to cut them off if possible, and take possession of them. They accordingly gathered all the force they were able, and began by plundering the house of a Mexican who lived on the borders of the river of the Salinos, and who has been friendly to the American cause from the very first hour that the flag was hoisted. According to his own statement this morning, they ravished all the women that were in his house, and committed many other outrages — though we have hopes that fear and vexation somewhat exaggerated the story. However, yesterday, about 4 o'clock in the afternoon, the Californians fell in with the party of Americans, who were thirty-seven in number, under command of Captains Forster and Burrows, and who were bringing four hundred fine horses. Captain Forster being in advance of the party about five hundred yards, was suddenly surrounded and his brains blown out. On the report of the piece, some more of the Americans rode up and a skirmish ensued. The Americans fired their rifles and charged on the Californians without loading, and drove them before them, though there were about five Californians to one American. A Delaware Indian belonging to the American party offered his services to bring notice of the dangerous situation in which the company was in, to Col. Fremont, the Californians still rallying, though with more the appearence of acting on the defensive.

---

3. Larkin had left Monterey to see his critically ill daughter Adeline in San Francisco when he was captured by Manuel Castro on November 16. *Larkin Papers*, V, xv, 287–288 (Larkin to his wife, Rachel, describing his capture).

4. Garner is describing the Battle of Natividad, the only sharp encounter between the American and Californian forces in northern California.

1. Larkin was, in fact, treated well. From Los Angeles he wrote his wife on

The Indian accordingly started, but had got but a very little distance when he was pursued by five men; the former of these made a thrust at him with his lance, which the Indian, in trying to parry, received through his hand, and with the other hand he immediately seized his tomahawk and split the offender's head from the crown to the lower jaw. By this time the other four had come up and the Indian fought so bravely as to kill two of them, and the other two fled. He then rode on towards Monterey, but his horse tired with him and he had to walk about seventeen miles. On receiving this information Col. Fremont started, with about 350 men and five pieces of artillery. The Indian says he supposes about 13 Californians were killed.[4]

November 18, 1846 — From information received this afternoon, it appears that the Californians are still hovering in the vicinity of Monterey; one of them was seen within a mile of the town, gathering up the worn out horses which Col. Fremont had left behind, and nine more were seen about five miles from town. Their object is not known. Capt. Maddox went with a company of twenty-five men to see if he could fall in with any of them, but returned without having seen them.

We likewise hear that Thomas O. Larkin, Esq., has been sent to the head quarters of the Californians at the town of the Angels. This person, of course, is to the enemy a prisoner of great importance, and they being aware of this it is hoped will not attempt his life, though there is no doubt but he will have to put up with a great deal of abuse from such men as Torres and a few others.[1] The horses which were coming down for Col. Fremont are now safe in his possession, the Californians not having been able to carry out their intention of getting possession of them.

December 14, "From Don Manuel Castro and in particular from Don Francisco Rico I rec'd every treatment I could expect. Whether it was the only thing to eat, or the only bed, I always had it. They were even afraid I might fall in riding in the night, partly from friendship of old and partly that my Countrymen may not find me dead in their possession, which might lead to retaliation." *Larkin Papers*, V, 311.

The bark Don Quixote of Oahu is now lying in this port, bound to the Sandwich Islands, and many people are trying to engage a passage in her. The women are beginning to get very much alarmed, and some Mexicans are trying to sell off their property at half cost.

It is very doubtful whether Col. Fremont will be able to get within shot of the party now under command of Manuel Castro. They are all young men and excellent horsemen; not only that but they are so well acquainted with every hill and valley, every bad pass, and in fact every piece of ground in California; they will keep dodging about backwards and forwards, and still keeping in their sight from different mountains all the movements of the Americans; besides, they are at no loss for resources, nor will they be for some time, so far as provisions are concerned. Give a Californian his horse, his lasso and his knife, and he will never go hungry, and he can always find people living in the interior who will give him clothing and money for the hides he steals.

As for living or sleeping in the open field, it is nothing more than what he has been accustomed to all his life, for no male child after it was three years old, was allowed to sleep inside the house of his father formerly; such a thing would have been looked upon as a great indelicacy, and even a sin, and would have been severely censured by the priests; indeed, so far from the male relations sleeping in the same house where female relations slept, brothers were scarcely permitted to converse with their sisters, unless in the presence of the father and mother, or some third person being present, and that third person was to be an elder.

A bed was a luxury the males were never allowed until the day they were married, and then I have often known them to go to bed with the bride without taking off even their riding boots. It is only within the last twelve years that beds for male persons not being married have been in vogue; consequently a Californian is as much at home when living in camp as when he is at his house. They are good watchers, and it is hard for an enemy to surprise them in camp. — Much of this may be attributed to custom also, as they go every year to run elk and wild horses, when they are obliged to keep good watch on account of the wild Indians.

November 19, 1846 — The women are all coming in from the country for protection, leaving their houses alone. Yesterday morning upwards of a dozen families arrived at this town; their situation is really distressing, but their husbands and sons seem to care little about them; instead of striving to alleviate the difficulties which inevitably are the constant attendants on a country in a state of war, they, on the contrary aggravate them by all the means in their power. This can be nothing but the result of ignorance; had the natives of this country been allowed to receive such education as the poor of all other civilized nations do receive, instead of having been taught nothing in the world but to believe Priestcraft, they would have had some sense of honor, and consequently would not so readily have forfeited their words pledged to a great nation; but it is, and always has been, the rule with the Californians, *to attain their end*, and it matters not to them by what means; they care not how dishonorable an act may be, where they think they have an interest; honor is out of the question, and they go headlong into it, saying to themselves, "if they gain their ends, well and good, if not, there is nothing lost."

They have not the least forethought, they will not look one day ahead. The greater part of the natives, I think I may say without exaggeration, nineteen-twentieths of them think of nothing in the world but gambling, dress, horse-riding, women, and stealing to maintain these vices. There are many persons who have tremendous large tracts of beautiful and fertile lands, containing from three to eleven square leagues, and the man who cultivates twenty acres of it, without taking the trouble to fence it, is considered among themselves an extraordinary industrious man, and at the same time, were it not for the Indians who work about the farms for little or nothing (and generally get cheated out of that), there would be no land cultivated in California; and I have never seen in any part of the country, since the missions have been secularized, a superabundance of provisions, not because the ground will not produce, but because the people are so indolent and careless, that they will not take the trouble to look after it; and more than half the produce is eaten up by the cattle before it becomes ripe.

The current price of wheat for the last eight or ten years, has been, and now is, two dollars per *fanega*; a fanega being nearly two bushels, and flour two dollars for twenty-five pounds, or per *arroba*. One fanega of wheat will give one hundred pounds of flour. The expense of grinding, bolting, &c., seventy-five cents, and one arroba of flour made into bread, will turn out three dollars and fifty cents; here we see one hundred pounds of flour, or rather one fanega of wheat turn in thirteen dollars and fifty cents, exclusive of bran, &c. Now if we deduct the cost of the wheat, which is two dollars, and one dollar and fifty cents for expenses of grinding, baking, &c., we shall find a clear profit accruing to the owner, of eleven dollars on one fanega of wheat.[1] No doubt my readers will say, how is it possible that any body can be poor in this country? I answer the same as before, that industry is unknown in California. If a native should be going any where on business of life and death, and there should happen to be a fandango at any house on his road, he would as soon think of committing suicide as to pass without stopping.

November 21, 1846 — In my letter of the 17th inst. I was not able to give an account of the skirmish which took place on the 15th inst. between the Californians and Americans, for want of authentic notice of the circumstances. Since that time, we have been able to procure a true account of it· though there is little to be added to what is there stated, and which is, that four Americans were

---

1. Garner seems to have made an arithmetical error here.

1. The American losses at Natividad, as at San Pascual, were relatively heavy because they succumbed to the usual ruse of the native horsemen of pretending to flee and then rounding upon their pursuers with lance, pistol, and *reata*. The number killed and wounded on each side has never been ascertained, but Garner's account is the best contemporary source. The discrepancy in other reports may be attributed to the fact that only white American casualties were counted, not those of their Indian scouts. Garner's statement tallies closely with that of Vicente Gómez, at whose father's ranch house some of the dead were buried, that ten of the American force were killed and nine wounded. (Vicente P. Gómez "Lo Que Sabe sobre casas de California," 1876, MS, Bancroft Library, 316 ff.) The losses of the

killed and six Indians, all of whom were subsequently found by
Colonel Fremont, and their bodies buried near to the spot where
the skirmish took place. There are likewise five Americans
wounded.[1] It is impossible to say how many Californians were
killed and wounded, because their comrades took them all away
excepting four, three of whom were killed and not natives of
California; the wounded man was a native, and escaped to a
farm house hard by. He has since been brought to Monterey by
his father, and the ball which had passed up his thigh and lodged
in the buttock, was extracted.[2]

On the 17th inst. the party of Californians, excepting a few who
remained to observe the movements of Colonel Fremont, started
for the South, taking T. O. Larkin, Esq., in their company.
Whether they will not try to stop Colonel Fremont's horses or
cut them off by lying in ambush in some of the bad passes, is
doubtful. It is very probable they will try this scheme. Colonel
Fremont divided his battalion into three companies of about one
hundred and thirty men in each, and spread them abreast, so as
to sweep the country near the coast. Either of these companies will
be sufficient to destroy any force he is likely to meet with between
San Juan and Santa Barbara. The only danger is, that the enemy
will elude his vigilance.

We have now in Monterey eleven prisoners of war, three of
them are men of high standing as civilians, though none of them
are military officers. However, their being prisoners in our possession, may prevent the enemy from killing or ill-treating the
Americans whom they hold.

The winter is now set in, and it is very much to be feared that

---

Californians were never determined, but most sources give about three or four
killed and five or six wounded.

2. This was probably Juan Ignacio Cantua, whose father was foreman of the
Rancho Patrocinio at Alisal (Salinas). Colton, *Three Years in California*, p. 104,
says he was attended to by the U.S. surgeon.

A more slightly wounded man, José Antonio Chavez, came back to Monterey
and was so cleverly hidden in her baby's bed by Doña Angustias de la Guerra de
Jimeno that when the Americans searched the house they did not find him. He
escaped on a horse the next day. (Angustias de la Guerra Ord, *Occurences in Hispanic California*, pp. 60–64.) Colton, pp. 144–145, gives a gently risqué version in
which Chavez is hidden in a bed between two sleep-feigning ladies.

the Californians will keep this country in a state of war until
the spring is well set in, they having the greatest number and the
best horses. The grass is beginning to spring up, and every mouth-
ful of this young grass that a horse eats, weakens him very much,
so that one day's work lays a horse up until the grass begins to
get substance, consequently the land forces will not be able to
travel so much as will be necessary to keep up with the movements of the enemy; not only this, but a Californian will ride a
horse twenty miles farther than most of the people Colonel Fremont has, without tiring him.

On the other hand, the ships of war cannot lie safely at anchor
any where between the ports of Monterey and San Diego, until
the month of April is well set in; San Pedro, Santa Barbara and
San Luis being nothing but open roadsteads where vessels lie
exposed to every wind that blows. So that the co-operations of
Colonel Fremont and Commodore Stockton will be very difficult,
if this co-operation can be effected at all.

The strictest vigilance is maintained in this town. No person
whatever is allowed to enter it without the strictest inquiry being
made as to his business, and even then, if he has no passport, he
is confined until a satisfactory account of him is procured. Neither
can any person leave the town without a special passport from the
Military Commander.

November 22, 1846 — Having given some information in some of
my former letters of the fertility of the soil in most parts of California, I have to observe that whatever I have mentioned on this
head is the result of twenty-two years experience that I have had
in California, and I feel myself bound as a lover of truth to warn
all and every persons wishing to emigrate to this country, to be-
ware of some pamphlets that have been published, both by Americans and Mexicans, within the last three or four years concerning
the extraordinary fertility of the soil, otherwise on their arriving
here they may be disappointed.

I was led to mention this warning, from having a pamphlet,
now before me, written by Don Manuel Castanares, who went to

Mexico in the year 1843, as representative of California.[1] This gentleman does not scruple to say, "the land of California is so surprisingly productive that wheat commonly yields crops of from four hundred to six hundred for one of sowing, and maize or Indian corn from one thousand to twelve hundred bushels for one of seed, and beans from five hundred to seven hundred for one of seed." Now as I should be very sorry for any family well situated in life, to sacrifice their property in America for the purpose of emigrating to California, under the expectation of making an independent fortune in one or two years by agriculture, from having read such a pamphlet as this, which will no doubt find its way to America, in a very short time, if it is not already there, I should wish this gentleman, as well as some who have published before him, had been a little more explicit. For instance, if he had said he had seen a grain of wheat yield one thousand or two thousand fold, or a grain of corn yield three thousand fold, or a bean yield three hundred fold, and all these I have seen myself; but still it does not follow that a field sown with either of these different kinds of grain should yield in the same proportion. That the soil would yield, under the hands of an American agriculturist, double the quantity of produce from the same quantity of seed it at present yields, I have not the least doubt, but still the account given by Castanares is exaggerated at the very least cent per cent.

Not only this, but all parts of California are not equal in the fertility of soil. To the southward of San Luis Obispo, the farmers consider they have a good crop of wheat if they gather thirty bushels for one of seed. Beans, corn, peas, melons pumpkins, &c., &c., yield well all over California, but the most fertile land is from San Luis Obispo to the northward.

I have mentioned the above as an example that people may be on their guard, because I have already seen some of the persons who came over in the last emigration, who stated to me that they had been persons well to do, and that nothing in the world had

---

1. The title of Don Manuel's book is *Coleccion de Documentos Relativos al Departamento de Californias.* (Mexico, 1845), 70 pp.

tempted them to sell off their property and emigrate to California, but the reading of a small book published by an American who had visited California, and that they had been most egregiously disappointed.[2]

That the fertility of the soil in most parts of California is most extraordinarily rich no person can deny, or that its variety of soil and climate, which last is in all parts excellent, will enable it to produce an innumerable variety of vegetation is likewise not to be denied, but as I wish to represent things as they really are, and as I have no interest whatever in deceiving any one, I shall contradict such absurdities whenever I fall in with them.

November 23, 1846 — We yesterday received private information that some of the Californians who had been taken perforce by their countrymen previous to the skirmish of the 15th inst., and who were engaged in that skirmish, made shift to run away as soon as it was over, and have since been lying by, waiting for an opportunity to come in to this town to surrender themselves to the U. S. authorities.

Two of these persons have availed themselves of a friend, asking to make enquiries how things stand, and at the same time stating that if the authorities of this town, or rather the commandant will give them his word that they shall not be injured in their persons, and will send them a passport they will immediately come in and surrender themselves prisoners of war. On this being communicated to the commandant, he went to see the persons who had been authorized by them to negotiate for them, and said that he could not promise so much as was desired, because he did not know the persons names who wished to come in, and as so many of the Mexican officers who had taken their paroles, had set honor aside, and forfeited their words, he was doubtful about putting confidence in any of them. On this gentleman being in-

---

2. The small book that influenced the 1846 emigrants was probably Hastings, *The Emigrants' Guide.* On pages 86–89 he mentions clover in California as generally two to three feet high, and four to five feet in some places; wheat with an average crop thirty to forty bushels to the acre but from fifty to seventy frequently,

formed who the persons were, he gave his word that they should
be treated with all the lenity that the circumstances would permit.
The terms were accepted and a passport given by the commandant for their safe journey into Monterey. This is exactly what I
have supposed from the first break out of the insurrection would
take place.

It is impossible for a party of Californians to remain away from
the settlements over two or at most three months; by that time
they begin to get discontented among themselves. (I speak from
experience, having made several campaigns in company with
them, in pursuit of the wild Indians.) They begin to think they
would be more comfortable at home. They do not like to be
ordered about or commanded by persons who they know are in
nothing their superiors, and who are merely using them to work
out their own private ends. This is and always has been invariably
their manner of reasoning; and the very moment one or two of
them leave any party, it matters not what the original object in
accumulating that party may have been, the rest soon begin to
follow, and the original intention is abandoned, at all events until
they again feel in the humour to proceed or to resume it.

Now the example is set; some of them have deserted, and
should they come in and surrender, and receive no harsher treatment than they have a right to expect, the word will fly through
California from one end to the other, and with a little discreet
judgment on the part of the authorities at the different towns,
I think I may almost affirm that in one or two months the United
States would have no person to contend with in California. Of
course all those persons who have taken their paroles would fly
from the country as soon as they began to find themselves deserted. *They* have sense enough to know that their words of honor
would not be taken a second time, and even now many of them
have been heard to say, that they may as well die on the field of
battle as to be taken and shot.

---

and on some land, 120 bushels at first sowing and a volunteer crop of sixty the
following year; corn, fifty to sixty bushels to the acre; oats, eight feet high, stalks
one-half an inch through.

November 24, 1846 — Colonel Frémont has returned to San Juan. The state of California is getting still more alarming: a devastating war in its centre, with little hopes of its coming to a speedy conclusion — the inhabitants destitute of provisions, or the means of procuring them, as no stock of provisions has ever been kept on hand but just as much, and scarcely as much, as would last from one season to the other, and this year not even that.

Besides this scarcity here, one way or the other, there are about three thousand more persons in California now than there ever has been before. These have all to be maintained; and in preference to those who do not carry arms, all sorts of provisions coming from the country to the towns are seized for the support of the troops, whether Americans or Californians. Bread is now worth eighteen cents per pound, and flour cannot be bought at any price, because those who have a little more than they actually need for their families, are, on account of the scarcity, making it into bread for sale, by this means increasing their profit.

Although California surpasses all other countries in the world as a cattle country, a bullock of the meanest kind cannot be bought in Monterey under twelve dollars at this time — and then it cannot be found for sale when it is wanted, once in ten times. These things a year ago would have been thought impossible, still it is at the present time true. This being the state of the country now, we may easily conceive what it will be six months hence, should the war last that length of time, and the natives hold out (which I by no means believe); they, however, will not feel the want of provisions, because they have driven all the cattle away back inland, and there they have an inexhaustible resource at no expense, while the peaceable inhabitants who remain in the towns, though provisions may be plentifully brought on by shipping, still have not the means of purchasing flour at sixteen and eighteen dollars a barrel, or potatoes at seventy-five cents, and from that to a dollar, for twenty-five pounds.

However, there is no fear of any family starving in Monterey, for every house has from two thousand to ten thousand square yards of land belonging to it, and for the most part walled or fenced in, so that each family, by industry and economy, can maintain itself for a length of time — and in case of emergency, the coast of California abounds in most exquisite fish: in short, California affords a remedy for every difficulty that can present itself.

An Indian came into this town this afternoon, who had been taken by the Californians about five weeks since, and was kept by them until last Wednesday evening, or the 18th inst., when he made his escape. He says the Californians are waiting near a bad pass in the road towards San Antonio, for the purpose of cutting off Col. Fremont's horses. Of course this is important news, as it will put this gentleman on his guard in such a manner as to enable him to act on the offensive, and let them fall into their own trap should they persist in laying in wait for him where they now are. This Indian likewise states that many of the Californians in La Torre's party have neither musket, pistol, carbine nor rifle, nor any other kind of weapon — but a butcher knife.

November 25, 1846 — I shall now give you an account with the descriptions of the principal classes of timber in California, beginning with the red pine tree. This tree commonly grows from two hundred and fifty to three hundred feet high. I have measured one when felled that was three hundred and twenty-seven feet from the butt to the point or head; this was by no means an uncommon sized tree, being but nine feet in diameter where it was cut off, and the largest ever I saw measured while standing was forty-two feet in circumference. I have heard of much larger ones, but never saw one; these trees all run very regular in their dimensions from the bottom to the top. The heart of a young tree begins to turn red at about six years old, the outside from two to three inches in thickness, always remaining white; the bark is stringy and difficult to cut through, even with the sharpest axe; it may well be compared to the husk of the cocoa nut. The leaf and burr are very similar to those of the spruce tree; it contains some rosin, and I have seen several trees felled in the spring of the year which have discharged as much as a barrel of water the moment the axe has struck the heart of them.

The timber which this tree produces is invaluable for its dura-

Workmen Engaged in Felling the Mammoth Tree

bility, the worm does not enter it after it has been put to use, though while the tree is standing there is a worm which is very injurious to it, always entering at the bottom of the branches where the knot is almost equal to a flint stone, and always eats upwards, so that a tree is very often found to be sound and good as high up as the first branch, and above that is sometimes found greatly injured by the worm, but whenever the tree is cut down and dried this worm dies, and no other insect ever enters the wood, and if it is properly seasoned before being put to use, I cannot say if ever it rots at all, unless it is put in some place in

---

1. Garner's description of the coastal redwood (*Sequoia sempervirens*) is the fruit of many years experience as a lumberman and is almost unique for this early period. His mention of a boring insect is therefore all the more curious, for damage by insects is rare in redwoods, and his letter of Nov. 3, above, states that "this wood is not subject to the worms." There are some very small bark beetles, but they are of superficial importance and have no effect upon growth or lumber quality. Professor Emeritus Woodbridge Metcalf of the School of Forestry, University of California, Berkeley, suggests dry-wood termites in fire-damaged or lightning-struck trees, but even here, infestation is rarely serious.

2. Garner had many opportunities to listen to botanists in Monterey before 1846. Although he probably had little contact with the naturalists of Captain Beechey's expedition in 1825–1828, there were at least six other scientists with whom he may have talked. David Douglas, plant exploring for the London Horti-cultural Society, was in Monterey at various times between 1830 and 1832, and was

the ground where it is exposed to the wet and dry seasons alternately, and even then it lasts an immense length of time. I am well acquainted with a rich farmer in this country who built a cattle pen of this wood in the year 1824, and the stanchions, where none of the outside or white part of the tree has been used, are not the least decayed. Several of the old houses in the Mission of San Carlos were pulled down this year for the purpose of getting the timber they contained, and which was red wood, and the beams and lintels were as sound, to all appearance, as the day they were put into these houses, which must have been some sixty or seventy years ago, and yet by driving the plane once over them they showed as beautiful and bright a red as the day they were cut down.[1]

For shingles this timber has not its equal, either for the ease with which it is worked or for its durability. I have seen a man make by hand, that is to say split, shave and joint, fifteen hundred a day for two months at a time.

This tree is fond of hilly ground; it is seldom found on level places, but in the valleys and on the sides and tops of mountains, it grows in immense groves, and the great demand there is for it both in this country and at the Sandwich Islands, proves the superiority of it to all other kinds of timber on the shores of the north Pacific Ocean. I have called it the red pine, because I have heard many disputes between botanists as to its proper name, and it appears to me to resemble some species of pine nearer than any thing else.[2]

Garner's fellow militiaman in the Compañía Extranjera. Thomas Coulter, discoverer of the Coulter pine, was collecting for the Swiss naturalist De Candalles and botanized with Douglas in Monterey in 1831. Thomas Nuttall, Philadelphia Academy of Sciences, was in Monterey in 1836. Frederick Deppe of Berlin, a friend of Douglas, was often in Monterey between 1829 and 1837. He was supercargo on several Mexican trading vessels and used his time ashore to collect specimens for the Museum of Natural History in Berlin. An engaging Swedish scientist, G. M. Waseurtz af Sandels ("The King's Orphan"), whose search for botanical and geological specimens near Monterey in 1842 made the simple people believe him a doctor, was greatly interested in the redwood forests and visited Larkin's cuttings in Santa Cruz where Garner may have been in charge. Another little-known botanist, Carl Theodor Hartweg, a plant explorer for the London Horticultural Society, arrived in Monterey from Mexico on June 7, 1846. He explored the Carmel and Sacramento Valleys and the Santa Lucia Mountains and investigated the red-

November 26, 1846 — In resuming my discourse on the pine tree, or as it is called here the red-wood tree, it merely remains to say, that from ten leagues to the southward of Monterey up to forty degrees north latitude, California abounds in it, and the exportation market has increased to such a degree that at the present day a board of this specie of wood cannot be bought in Monterey for any price, and several buildings have been stopped this year for want of this class of timber. Since July last there have been no less than five ships in Monterey looking for a cargo of red wood boards, joist or shingles; and none of them were able to procure as much as they required, merely for the want of laborers or capitalists who could turn their attention to this branch of commerce and industry.

Monterey is half surrounded by groves of pines which extend in some places about ten miles back, in others two or three. These are of an excellent quality for ship masts and yards, when cut in the proper season; they are principally a sort of white pine, very tough, and run generally from thirty to one hundred and ten feet high, and from one to four feet in diameter, seldom exceeding the latter; the timber makes excellent flooring, but must be cut in the winter, and must be well seasoned before being

---

wood forests, mentioning the presence of the Douglas fir (*Psuedo-tsuga douglasi*) and "mountain oak" among the redwoods, as does Garner. His outstanding feat was the naming and scientific description of the Monterey cypress (*Cupressus macrocarpa*). How this characteristic and unique tree escaped cataloging by earlier scientists is a marvel. Hartweg, his studies hampered by war restrictions and lack of horses, left for England on February 3, 1848.

1. The "white pine" (*Pinus radiata*) is the characteristic Monterey pine. In Garner's time it was almost entirely confined to the foggy hills of the Monterey Peninsula, and very small stands at Pescadero and Cambria. Monterey Pine is so hard and durable that the early streets and sidewalks of San Francisco were paved with it (Jack Swan, *Monterey Weekly Herald*, Oct. 16, 1875).

2. Garner means the Douglas fir, which is commonly seen with the redwoods all along the coast from Santa Cruz northward, rather than to what is today called "yellow pine" or Ponderosa pine (*Pinus ponderosa*), which has only very small stands near Santa Cruz.

3. The French ship *Le Lion*, under Captain Bonnet, came to Monterey in June 1844 to trade for cattle and provisions for the French in the Marquesas Islands. It sailed for the South Seas in April 1845, but lost 350 out of 400 cattle on the voyage. The ship came back to California late in 1846 to get more cattle. (Moerenhaut, "The French Consulate" 12 [1933], 348).

used.[1] Across the bay, at Santa Cruz, and to the northward there are immense quantities of yellow pine.[2] Samples of the red wood and white and yellow pine were last year taken to the Marquese islands by the French missionary ship Lyon.[3]

There are likewise several kinds of oak in California; the large black oak tree is very plentiful, though the trunks of none of them grow very high, yet there are some few places where the trunk of these trees grow as high as fifty feet clear of branches, but the common growth of them is from fifteen to thirty feet, seldom exceeding the latter clear of branches.[4]

About twelve miles to the southward of Monterey is a large cypress grove; this is another very valuable class of timber, both for its beautiful clear grain, and for its durability; this tree does not grow large here; they run commonly not over seventy or eighty feet high, and at about twenty-five or at most thirty feet from the ground they begin to branch out, consequently the timber above that height is unserviceable.[5]

Buttonwood, willow, poplar, alder, cotton wood and black and white ash, are very abundant all over the country; and some of these grow to an immense size, but are very little used except for fencing or building wooden huts in the roughest style.[6] There is

---

4. The black oak (*Quercus kelloggii*) is found high up in the Santa Lucias near Chews Ridge and on the eastern slope of the Santa Cruz Mountains. As a lumber tree it is not plentiful. Garner may be referring to the tanbark oak (*Lithocarpus densiflorus*) which is common in redwood territory. It is scarcely a dark-colored tree or wood, but it can reach a height of 150 feet with a diameter of four feet. It is not a durable wood if left exposed but makes good flooring and furniture.

5. The Monterey cypress (*Cupressus macrocarpa*) is unique to the Monterey Peninsula. The wind-tortured shapes of these trees clinging to the rocky shores of Point Lobos and the 17 Mile Drive are famous. The cypresses were never commercially exploited to the extent of the pines and redwoods. Hartweg describes trees sixty feet high and nine feet in circumference; William H. Brewer noted many trees ten feet in circumference. One cypress was eighteen feet, eight inches around "as high as I could reach," and another, measured two feet above ground, was twenty-three feet in circumference (Brewer, *Up and Down California in 1860–1864*, ed. Francis Peloubet Farquhar [New Haven: Yale University Press, 1930], p. 107). These forests are protected and are still largely intact.

6. Buttonwood or California sycamore (*Platanus racemosa*) was highly regarded for its furniture qualities by the Americans in Santa Barbara in the 1830's. See Thomas Nuttall, *North American Sylva*, 2 vols. Philadelphia, 1865. The arroyo willow noted by Hartweg in the Carmel Valley reached a height of twenty-five to

likewise a species of shrub oak growing in this country very abundantly, but I know of no other use it can be put to but fire wood, and for this purpose it is excellent, though many people say the bark is very excellent for the purpose of tanning; the tree scarcely ever grows eight feet straight up; it generally begins to grow crooked from its very root; sometimes vessels use it to make knees, but I do not believe it is durable, and the maggot generally gets into it the first year after it is cut down.[7]

On the borders of the Sacramento river and in the Sacramento valley, besides the different species of timber already mentioned will be found the walnut, hickory, maple and several other kinds of useful timber.[8] In short, if California was as well watered (though this is not scarce) as it is wooded, it would surpass every country in the known world.

November 29, 1846[1] — Bear hunting is one of the most prominent diversions in California, and it is worthy the entertainment of an Emperor, when it is conducted by the natives of this country, and after their own fashion.

Whenever a Californian wishes to catch a bear, and which at any time he is ready to undertake for the sake of the diversion, he goes, in the first place, and looks well over the ground for

---

forty feet, but, in general, willow was used by the Californians only for making saddletrees. The withies and bark were used by the Indians for making baskets. The cottonwood (*Populus Fremontii*) and the poplar are common along streams but are too soft for anything but boxing. The alder (*Alnus rhombifolia*) grows fifty to sixty feet high but only eight to twelve inches in diameter. It is found along streams in the Coast Ranges to Santa Barbara. Garner's use of the terms "black and white ash" is puzzling. The only specie of ash native to California that has any commercial value is the Oregon ash (*Fraxinus oregona*), an excellent hardwood not abundant south of the Golden Gate.

7. The shrub (scrub) oak or *encina* of the Californians is the familiar coast live oak (*Quercus agrifolia*). A much better, heavier, stronger wood for ships' knees, wagon wheels, and axles came from the canyon live oak (*Quercus chrysolepsis*).

8. Garner may have had Captain Belcher's *Narrative* at hand when describing the trees of the Sacramento Valley. During Captain Belcher's tour of discovery up the Sacramento River in 1837, Richard B. Hinds, surgeon-naturalist to the expedition, saw the walnut trees that now bear his name (*Juglans hindsii*). These are magnificent trees, measuring up to six feet in diameter and clear of branches for forty feet, but the kernels, although sweet, are so small and the nuts so hard that they are hardly worth struggling for.

about two miles all around the spot where he intends to lay his bait. This is done for the purpose of reconnoitering every step of ground that he thinks he may have to ride over, for the purpose of ascertaining if there are any squirrel holes or ravines, and likewise to form a judgment which way the bear will be most likely to run from the bait, on her being surprised. At least one of his companions accompanies him on this excursion.

They then go and catch a mare, (it matters not much who is the owner,) or if this is difficult, a stray horse will answer the purpose. As soon as they have lassoed their victim, they take it to the place previously selected for laying the bait. On this spot they strangle the animal, and then let out its entrails, that the bear may scent it at a great distance. They then cut off one quarter of this animal, and drag it all over the ground for a half or three quarters of a mile round the spot, then take it back and leave it with the carcase, always covering it over with some grass or bushes that the birds may not devour it before the bear makes his appearance.

The bait being left in perfect order, and the ground well reconnoitered, they go away, and do not trouble the bait for the first night, because if the bear comes the first night, he will be sure to return if he is not troubled, and most likely with two or several

---

This species is quite restricted in habitat, only three stands being known at that time: on the Sacramento at Walnut Grove, at Walnut Creek in Contra Costa County, and at Wooden Valley, east of Napa. There is also a shrubby black walnut (*Juglans californica*), which is rarely large enough for lumber but does have a heavy-shelled nut. Captain Belcher says that he ate "hickory" (*Juglans californica?*) and walnuts on the banks of the Sacramento, and I take this as evidence that Garner was using him as a reference for this letter. There is no hickory anywhere on the Pacific slope and Belcher is the only traveler who reported any. See Edward Belcher, *Narrative of a Voyage Round the World . . . 1836–1842*, 2 vols. (London, 1843), I, chap. 5.

The big-leaf maple (*Acer macrophyllum*), a fine hardwood, is probably indicated here. It is readily found in the Santa Cruz mountain area where Garner was logging and in the Santa Lucias at less accessible spots. It is rather slender in California, but reaches a larger size in the Northwest.

1. This letter is the best known of Garner's writings. It was republished for the first time only three weeks after it appeared, in *Littel's Living Age*. One of its latest uses has been in Tracy I. Storer and Lloyd P. Tevis, Jr., *California Grizzly* (Berkeley: University of California Press, 1955), pp. 133–135.

more. Consequently the second night is the best hunt. — The owners of the bait then invite, in secresy, four or five choice friends. They do not invite too many, because, through too much excitement amongst many persons, or eagerness to get the first chance to throw the lasso, the bear gets wind that all is not right, and being a very cunning animal, if he once begins to suspect that the enemy is near, he keeps so good a watch that it is impossible to catch him. — This company catch the very best horses they can find. It is not the fleetest horse that is considered the best for this employment. It requires a tame, lively horse, with a good government in the mouth, and a strong back.

Every thing being prepared, men, horses, saddles, and lassoes, they all start at sun down or dusk, and keep carefully to windward of the bait, which must be placed on a piece of ground clear from rocks, trees or bushes, and near or within about eight hundred yards of one of these, for the purpose of hiding themselves, that the bear may not see them when he is approaching the bait. A horse that has been catching bears three or four times, will keep a strict watch for the approach of the bear at the bait, and will invariably let his rider know, — not by any noisy motion, but by deep suppressed sighs, and pricking up his ears. Whenever one or more of the horses do this, the men who have been lying by on foot, mount as quietly as possible, and when all are ready with their lassoes in their hands ready to swing, they put spurs to their horses, which at that moment is very little needed, that noble animal appearing to all intents and purposes to be as anxious as his rider to capture the savage animal. The horse, being swifter than the bear, if the plan has been well laid, is sure to overtake him before he can get to any bush. The foremost rider throws his lasso, and seldom fails of catching the bear, either by the neck or round the body or one of its legs. Should he miss, there are several more close at his heels to throw their lassoes. As soon as the bear finds himself fast he rears and growls, taking hold of the lasso with his two fore paws. At this crisis the lasso must always be kept tight; if not, the bear will extricate himself immediately. Now comes in play the sagacity of the noblest of animals. The horse, from the very moment the bear is lassoed,

The Pull on the Wrong Side

Grizzly Bear Hunt

keeps his eye on every movement, and appears to do, or rather I believe actually does do all in his power to protect and defend his rider as well as himself; as it often happens, that from care-lessness or inattention on the part of the rider, the bear will en-tangle the horse's legs with the lasso, and in such cases, if it is a horse that has been used to lassoing bears, he will with the greatest agility clear himself, without the least motion from the bit. I have several times seen a horse when the bear has been ap-proaching him from before, instead of turning round to run away or to run on one side, wait until the bear got close to him, watch-ing him all the while with a steady eye, and all of a sudden take a leap right over the bear, and then turn suddenly round and face him again. This feat of course is only done by such horses as are well acquainted with bear hunting. I never was in either a military or naval engagement myself, but I have heard hundreds say that fear exists in the breasts of warriors no longer than till the first volley is fired. The same may be said of the horse in bear hunting. From the moment a horse sees the bear, it matters not at what distance, he begins to tremble, and his heart beats so loud that his rider can distinctly hear it. But this lasts no longer than the first momentary onset; for as soon as the horse feels by the strain of the lasso that the bear is lassoed, his fear leaves him, and he is from that moment to all appearance in his highest glee. If the bear is a very large one, two or three more persons will throw their lassoes on him, because an old bear will be very apt to take the lasso in his mouth and bite it off, or bring such a strain on it as would break it.

The bear being now well secured, with three or four lassoes on him, the horses arching their necks and snorting with pride at their prize, walk away with the savage animal, which is rearing, plunging, and growling. Each motion from the direction in which it is the intention of his captors to carry him, is checked by the horseman on the opposite side; and if the intention is not to kill him at once, but to make him fast alive, for the purpose of baiting him next day with a bull, then the most dangerous part of the business has yet to be performed, which is that of making the bear fast alive, in such a manner as is least likely to injure him or affect his agility for the ensuing combat with his savage antagonist.

When it is the intention to keep the bear alive for the purpose of baiting him the following day, they take him as near to an oak or some other sturdy tree as they can well get him; then two horsemen try to get their lassoes over his head and one arm, and other two lasso each one a leg. These latter horsemen then drag the bear, going on opposite sides of the tree, until they get his after parts close up to the tree, with a leg on each side of it. All four horsemen now keep a tight strain with three turns round the loggerhead of each saddle, turning their horses so as to face the bear and hold back, a position which all the Californian horses are well accustomed to, and in which position they hold the greatest strain. There must now be a man on foot, who takes a good strong lasso and makes one end fast to one of the bear's legs just above the ancle, in such a manner that it will not jam or draw tight around the leg. He then leads the same lasso to the other leg, and makes it fast after the same manner, and so keeps on from leg to leg, until he has eight or ten turns. He then takes the lassoes which the two hinder horsemen have fast to the bear's legs and casts them loose. The bear being now well secured, with the tree between his legs, and the lasso behind the tree, the forward lassoes are taken off by slacking them with long poles, pushing the sliding parts with the ends of these poles. This is a dangerous piece of work, and the lassoes are sometimes left on the bear. When this is the case, he invariably takes them off himself, though they are seldom of any service afterwards, on accounts of their being generally bitten to pieces.

The bear is now left with all his body perfectly free, so that he can move round and round the tree. Care is always taken not to irritate him unnecessarily, because it often happens that these ferocious animals die with rage; and sometimes water is thrown on him to freshen him, — though, as this is some trouble, and consequently contrary to the inclinations of these people, it is seldom done.

This method of hunting the bear is one of the noblest diver-

sions with which I am acquain[t]ed. There is no cruelty annexed
to it, so far as the catching is concerned. The cruelty consists in
the baiting the animal, of which I shall give a description here-
after; but there is something extraordinarily grand in this exercise, which requires courage, skill, and activity. It requires an
extraordinary degree of courage for a man to ride up beside a
savage monster like the grisly bear of this country, which is
nearly as active as a monkey, and whose strength is enormous.
Should a lasso happen to break, which is often the case, the bear
invariably attacks the horse; and it requires very often the most
skilful horsemanship to prevent the horse or its rider from being
injured. It requires also great skill to know when to tighten the
lasso, and to what degree, to prevent it from being suddenly
snapped by too sudden a strain. The rider must have his eye
constantly on that of the bear, and watch his every motion. Sometimes either through fear, carelessness or inadvertence, a man may
let go his lasso. In this case, another, if the bear takes off, (which
he is likely to do,) will go as hard as his horse can run, and without stopping his speed, will stoop from his saddle and pick the
end of the lasso from the ground, and taking two or three turns
around the loggerhead of his saddle and checking his horse's
rein, again detain the bear.

In short, from the moment that a person arrives at the spot
fixed upon to lay wait for the bear's coming to the bait, until he
is fast to a tree or killed, he feels himself elated. Every motion of
those noble animals, the horses, which seems as if they were doubly
proud when they feel the strain of the lasso from the saddle, and
appear to take as much delight in the sport as the riders themselves, is grand beyond my power of description.

I have dwelt at length on this subject, because it surpasses every
thing of the kind on horseback that ever I either saw or read or
heard tell of.

*   *   *   *   *   *   *   *   *   *   *   *   *   *   *   *   *

In a night skirmish the lasso is a dangerous article. A Californian will lasso a man and drag him off his horse and choke him in

one minute; and, without getting off his horse, he will take his
lasso off the neck of his vanquished foe, and in two minutes will
be prepared for another. I have seen a man do this when fighting
the wild Indians; and a man pursued by two others with a brace
of pistols each, would stand a better chance of saving his life,
than a man pursued by one Californian within lassoing distance;
because the party pursued by those with the pistols might possibly dodge and destroy the aim of his pursuers, but he who
should be pursued by the Californian with his lasso, would have
no means of escape, because the lasso when thrown at any thing
that is running, is as true in the hands of a Californian as a rifle
ball from a good marksman's steady aim.

November 30, 1846 — Nothing in this world can equal the antipathy of a Californian to the Mormon tribe. As soon as it was
mentioned here that several Mormon emigrants were expected,
the women considered themselves as lost. They began to entertain the idea that it would be impossible for them to preserve
their religious principles, while living in contact with a class of
beings whom they supposed to be no better than the worst class
of infidels, and I have heard many of them say that they would
sooner live in a house where some contagious distemper was
raging, than come in contact with a Mormon.

Some few days ago, a woman came to the magistrate's office,
and complained that in her absence a gentleman had taken it
upon himself to beat her son severely. She stated that she did not
feel so much hurt at the gentleman's having beaten her son, because he might have deserved it, but the gentleman had gone
beyond that — he had the assurance and the impudence to call
her son a *Mormonito*, or little Mormon — which word she said
was no better than if he had told her son that he was an outcast
in this world, and condemned to all eternity in the world to come.
The mother appeared to be almost inconsolable for the opprobious
epithet which had been bestowed on her child. The magistrate
kindly remonstrated with the woman, and tried to persuade her

that no harm had been intended toward her or her child, but it was of no use; she still kept harping on the word Mormon, until she exhausted herself, and then ended in saying that if by the Mormon emigration her soul should be lost, it was not her fault, and that God would not punish the innocent for the crimes of the guilty.

I am myself not at all acquainted with the religious tenets of the Mormons, but I have seen some few gentlemen among the emigrants to this country who have been pointed out to me as Mormons, and all I can say of them is, that I have found them to be well educated, sociable, and upright men, so far as my short acquaintance with them has allowed me to form an idea of them.

The antipathy which the Californians bear toward the Mormons, was occasioned by the representations given of them by the persons who first brought us notice of their intended emigration, and it has kept rather on the increase ever since. This, however, may be attributed to the circumstances in which this country is at present placed.

If a Californian wishes to express his disgust of any person, action or thing, he immediately says that person is a Mormon, or that is a Mormon thing, or such a thing is of Mormon extraction. Yesterday another circumstance took place, shewing the antipathy these people bear to every thing like Mormons.

A young man, who is an Englishman by birth, applied to the priest of this town for a license to marry a young girl, whose consent he had previously obtained, (contrary to the custom of the country.) It appeared, however, that the priest had noticed him some days ago, in company with some of Col. Fremont's men — who are all supposed by the natives of California to be Mormons. The priest accordingly told the young man that it was impossible for him to get married to a daughter of the only true faith, unless he abjured his present heresy, and acknowledged the Roman Catholic church as the only true church of God, and which would infallibly conduct him in the right path. The priest then sent for the maiden, and reproved her in the strongest terms, at the same time telling her that she must immediately confess the sin of

which she had been guilty, in having promised to give herself
away to a Mormon, which was only a nickname for the devil.[1]

---

1. In all the places where the California-bound emigrant trains were formed,
violent anti-Mormon sentiment existed. Mormon and non-Mormon settlers in
Missouri and Illinois carried on a virtual civil war from 1832 to 1845, and politicians, anxious to rid their areas of turmoil, urged the church leaders to go
farther west. Governor Ford of Illinois told Brigham Young in 1844, "California
now offers a field for the prettiest enterprise that has been undertaken in modern
times. . . . Why would it not be a pretty operation for . . . your people to go
out there . . . and establish an independent government?" (William Mulder
and A. Russell Mortensen, eds., *Among the Mormons: Historic Accounts by Contemporary Observers* [New York: Knopf, 1958], pp. 163–164). The prophet
Joseph Smith proposed a refuge-seeking expedition to Oregon or California in
February 1844.

The expulsion of the Mormons from Illinois in the winter of 1845–1846 and
their decision to "flee out of Babylon" and into some undefined haven beyond
the Rockies alarmed the Californians. On March 2, 1846, Governor Pico warned
the Assembly that ten thousand Mormons were on their way (Archives of California, IX, 16–17). He could not have known it, but Elder Samuel Brannan had
already sailed for California from New York on February 4, 1846, with a colony-
nucleus of 238 converts.

Brannan arrived in San Francisco Bay on July 31, only to find the American
flag flying over the presidio. He sent out scouts to seek a good place for the new
colony but at the time of Garner's letter, most of the Mormons were concentrated
in the Marin lumber camps and near the mission of San Francisco. The great
majority of them were honest, sober, industrious people, and there being no
polygamy among them, they were accepted by the Californians.

DECEMBER 1846

December 1, 1846 — The grisly Bear of California is the most savage animal to be found in it. It is a very dangerous animal when attacked, but in all my travels in California, in the course of which I have seen several hundreds, I have never known a single instance of a bear attacking a man, unless the man has in some way or other molested the bear, either by coming upon him suddenly, or disturbing the animal in some way or other. I have heard of men being attacked by bears or a bear, without the man in the first place having given any provocation, but I have so many reasons to doubt the truth of these stories, that I can almost assert that such is not the case. I have invariably seen them run from a man whenever they could see him or smell him at a distance.

I know perhaps of some twenty or thirty instances of men having been attacked by bears, but in every instance the bear has been provoked in some way or other, or surprised by his adversary.

A full grown Californian he bear, when lying stretched out on his back, will measure from his nose to the claws of his hinder feet about ten feet in length, and they are about five feet round the body. They have great muscular strength, and their color is generally a dirty gray or a dirty dun. The hair is very coarse and about 5 inches long all over the body, and when the animal is surprised or excited, every hair on his body stands on end. They live chiefly on berries, but sometimes kill cows and calves and eat them. In the winter season they live entirely on acorns, which abound in this country, and then they get very fat. I have seen fifteen gallons of oil taken from a fat bear, though this is not common, but ten or twelve gallons is often taken from them.

The she bear generally brings forth two or three cubs at a litter, but a she bear has never been killed during her pregnancy. The opinion of the people here with regard to this singular circumstance is, that the moment the she bear finds herself pregnant she hides herself away, and never comes out of her hiding place until she has brought forth her young; and that during all this time she is fed by the male. When the female has young ones she is very savage, though not very daring. I have seen the young ones lassoed several times, when the mother would remain at a distance from the horsemen, traversing the ground backwards and forwards, tearing it with her claws and snorting and puffing, her eyes red as fire, and every now and then she would dart forward as if with a determination to defend her young, but on any horseman turning his horse towards her, and making a motion with his laso she would again retreat to a distance.

They are excellent climbers, when the tree they wish to climb is large; they will go up a large oak tree as nimble as a cat, and if they cannot find as many acorns on the ground as they want, they climb an oak tree which they have previously observed to be well stocked with acorns, and go out on the richest branch that is on the tree, and taking hold of the branch with their fore claws, they let their body hang down and keep jerking and shaking the branch until it breaks, when bear, branch and acorns all come down together, and the bear makes his feast. They likewise, when berries are scarce, dig up moles, squirrels, &c. The flesh of the California bear is not good eating, unless it be the feet and the hams. These are excellent, let them be cooked what way they will.[1]

---

1. Colton's entry for Dec. 11, 1846, in *Three Years in California*, pp. 118–120, copies verbatim many of the sentences of this letter and embellishes others to fit his more florid style.

Bull and Bear Fight

December 2, 1846—Bear-baiting, bull-baiting and horse racing were formerly the constant diversions on all *great feast days*, but have latterly been for the most part done away with since the country has been turned upside down by civil contentions.

The two former of these diversions were barbarous in the extreme. When a bear was to be baited with a bull, they were both brought into an area fenced in, about two hundred yards square, and the bear's hind leg was made fast to the bull's fore leg, with a scope between of about twenty-five or thirty feet; the animals being fastened in this manner, if either of them shewed a disinclination to the combat, a horseman would throw his lasso over the bear and drag him toward the bull, and they would keep doing this until the bull got exasperated, when he would universally kill the bear with his horns.

While they are fighting, the bull always appears to pay the most attention to the defence of his fore feet, which the bear invariably tries to get hold of with his teeth. I have seen a bear get hold of a bull between the horns with his teeth and hold him there with the bull's nose on the ground for the space of ten minutes, and on being hauled off by the horseman, again catch the bull by one of his fore feet and bite it or tear it completely off by the lower joint.

Should the first bull not kill the bear, which he is sure to do if it is an old mountain bull, a second one is brought in, and sometimes a third, but the bear never has fair play; as he is made fast by the hind leg, he gets entangled and often loses what would be a mortal grasp to the bull; but as the bear is destined to be killed whether he conquers or not—the people, as they have no feeling for dumb animals of any kind, take a delight in torturing him. To be sure the bull does not fare much better, for it seldom happens after he is let loose that he is able to go a mile before he is overtaken by some men who are always lying in wait for him, and his hide is taken off and his carcase thrown to the dogs.

Bull baiting with horsemen is another barbarous diversion, of which the natives of this country are very fond, but neither in this does the animal get any fair play. Before he is let loose in the ring his horns are sawed off; he is then allowed to get on his legs in the midst of from fifty to one hundred men on horseback, who ride before and behind him, with their blankets or ponchos on their arms, holding them out ready to blind the bull with them should he make after them. If it were not for the precaution which they take in cutting off the bull's horns, many a noble creature would be slain on these days. The principal feat in this cruel diversion consists in taking the horse as close to the bull's head as possible and watching his motions, and as the bull makes a spring, to clear the horse by a dexterous and agile movement, which most of these people know how to make in a most admirable manner.

This is all that California bull-baiting consists of — being nothing more than a worrying of the animal until he is completely exhausted, when he is turned out to lose his life and his hide, and another one is brought in to share the same fate, in the same manner.

The owners of these bulls of course are the owners of their hides, but they must be extraordinarily vigilant if they get one hide out of four that are taken off.

December 3, 1846 — There is a diversion very much in vogue among the natives of this country, called 'Drawing the Cock.' This is amusing so far as showing off the horsemanship of the Californians, but as there is a degree of cruelty attending it, a humane person cannot derive much pleasure from the exhibition.

A live cock is taken and buried in the ground on some level spot up to his neck, and a prize is put up for the person who draws him out of the ground from his saddle — the horse being at the same time at his greatest speed. Any person whatever may contend for the prize, and I have on some occasions seen from ten to twenty cocks drawn from the ground in this manner as fast as they were buried.

In performing this feat, a horse that has good government in the mouth is necessary. The cock being placed about seventy-five yards from the place where the horse starts, the rider gives him the spur, and when he comes within about 10 yards of the cock he takes hold of the horse's mane with one hand, and as he

Drawing the Cock

hangs himself over, with the other hand makes a grasp at the cock, which a good rider will seldom fail in drawing from the ground. The cock he likewise claims as his prize, and generally twists his neck as soon as he gets him.

There is yet another diversion which the Californians are very fond of, and will leave any kind of business they may have on hand to attend it: this is throwing a bull or a mare by the tail — a parcel of men will get together and go to some place where there are a number of wild bulls, the wilder and more fierce the bulls are the better they are for the purpose. For this as well as all other diversions, they take the best horses they can find, and having arrived at some place where there are plenty of cattle, they part out the largest bull they can see, and start after him; as soon as they overtake him a scuffle ensues for the first hold of the tail, and he who gets it takes a turn over his right hand, guiding his horse with the left; he then places his right hand above his right knee, so getting the tail of the bull under his knee; as soon as he has the tail well secured in this manner, he guides the horse off the bull, which is on his right, to his left, and by a sudden prick of the spur increases the velocity of the horse so suddenly, that the bull is thrown over and over; and I have seen the largest kind of a bull rebound two feet from the ground, the rebound being occasioned by the force of the fall. The harder the animal runs, the easier he is to be thrown.

It is not strength of muscle that is necessary to throw a heavy animal in this manner: it is art. It is principally necessary to know what impulse to give the horse, and at what moment, and in what position to place the body, so as to assist the horse and give more force to the arm.

I have seen high wagers bet at this amusement, and it engages the attention considerably, particularly as there is no great degree of cruelty attached to it; to be sure the falls the bulls get may bruise them a little, but it is very seldom they get seriously hurt, perhaps not more than one time in a hundred. I don't know but the man has the worst of it, for he is sure to get his right hand skinned, often to the bone, but that he thinks nothing of — he is on horseback and he is happy.

December 6, 1846 — A man arrived here yesterday evening from Santa Barbara, bearing letters from Thomas O. Larkin, Esq., U. S. Consul, and now a prisoner of the Californians. He states that he has been as well treated by the Californians as the circumstances would permit — he was sent down with an escort of five men, who will proceed with him to the town of the Angels.[1]

The man who brought these letters states that the Californians are about dividing themselves — the people from the Northern parts and those from the Southern not being able longer to agree together. There is nothing extraordinary in this, because they never have for the last ten or twelve years agreed on politics, six months at a time. The Northern party, it is said, wish to hoist the flag of independence, and then deliver the territory into the hands of the Americans, supposing that by so doing, those who have violated their parole will be free from punishment.

The prize schooner Julian is lying in this harbor, waiting for orders from Colonel Fremont, who is now on his road to the South, but he did not let any person know what road he was going to take; no person here knows where he may be found at

---

1. See above, letters of Nov. 17 and Nov. 18.

this time; though it may well be supposed that he cannot have gone very far on his way, as the rivers are all high from the rains and the weather for the last six days has been very stormy.

There is a report among the Californians who reside in this town, that the party of natives who attacked the Americans a few weeks ago, and took Mr. Larkin prisoner, are still hovering about the Mission of Soledad, distant fifteen leagues from Monterey; how far this report is true we do not know, but we are well informed that one of the principal men of that party joined two of the prisoners who escaped from the jail of this town on the 30th ult. and broke into a house about eighteen miles from hence, in which there was no person living at the time; the family having left it to come into Monterey as many more had done, for protection, and robbed it of everything they could conveniently carry away.

Martial law exists at present throughout California, but here as well as in the town of Angelos, it has been and is carried on in its extremest rigor; perhaps it is a blessing for us who reside here, that there are so very few Mexicans residing in this place; or we might expect a repetition of what had occurred in the town of the Angelos and from the self same causes.

Commodore Stockton in the U.S. frigate Congress is still in San Diego; the Warren and Portsmouth are at San Francisco, as likewise the Savannah, which ship is now fitting out for home. The Cyane is expected here daily from the Gulf of California, and it is expected she will bring on some money, which is here very scarce, it cannot be borrowed for the use of the United States Government, nor even at two per cent per month; and not because the people are unwilling to lend, but because they have not got it.

The prospect this year for a good farming season is superior to anything we have had in California for the last five or six years. The rains have set in early and abundantly which is a sure sign of a good season.

December 7, 1846 — In almost all the civilized parts of the world with which I am acquainted, as Christmas draws near, the price of hen's eggs gets high: but in California it is not so. Eggs are bought and sold here at the usual price, vig: five or six for a shilling, (this being the smallest coin we have,) but then you have the advantage of selling the shells for more than the first cost of the eggs, shells and all. Nay, I have seen egg shells filled with cologne water, or small pieces of colored paper, sell for thirty seven and a half cents each; and in one or two instances as high as fifty cents. This account of the value of egg shells in California will, to persons unacquainted with the customs of these peaple, appear incredible; but a little patience, and I will shew the reason why they are so much valued.

There is a custom very much in vogue amongst the people of this country (whether it is the same in other catholic countries or not I do not know) of breaking egg shells filled with some kind of scented water, or small slips of paper, over people's heads.

This amusement (if so it may be called) always begins on the 6th day of January, directly after church, and lasts without intermission until Ash Wednesday morning before church. What the signification may be I have never been able to learn, though it is something, I am aware, which appertains to the Roman Catholic religion exclusively.

The eggs for this purpose are pricked at both ends, and blown in the same manner that our boys blow birds' eggs for stringing; then one end is stopped up with a small piece of wax, or if this is not to be procured, a piece of pitch will do, and I have sometimes seen tallow used; the egg shell is then filled with scented water, it matters not much of what kind, and the end from which the shell was filled is stopped up in the same manner as the former; the egg shells fixed in this manner will always sell for six and a quarter cents each; but there is another way of fixing them, and which is more costly; this is by filling the egg shell with very small pieces of colored paper, or ribbon, and painted, or rather besmeared with some sort of coloring matter on the outside; these shells so fixed will sell for the space of eight days before Ash Wednesday, at one dollar each — its cost, at the very outside, cannot exceed twelve cents.

The season for breaking egg shells having arrived, the young men and women procure as many of them as they can, and woe betide the young fellow who breaks an egg on a female's head where there are four or five young women, they will be sure to take ample revenge by breaking as many on his head as they possibly can find an opportunity for, generally drenching him from head to foot with cologne water.

During the season I have mentioned, a public dance, or fandango, is got up about every two days, for the special purpose of breaking these egg shells on one anothers heads, and I have actually seen a man pawn his horse and saddle, when he knew that he had not the means of redeeming it, for money to buy egg shells, and I am certain I may say without exageration that in the six towns which Upper Colifornia contains, there are spent at least three thousand dollars for egg shells prepared as I have described, during two months in each year.[1]

December 9, 1846 — This country has for a long time been distracted by the incursions of the wild Indians from the mountains commonly called *Tularenos*; and even yet, although this part of the country is under the government of the United States of America, and they are well aware from what they have formerly experienced from American trappers, that such depredations will meet with the most rigorous punishment, they occasionally pay a visit, taking off with them any stray horses or mares that have been left by either of the parties now at war.

The manner in which these excursions were made is as follows In the first place, some Indian who lived on a farm and was well acquainted with the grazing ground of the horses belonging to some person who had a large quantity of these animals, would go out to the Tulares, and inform some tribe with which he was friendly, that a lot of horses might be captured; but before telling

---

1. Sherman says that in 1847 the cost of an eggshell filled with tinsel stuff ran "as high as one or even five dollars. . . Here they do not like the shells filled with perfumed water as it produces stains on the dresses, and also colds to which these people are very subject" (*Home Letters*, pp. 110, 111). Cf. the similar de-

them from whence, he would stipulate with them the share he was to have for his information and assistance.

This being settled he would give all the necessary information as to the quantity of animals that might be taken, the risk to be run, and the road by which they were to enter, as well as those by which they were to return, &c. All this information having been eagerly attended to and well understood by the tribe, their next business is to go to work, making grass ropes, moccasins, and bows and arrows, taking care to have all these things in readiness a little before a full moon, as likewise about two quarts of meal for each man; all things being thus prepared, as the time approaches for the excursion, the chief would select eight or nine volunteers out of many who would be ready to offer their services, and send them into the settlement, with the man who had gone to them with the information, as head of the party.

They would manage to be down in sight of the farm where the robbery was to be committed, one day at least before the attempt was made, for the purpose of reconnoitering well the ground, and if the owner should have taken the precaution to put his horses in the *corral*, on the evening in which it was the intention of the Indians to steal them; it is so much the better for them, as it saves them the trouble of running around the farm on foot to gather them up. The Indians then creep up when they think the people of the house are asleep, and one or two goes to each door of the house, placing themselves there as sentries, to prevent any person from coming out: (several people have been killed on coming out of their houses when they have heard the Indians stealing their horses;) the rest go to the corral, and let down the bars of the gate with the least possible noise, and then stand off, or kneel, or lay down on the opposite side of the gate from that on which it is their intention to drive the horses, and about ten or fifteen paces from it.

---

scription of egg-breaking that Garner sent to the *Journal of Commerce*, Dec. 29, below, and the Reverend Colton's thoughts on the subject quoted as footnote 2 of that letter.

In a minute or two, the horses seeing the gate open, walk out quite slowly by themselves, and the Indians who opened the gate begin to drive them slowly until they get them about a half a mile away from the house, when their companions having been watching every moment, and as soon as these perceive that the horses are moving off a little distance, they go and join the drivers.

One half of the party now have their bows well strung, and three or four choice arrows in their hands for defence in case of attack, and the other half have their bows strung and two or three arrows in their hands, which have two pieces of stick tied crossways on to the point, or an inch below the point of each arrow. These are intended for driving the animals, should any one of which start on one side, or in any way wander from the direction in which it is the intention of the Indians to drive them. One of these arrows are shot at him with great force, whereby the horse immediately takes his place again in the band, and it is very seldom that the Indians are obliged to punish one unruly horse twice for that offence — the horse which has thus been shot at seldom keeping behind afterwards, or running out on one side.

As soon as they get well clear of the house, they drive the horses towards some deep ravine, if there is one near, and all the Indians but one surround the horses, while this one, who is always the best hand with the lasso, goes into the band, and catches a horse for himself and each of his companions, always taking care to catch the best horses that are in the gang; or if a ravine cannot be found suitable for their purpose, one Indian, or two, will get up into a branchy tree with their lassoes, and their companions drive the horses slowly under the spreading branches of the tree. They drop their lassoes over such of the horses' necks as they wish to catch, and keep on doing until each man has a horse to ride upon.

When they are all mounted, they start off at a full gallop, and keep on at this rate until daybreak, driving all the time through the worst thickets and most intricate roads they can find, and turning round several times, for the purpose of deceiving their pursuers. Should they, on the appearance of daylight, not perceive they are pursued, they drive the horses into the most secret place they can find, and dismount for the purpose of breakfast-ing, and letting their horses take breath. For their breakfast they select a fat colt, if there is one in the band, but should there be a mule, this is to them by far the most preferable. If they think it safe, they remain in this place the whole day, and proceed on their journey in the night, on the first approach of which they all mount again, and drive as fast as possible. Should they not be overtaken the second night, they consider themselves safe, and it is very seldom they do not get away out of danger by that time.

When the horses belonging to a farm are allowed to run out all night, the owner certainly has a better chance of having some horses in the morning, either to pursue the thieves, or to apply to the neighboring farms for assistance; because horses in the night time are very apt to scatter and stroll about, some one way and some another; so that it becomes very difficult for the Indians to gather them. But still, on the other hand, there is one great advantage in having them shut up, which is this: that when the horses are shut up in the evening and are stolen during the night, the owner is aware of his loss at daylight the next morning, and by using a little energy in getting assistance, by following up the trail, will undoubtedly fall in with the stolen horses, and five times out of six will get them back again; though this likewise depends on the bravery of himself and company, and sometimes on the pusillanimity or cowardice of the Indians who have taken them.

It often happens that the Indians on perceiving they are pur-sued, drive the horses on as hard as they can, until they come to some thick woods, or a bad pass in the road and then they drive the horses on beyond this spot, and dismount all but one, or at most two persons, according to their strength, the rest of them lying by or in ambush until their pursuers come up, and should these be few, the Indians will come out of the bush into the road, and dispute the pass with their adversaries. But they more com-monly lie by, and shoot their arrows from their hiding place at the first horseman that presents himself within their range. This method invariably checks the ardor of the horsemen, who seldom have the courage to advance, rather choosing to lose their horses than risk their lives in the dangerous pursuit.[1]

Neither must it be supposed that the one or two persons who go on with the horses, remain idle while their companions are skirmishing with or entertaining the foe; on the contrary, they are doing an active duty, by driving on as fast as they can, well aware that their companions will follow them on foot, and find them in a short time in some preconcerted spot.

As soon as the robbers arrive at their village with the animals they have stolen, they begin to slaughter the horses, unless they are aware of some trapping company being in the neighborhood, and in that case they barter them for blankets, cloth, and various other articles; but when this is not the case, they merely separate a few of the fleetest horses, which they keep for the purpose of hunting the elk, which abound in the Tulare valley.

So frequent had these depredations on property become, that many farms were left without a horse, and several people wounded and some killed. It is true a great many Indians were killed also by the Spaniards, who seldom took any pains to discriminate, and in many instances the innocent suffered instead of the guilty. This in a measure exasperated the Indians, and they became still worse, having latterly been seen about the farms in large parties, consisting of from one to two hundred men.[2]

The evil I have spoken of in this letter, would by this time have been remedied in part, if not entirely, by the very wise disposition of the present Governor General of California, had the insurrection in the Angelos not drawn his attention thitherward, as well as that of Colonel Fremont, there having been a company of eighty riflemen destined to quell the invasions of these marauders. However, we have every reason to hope and believe that these

1. Consul Larkin's 1846 report confirms Garner's letter: "Some few farms are being vacated by the Californians, from fear of further depredations of the wild Indians, who yearly steal thousands of Horses, even out of the enclosed yards near their dweling houses. They are now (almost every week) committing depredations of this kind. The whites seldom follow them to regain their property; the Indians are losing all fear of the Inhabitants and with their arrows have

outrages will soon be effectually stopped, as it certainly will not require either much expense or trouble to make the Indians who now inhabit the Tulares and the borders of the different rivers, become useful members of the community.

There is an immense deal of work to be done in California by the American government, wherein occupation may be found for every Indian in the country; and I am sure from the knowledge I have of their present situation and manners, that nothing more is requisite than some kind of employment suitable to their contracted ideas, to make them forget their present misery and become, as I said before, useful to the commonwealth.

December 12, 1846 — A scouting party was sent out yesterday by the military commandant of this town, in search of some Californians said to be lurking about the river of the Salinas. We have many reasons to believe that those men are nothing more than some plunderers who, taking advantage of the loneliness of the farms all along the banks of the river Salinas, are killing cattle for their hides, which they either bring into town in the night time, or are hiding them away until they can get an opportunity to dispose of them, and such opportunities but too frequently occur.

To-day, at 11 o'clock, a sloop of war bearing the United States flag, came into the harbor with a very strong breeze from the southward. As soon as she got round Muscle [*Mussel*] Point, and within half a mile of the anchorage she wore ship, shook two reefs out of her main and fore-topsails, set top-gallant sails and topmast studding-sails and went away under a crowd of sail with half a gale of wind, to the northward, without either sending a boat, or holding any communication whatever either with the vessels lying in the harbor, or the shore.

---

shot several of them during the years 1845 and 1846." *Larkin Papers*, IV, 306. For the Indian attack on Garner in the Tulares see the biography above.

2. This is by far the best extant description of the horse-stealing technique of the Central California Indian raiders. Cook, "Expedition," contains translations of the reports made by official military expeditions against the horse-stealing Indians and the reminiscences of some rancheros who conducted private retaliatory raids. The brutality of this conflict is nowhere so clearly delineated.

This circumstance has created considerable excitement here, nobody knowing how to account for such an extraordinary movement. It is now some time since we have received any certain news from the leeward, consequently are not aware of the situation of things in that part of the country, and every body here to the northwards feel that anxiety for the uncertainty of events, which may easily be imagined, but cannot be described. A thousand conjectures have been formed as to the object of this "flying Dutchman," who just shewed his nose in the harbor, turned about, and in a few minutes was no more seen.[1]

The scouting party that was sent out yesterday returned to-day without having seen any of the marauders. A man might just as well go and catch a fox, cut his ear off, and let him go; and in a month's time go and look for him in the prairies, as to look for a certain class of Californians that do not want to be seen; they are here, there, and everywhere in the shortest time imaginable.

Lieutenant Seldon, in the prize Julian, sails on Monday the 14th inst., for San Pedro. She will touch in at San Juan Capistrano to carry despatches from Colonel Fremont on his arrival there, to Commodore Stockton.

The brig Euphemia, from the Sandwich Islands, arrived here yesterday, bringing various articles of commerce, but although the importation duties have been reduced from cent per cent to fifteen per cent, we as yet derive no benefit from this alteration in the duties. On inquiry to-day I found the price of the very commonest kind of writing paper to be seven dollars per ream; coarse sandwich island sugar, sixteen dollars per cwt., and every thing else in the same proportion. Such prices are outrageous, but as there is no competition we are obliged to put up with them, and these coasting traders are never satisfied with any profit less than two hundred per cent, and from that upwards.

On account of so many persons having arrived in California within the last six months, provisions and goods of all kinds are

---

1. This was the *Dale*, ariving from New York with dispatches. Not seeing the commodore's pennant displayed at Monterey, the ship went on to San Diego to find him and returned to Monterey on December 30.

getting very scarce; and from the Euphemia we learn that no provisions can be bought at the Sandwich Islands. The natives are all in the war, the farms are without horses to look up their working oxen, and should a change not take place for the better before three months, we shall have nothing to eat but beef, without any hopes of being able to procure any thing else for some time.

December 13, 1846 — There is no toleration of religion in California but the Roman Catholic and Apostolic Church; this being the only one recognized as the Church of God and the Mother church of the people.

Before a person professing any other faith can join in wedlock with a native of California, he must join the Catholic faith; and not only join that faith, but give some satisfactory proof to the Priest *that he believes in all the tenets of the Roman Catholic Church, and in every thing that she teaches her children to believe in; and that he disbelieves and abhors all other religious doctrines in the world, of whatever denomination and from whatever source they may have sprung.*

He is obliged in the first place, to learn by rote, all the most substantial parts of the doctrines of the Roman Catholic Church. Having done this, which commonly requires about two months application if the person understands the Spanish language well enough to read it; where this is not the case, of course it will require from four to six months; he is then examined by the Priest, who questions him as to his motive in wishing to become a Catholic; if he has any temporal interest in being reconciled to the only true faith; if he has any pecuniary interest in it; if he has been persuaded to embrace the Catholic faith contrary to his own inclinations or opinions of right and wrong. In short, if it is for the love of God and the true belief that the Roman Catholic Church is the only one that can save his soul from eternal damnation.

Having answered all and each of the above questions, and whatever more questions may be put to him by the Priest, in such a manner as to relieve any scruples that might appear to hang on the conscience of the Priest with regard to the propriety of receiving the proselyte into the bosom of the Roman Catholic Church, a day is named for the ceremony of baptism, which is commonly the day after the examination has taken place.

The above preliminaries having been satisfactorily settled, the person to be baptized prepares himself with a godfather and god-mother, though the latter is not indispensably necessary if a male person is to be baptized, and they proceed to the church, where many other persons go at the same time for the double purpose of hearing mass and witnessing the making of a saint by baptism; they all believing that when a grown person embraces their religion by baptism, he is from the moment the water is poured on his head, to all intents and purposes, as free from sin as the new born infant when taken from the font; and they will embrace him and appear to be as joyful over the happy lot of that man who they say, has thrown from him not only the sin of heresy which he has maintained from his birth, but all sins whatever, that he may have committed during his life, let their number or magnitude be what they may, as they possibly could be were a saint or an angel to visit them on earth. And they heartily believe that if that person were to die suddenly within a few hours after having embraced the Roman Catholic religion, that he would go straight to heaven without so much as being singed by the flames of Purgatory. And I have many times seen the women and old folks ready to go down on their knees and pray for the death of the newly baptised person, that no opportunity might be allowed for him again to commit sin, after having been so miraculously saved from h——l by a timely warning from his Maker, to embrace the tenets of the only true Church, as the only means of conducting a soul in the path to heaven.

The confession comes on next as an auxiliary in case any thing should have remained in the mind of the proselyte, which by a slight reaction, might cause a relapse of former heresy; the penitence imposed for the first time, is generally very light, and the new made christian is ordered to return to the confessional in a month from that time, and although in the common run of life, a man may be supposed to commit but few if any very heavy sins in the course of that time, particularly after having been so recently baptized, he is generally obliged to undergo a severe penance, and I have known two or three instances of young men having been flogged or rather obliged to flog themselves with sticks in the presence of the Priest. This is by no means common, but it was done in the Mission of Santa Cruz, and some of the persons are still living in the same place.

It will readily be supposed that when a foreigner had cast his eye on a lovely Californian female in such a manner that love in the course of a short time took possession of his victim, that he would be obliged to have recourse to much dissembling before he could arrive at the consummation of his wishes by the holy and sanctified bond of matrimony. There is an old adage very much made use of in this country, and which with good reason is often applied by the natives to such foreigners as have in a certain superficial manner passed the ordeal and formally and lawfully taken possession of his highly prized and well pleased domestic companion. The adage is this, "An old Turk will never make a good Christian," and certainly, in this country at all events, an old Protestant will never make a good Catholic; he may go regularly to church or mass and to confession, but the first is a mystery which he does not understand, and the second, when he retires from the confessional he generally forgets the penance imposed. It is very difficult to make a man forget and disbelieve what from his infancy he has been taught to remember and believe, and to adopt in its stead other ideas and opinions which in themselves are mysterious, besides being exact contrary and opposite to those already engraved on the heart.

I have known two instances in California where one certain Priest, who was an old Spaniard by birth, would not baptise two persons who applied to him for admittance into the pale of the Catholic Church; but the reason was, that one of these persons could talk good Spanish, and made the Priest fairly understand that he had been baptized when an infant, with *pure water*, and in the name of the Father, Son, and Holy Ghost. This explanation satisfied the Priest, and consequently he did not rebaptize him, but merely went through some minor ceremonies, for the purpose of turning the person over to the Catholic religion. Some time after this another foreigner, who wished to be married, and consequently to be recognized among the sons of the Catholic Church, asked me to go with him to the Priest, and explain for him his wishes; I did so; he was ordered to learn by rote the most substantial parts of the Catholic doctrine in Spanish, which he soon did, and in a very short time became as good a Catholic as all the rest of the foreigners, without being rebaptized.[1]

Since the old Spanish Priests went away and the Mexican Priests took their places, there has not been so much scrupulosity — money being with them an all-powerful object, such trifling scruples of conscience are merely exhibited where poverty exists, and fly like lightning from the miraculous enchantment of riches, so that now a man who has plenty of money may marry who he pleases if he has got the consent of the party that does please him.

December 16, 1846 — We have lately had another sad example of the audaciousness of the Californian Indians. I informed you in a former letter of the goodness of Colonel Fremont in having left a considerable number of horses to be divided among the farmers who stood the most in need of them: this has been of no avail. On the 14th inst. a large body of Indians came down and swept every horse they could find a circle of about twenty-five or thirty miles, and left the farmers without a single horse to hunt up their working cattle. This circumstance is really distressing, and I am sorry to be of the opinion that nothing but the extermination of many of the Indian tribes will ever prevent these outrages.

It is generally supposed, from the information received, that the late plunderers were Indians who had left this town for the Tulares — as some Indians who have been living here for years,

---

1. The motive for conversion among the deserting sailors, trappers, and traders was most frequently one of convenience in marrying and getting land. Some converts were wholeheartedly sincere; some, like Garner, were only half-hearted. Most, in the words of Sherman, "laugh if you ask them if they are not real Catholics" (*Home Letters*, p. 93). The first case Garner cites of conditional baptism is his own, given by Padre Felipe Arroyo de la Cuesta at the Mission San Juan Bautista on June 7, 1829. See Appendix I for the document.

were seen at the farm belonging to D. Francisco Pacheco, from whence the greater part of the horses were taken. This gentleman is owner of about thirteen or fourteen thousand head of cattle, and is now left without one horse to gather them with. What an immense loss he will have to suffer if the war continues six months longer![1]

The military authorities having assumed the functions of the civil authorities in this town, whereby the Indians were laid under many restrictions to which they had not been accustomed, and in consequence have left the town, and as they would not be well received by their relatives and friends in the Tulares, if they went empty handed, and having nothing else to take with them as a peace offering, thought that taking a quantity of horses would serve a double purpose, which is this: instead of having to walk from 150 to 200 miles and meet with a cool reception, or something worse, they would be able to ride that distance and have wherewith to make themselves independent when they got there, unless they should have the misfortune to be met by a stronger party on the road, who might take it in their heads as they often do, to rob the robber.

It may with reason now be feared, that these depredators will attempt to put in execution an act they have often openly threatened; and that is, of coming down from the mountains in a large body and carrying off cattle. This they may very easily carry into effect, there being no horses in the settlements to follow them with — The reason they have not done so before, is because cattle travel but slowly, and people on horseback would very soon have overtaken them; but now they having nothing of this kind to fear, and should they once undertake it, and be successful, there would be an end to farming in California, at all events until

---

1. Francisco Perez Pacheco was granted the Rancho Ausaymas y San Felipe, between the present-day San Juan Bautisa, Hollister, and Gilroy, on or before April 1, 1836, the Rancho San Justo along the San Benito River on July 26, 1844, and the Rancho San Luis Gonzaga, on both sides of Pacheco Pass, on October 3, 1843 (or perhaps to his son Juan?). In 1859 he received patent to 35,504 acres from the U.S. Land Commission.

peace and the Government shall be established; and in the interval many farmers would be ruined.

However, as there is little doubt but the Tulare Valley will be the first place pitched upon by emigrants for settling, we may reasonably hope that the outrages which for so many years have been committed almost with impunity, will, in the course of a few months, come to an end, and whenever that is the case, California will again become rich, and a property owner will be able to live on his farm without being in hourly dread of being robbed or assassinated by these desperate outlaws, who have but two ideas that engross all their time and attention, and these are, one of stealing and the other of running away from wherever he may be placed.

December 29, 1846 — It is the custom of this country to ring the church bells at midnight on Christmas Eve, for the purpose of waking up all those persons who wish to hear High Mass before day light; it being customary to sing this mass about one or two o'clock on Christmas morning. The church is then illuminated outside, and brilliantly lit up within, — as much perhaps for the purpose of being able to read the church service, as to see plainly the masquerade which takes place at the end of the Mass.

This masquerade, or perhaps farce would be the better term, is intended to represent the adoration paid by the shepherds to our Savior at his birth; but there has been introduced a certain *dramatis personae* which entirely destroys the effect the representation was originally intended to produce. The superfluous characters are the Devil, the hermit, a woman as shepherdess, old Bartholomew, and the Archangel Michael. These, with five shepherds, make up the actors; and these last are dressed in their common daily clothing, with a piece of printed calico drawn over each of their shoulders like cloaks, and a staff for a crook dressed up at the head with many various colored ribbons, lace, beads, &c.

The boy who represents the angel is dressed in a sky-blue silk tunic, drawn up on the outside part of each side as high as the knee; short sleeves, and open at the breast; a paper crown, set off with false pearls, gilt paper, and various ribbons of various colors curiously worked in; a pair of large wings are fixed to his shoulders, elegantly worked over with rich lace; between the wings and down the back a red scarf is hung, to give the light blue of the tunic a more striking appearance. On his feet he has a pair of red or blue satin shoes, and plaid silk socks half way up the leg. This, with a small sword, completes the costume of the Archangel.

Satan is dressed in black, with a red sash over the left shoulder and knotted under the right arm, with a large sword, a most terrific looking mask, and a cap of black feathers. The hermit is dressed in a friar's old cloak: he has a book and a bag in his hand, and wears a mask made of sheep skin, with the wool shaved off that part intended to represent the face. Old Bartholomew has likewise a sheep skin mask, is dressed as a poor wayfarer, with his budget at his back and a staff in his hand, with some old tin pots or rags made fast to the top of it, intended to form a contrast with the gaudy staves of the shepherds. For the full performance of this farce two more persons are indispensably necessary. These are, a fidler, and a person to play the guitar.

Their first performance is always in the church, and consists of a Christmas carol spoken by the shepherds, or rather sung, at the same time striking continually on the floor with the lower ends of their staves, and this in a measure drowning their own voices. Satan, the hermit, and Bartholomew act their parts almost without interfering with the shepherds, having very little connexion with them. Finally, the Archangel overcomes Satan whilst he is tempting Bartholomew and the hermit to sin, and after a few more verses are sung by the shepherds, a dance is arranged in the following style.

A man sits in a chair in the middle of the room, holding a staff, to the top of which are fixed six scarfs of different colors. Each of the Shepherds, with the shepherdess, takes hold of the lower end of one of these scarfs, and the fidler plays up a Spanish reel, — the six persons dancing round the staff until all the scarfs are fairly platted on the pole which the man in the centre is holding, and when they have but about a foot of the scarfs left in their hands, they turn about and dance back again, unplatting a turn every time each person dances round, until the whole is unplatted from the pole, when the whole affair comes to a conclusion. The dance is only made use of when the farce is performed at private houses, but never in the church.

After having performed in the church, they go to the alcalde and ask permission to perform in his house. This is done by way of compliment to the civil magistrate. After having exhibited at his house, they go from one house to another until they have visited all the principal houses in the town. If any person sends for them to perform at his house, they expect to be paid for it at the rate of at least $1 for each performer; but when they visit a house of their own accord, they are satisfied with a luncheon of cake, cheese, wine, &c. As soon as the time for this diversion is past, the ribbons, beads, and all other articles that may have been used for the occasion, are returned to the owners, generally speaking very little worse for the wear.[1]

The Pastores being over, egg-breaking comes on, and though it is not yet time for the latter, which ought not to begin until after old Christmas day, there have been already some thousands broken on people's heads; in short, a person can scarcely enter a house at present, where there [are] any young females, without being saluted with a slap on the head; and as the ladies of California are by no means weak in the muscles of the arm, it often happens that a person will receive a Herculean blow that will set his ears ringing for a whole day. Of course any or every person is at perfect liberty to return the compliment without the least affront being taken, the act being looked upon rather as a token of esteem than any thing else.

What this breaking of egg-shells originated from, I have not

---

1. Colton's entries for December 24 and 26, 1846 complement this letter. Their combined writings give the only full description of the characters, costumes, actions, and flavor of a California *pastorela*. Colton's account does not stem from Garner. The two men apparently attended the same ceremony, undoubtedly so that Garner could explain the drama, but Colton wrote his own impressions. Garner, however, seems to have written the article about *Los Pastores* that appeared in the *Californian* on January 2, 1847; the description of Satan is exactly like that of the letter, but the one of San Miguel is only partially so. Cf. Colton, *Three Years in California*, pp. 129–130, 132–133.

been able to learn; though I have often made the inquiry from persons who I supposed ought to be able to give the information; that is to say, if it has any meaning at all; but I never could receive anything like a satisfactory account. However, the custom is kept up in this country to its extremest point; and from about a fortnight before, until Ash Wednesday, egg-shells, filled with slips of colored paper and ribbons, will sell for a dollar each. Even now the empty shells sell for six and a quarter cents. It is only by watching the hen that lays, and seizing the egg, that a person can get an egg for breakfast.[2]

---

2. Colton's entry of January 6, 1846, in *Three Years in California*, pp. 143–144, is also on this custom:

As I was sitting in the house of an old Californian to-day, conversing very quietly about the condition of the country, I felt something break on my head, and, starting around, discovered two large black eyes, lighted with their triumph. It flashed upon me, that the annual egg-breaking festival here had commenced. The rules of this frolic do not allow you to take offence, whatever may be your age or the gravity of your profession: you have only one alternative, and that is, to retaliate if you can. . . . The antagonist is always of the opposite sex. You must return these shots, or encounter a railery, which is even worse. Having finished my chat, I bade my good old Californian friend, and his daughter, my egg-shell opponent, good morning; but turned into a shop, procured an egg or two, and re-entered the mansion of my friend by a side door, where I watched for my victim. A few moments brought her along, all-unconscious of her danger. I slipped from my covert, and unperceived, dashed the showering egg on her head. Her locks floated in cologne. I was avenged, and now stood square with the world, so far as egg-breaking is concerned. This seems like children's play; but here you are forced into it in self-defence.

JANUARY AND FEBRUARY
1847

January 29, 1847 — It is really gratifying to see the joyous smile which now begins to shew itself on the countenances of the Californians in general, knowing as we do, that the smile is a benign answer to the very humane and generous steps already entered into by Commodore Shubrick, for the alleviation of many troubles and restrictions under which the inhabitants of this country have suffered during the three or four preceding months.

Our prospects already begin to brighten on every side. A devastating war has just been concluded; the civil authorities have again resumed their functions; martial law no longer exists here, and the natives are returning to their homes. The season is the best for agricultural purposes that we have had for many years past. Immigrants and troops are flocking into the country, to buy up the produce of the laboring farmer, and all men are again free to travel where gain or pleasure calls them without being subjected to those numberless heavy, and often disgraceful, restrictions, necessarily imposed on them in time of war.

What a contrast between this week and last! Eight days ago the town was almost deserted, and even those few persons who remained in it, were more like spectres than living human beings, and whenever any conversation happened to take place among them, it was for no other purpose than to bemoan their hard fate or heap heavy censure on those persons who they supposed had been the cause of the aggravation of the evils they were obliged to suffer.

Commodore Shubrick has been here but one week, and his kind and conciliatory manners have already gained the good wishes of all the inhabitants who have in any shape applied, or have witnessed the application of others, for redress.

The civil authority runs in its proper channel, and the magistrate's office is full of complainants and defendants, from eight in the morning till dusk in the evening, and no applicant for redress retires from that office without having first received such satisfaction as the justness of his claim may demand; while at the same time, criminals are sentenced with all the lenity that may be consistant with justice.

The gentleman who holds the office of Civil Magistrate, (or Alcalde, as he is here styled) in this jurisdiction, is too well known in the United States, for any thing that I can say, to add any more merit to his already highly appreciated character. Suffice it to say, that the Reverend Walter Colton, has, without departing from the strict line of justice and patriotism, entirely gained the good will of every inhabitant of California, and I may safely say, that had there been *six Walter Coltons* elected, or appointed, to the office of Civil Magistrates, in the six different towns or jurisdictions, of which Upper California was comprised, much trouble and expense would have been saved, both to the United States, and the inhabitants of the country.

However, the times are now daily improving, and we have every reason to hope, that the future good will far overbalance the late evil.

February 1, 1847 — The company of volunteers in this town, under the command of Lieut. Maddox, was disbanded on the 27th of last month; and several horses and saddles have been returned to their respective and lawful owners. In the *Pueblo* of Angeles, three commissioners have already been named, for the investigation of claims for property taken for the service of the U. States; and in a few days, three more will be appointed, for the same purpose, in the jurisdiction of Monterey, and thence for that of

San Francisco. This step will go a long way towards establishing a permanent peace in this country, and towards reconciling the minds of the natives to the change of government.

Seven persons have been nominated to form a Legislature. They are to hold two sessions this year; the first in the town of Angeles, in March; and the second some time in the autumn, at Monterey. The persons nominated to form this Legislature, are the Ex-Governor of [California, Juan B.,] Alvarado, Gen. Valleyo, David Spencer, Esq., Thomas O. Larkin, Esq., Don Juan Vandine, Don Santiago Arguells, and E. Grimes, Esq. It is very much doubted if either of the three first mentioned persons will accept of the office to which they have been appointed; neither does this proceeding meet the approbation of the community. Perhaps it would have been better, if legislators had been *elected*: and there is some expectation that ultimately such will be the course pursued; at all events, it is the method most desired.[1]

People are still coming from the South, to their homes in the North; and they all appear to be well aware that opposition on their part for the future must not only be unavailable, but attended with certain destruction to themselves. Some thirty or forty Californians have gone to Sonora with Gen. Flores, but there is little doubt that they would have taken a different step had they been certain of a full pardon for having violated their paroles. Several of those who returned here, state, that it was not originally their intention to come home after the battle in the Angeles, — they generally supposing that they would meet with a harsh reception from the Americans in authority here; but they fell in with Col. Fremont, who treated them with all the kindness and hospitality due to a conquered foe; and promised them, that if they would return to their homes and pursue their domestic occupations, they should be treated with all the respect and liberality due to the citizens of the U. States of America.

---

1. Commodore Stockton issued commissions as governor to Frémont and as secretary of state to William H. Russell on January 16, 1847. On the same date he appointed the seven men named by Garner as a legislative council and set their first meeting for March 1. The meeting was never held. On March 1 the

Since their arrival here, their confidence has not been abused. They have all been from first to last well received by Commodore Shubrick, and all those under his command; and the greater part of them, having been advised of the great demand there must be for provisions in the fall, have already put their hands to the plough, in hopes, with the bright prospects before them, to reap from the rich soil of this country, a more than common reward for their labor.

February 7, 1847 — Improvements are daily increasing in this town; the country has been for such a great length of time under the Spanish government, and little or no improvements of note ever having been made, either by the old Spanish or Mexican governments, every step advanced by the Americans for the benefit of the country at large, or any part of it, excites the most pleasant feelings in the breasts of the Californians.

By what few things have been done in one or two places by the Americans, the natives already begin to form a distant idea of what California in a very few years must become, by remaining in the possession of a nation that has the will, the power, and the means, to make it what it deserves to be.

Notwithstanding it is nearly a fortnight since the arrival of Commodore Shubrick, one or two improvements have been put in operation in this beautiful bay, or rather in the town of Monterey, which, though trifling in themselves, so far as expense or workmanship are concerned, are nevertheless of such a nature as cannot but demand the attention of all vessels arriving on the coast of California.

A dam has been built on a small ravine near the landing place in this bay, and a cistern made, capable of containing twenty thousand or more gallons of excellent water. Shoots [chutes] made of two inch red-wood plank conduct the water from the cis-

---

presidential order naming Gen. Stephen W. Kearny governor of California was promulgated and that officer would not convoke the council, which was already rent by sectional rivalry.

tern to low water mark, a distance of one hundred yards, so that at half flood a launch can come under the end of the outermost shoot and fill her casks with water, without taking them out of their places, or any one man wetting his feet.[1]

Although this has been a work of great facility and little expense, the Mexicans never thought proper to undertake it whilst they had command, notwithstanding that they saw monthly some vessel obliged to leave Monterey and go to San Francisco, for no other purpose but that of procuring water, thereby losing many favorable opportunities of having specie introduced into this town — an article *at that time* scarcely to be seen.

Building lots in the town are sold by the municipal authorities according to the Mexican law, (i.e.) thirty-one and a half cents per yard of front line, so that a person can buy one hundred yards of front line for thirty-one dollars and twenty-five cents, and then he takes one hundred yards in depth which costs him nothing, making a plot of land of a hundred yards square, and containing ten thousand square yards. Such a building lot will cost the purchaser about thirty-four dollars, every expense included, even if he does not know how to write his own application.

February 13, 1847 — A Hint to Speculators. Whenever a stranger arrives in California, his first conversation with the inhabitants and his first questions are concerning the climate and the fertility of the soil. These being very interesting points, he is naturally led to inquire the size of a common farm in California, and the acres it contains; here the person questioned finds himself in a difficulty, either because he is no scholar, or else because he has never calculated, and consequently does not bear in his mind the number of acres contained in a Mexican league, and answers: "We do not measure farms here by acres — we only measure by leagues." "What," says the stranger, "do all the farms in California contain leagues of land?" "Yes," replies the farmer, "they all contain from one square league to eleven." Here the stranger looks around with

---

1. The water chute can be seen in the Hutton drawing used as a frontispiece. The stream that fed it was the northern property line of Garner's house lot.

a stare of incredulity, and after a moment's surprise, asks "What a tract of land of one league square may be worth in specie?" He is told perhaps, one thousand dollars. He becomes more astonished still at hearing of nine square miles of beautiful fertile land, that produce one kind of vegetable or another the whole year round, being sold for one thousand dollars.

A year, or a little less than a year from this time, many of the most splendid farms in this country, will have to go by the board. All the farmers are, with a very few exceptions, deeply in debt to American merchants. I think I may say without any fear of exceeding the truth, that half a million dollars would scarcely be sufficient to cover their debts. These people have no other means of paying those debts but by the sale of their cattle (that is to say those who have cattle) or their farms. The creditors are already making preparations for the recovery of money due to them by individuals in every part of California; they are appointing attornies, who will act with vigor in the performance of their obligations, and there is little doubt that many a noble tract of land will have to change its owner under the hammer.

And even this will be a benefit to this country, because those large tracts of land now held, in many cases, by individuals who never have made and very probably never will make any improvements on them, will fall into the hands of capitalists who will improve them for the purpose of indemnifying themselves.

As it is now almost beyond a doubt that Monterey, on account of its good harbor and central position, will be the capital of California, building lots in this place have for the last two months been in great demand. There are not more than eight or ten building lots belonging at this present time to the municipality — the rest have all been taken by individuals. The land belonging to the municipality of this town, extends two miles from the church in a circle, making a diameter of four miles and a circumference of twelve miles, nearly all of which has been sold to individuals.[1]

---

1. See Garner's fuller discussion of the merits of Monterey as the capital, and the editorial comment by the *North American*, in his February 27 letter below.

February 19, 1847 — There is not perhaps in the world another country or climate so well adapted to the breeding of sheep as Upper California. The reproduction of this most useful animal, and the facility [with] which it is reared here, may appear almost incredible to those who have not witnessed what every person who has resided in this country a few years knows to be the fact.

A ewe in this country never exceeds a year old without breeding; and at the expiration of every six months, or within that time, she will be seen with a new breed, and oftener with two lambs at a birth; though amongst the natives the latter is not considered profitable, because when a sheep has two lambs she is more likely to lose them both than she would be to lose one if she had no other to look after. I have frequently seen a sheep have three lambs, at a birth, but never knew a single example of the dam having reared the three lambs thus born.

The wool produced in this country is not of the finest quality, neither is it by many degrees the most inferior; but there is great room for improving the quality, and it can doubtless be done to a considerable extent. In almost every large flock of sheep in California may be seen four or five different qualities of wool, from very fine to very coarse. The cause of this is carelessness and inattention on the part of the owners; many of whom allow goats to run with the sheep. Thus the goat coupling with the sheep spoils the wool of the breed of all such sheep, and it in a very little time becomes coarse and hairy.[1]

Sheep are not subject to any disease whatever in California. Although I have known them, when the Missions were in their opulence, to run in droves of from ten to fifteen thousand, I never either saw or heard tell of one solitary instance of any malignant disease ever having been observed amongst them. There is no necessity here for washing and salving sheep. In

---

1. Although Garner's conclusion is erroneous, goats sometimes run with sheep, but the two animals are of different genera, and any union — if it did occur — would be infertile. What was actually happening was that the merino-improved

short, there is little or no expense whatever attending them. A farmer who is owner of eight or ten thousand sheep, will get an Indian boy, generally wild from the mountains; this boy will be sent out with the sheep about eight or nine o'clock in the morning, and the sheep are permitted to graze till about four or five in the afternoon, when they are brought home and shut up in a pen formed of a few oak bushes thinly scattered round a piece of ground sufficient to contain them. In the winter time this spot is nothing but a complete mud-hole; and every lamb that happens to be brought forth in this spot, invariably perishes almost as soon as it is born.

Such is all the attention that is paid to this useful animal in California; yet the increase in three or four years is surprising. They are often shorn twice in one year, viz: in April and in September; though this is by no means a good custom, — the animal quickly becoming old and the wool short; but if they are allowed to be shorn but once a year, they will average always two pounds and a half of wool, each sheep. Of this very interesting and serviceable animal, I shall speak more at length in another letter.

February 21, 1847 — On Friday, the 19th inst. despatches arrived here from San Francisco announcing the arrival of the Erie transport from Panama, with a civil Governor for California in case of the non-arrival of Gen. Kearney, who has been some time in the country, and who arrived at San Francisco in the U.S. sloop of war Cyane, on the same day with the Erie. Gen. Kearney will return to this place in the course of eight or ten days, and the very important question of who is to be the civil Governor of the territory of California will be settled.[1]

For several days past this question has given rise to some excitement and great difference in the opinions of the inhabitants.

---

stock was reverting to the basic churro breed. See Garner's October 1846 letter to the *Journal of Commerce*, note 3.

1. The prospective new governor was Col. Richard B. Mason. He did not take office until Gen. Kearny, the actual governor, returned east on May 31, 1847.

Col. Fremont was, some time ago, appointed by Commodore Stockton to the office of civil Governor, but there is great reason to believe that this appointment was not at all in accordance with the wishes of the people, on account of his having been connected with the flag which was hoisted in Sonoma a short time before the American flag was hoisted in Monterey by Com. Sloat.[2]

Next to Col. Fremont comes another person, who I believe, came across the land from the U. States in company with that gentleman. This man employed (after having been about eight months in the country, and without being acquainted either with it or the manners, customs, or necessities of the inhabitants) a shoemaker to go round and procure subscribers to a document he had drawn up for the purpose of becoming civil Governor of California. This document was subscribed to by about one hundred persons, most of whom had recently emigrated from the United States, consequently were not acquainted with either the country or its circumstances, or with the talents and capacity of the would-be Governor, who certainly is a very singular man, having it in his power to raise his head above all the heads of the people, *being full six feet eight inches in height.*[3]

The next person who it was thought would stand a good chance of obtaining this highly honorable office, was Thomas O. Larkin, Esq. This gentleman, besides being well acquainted with the inhabitants of California, their manners, customs and the necessities of the country, has great personal influence among them; and in the event of his being appointed or elected, would

---

2. Larkin reported to Buchanan on the rebellion, in which Frémont's role has never been determined:

On the 14th June at sun rise, thirty four foreigners, some of them Americans, took possession of the town of Sonoma, made prisoners of four of the principal men of the place . . . then took charge of the barracks containing eight pieces of cannon, three hundred stand of arms, and a large quantity of other munitions of war, . . . and forming themselves into a company under the command of William B. Ide, of the United States, fortified the town. On the following day, Commander Ide issued a Proclamation to the people and hoisted a new flag, having a white field with a red border, and a Bear and a Star in the middle; they continued in possession until the 10th of July (never having more than fifty or sixty men), when they lowered their flag and Lieutenant Revere

no doubt have filled the office with credit and honor to himself and the United States; but California *at present* must not be governed by any person who has long standing friends and acquaintances in the country, much less by any merchant, and still less if that merchant has out-standing debts scattered through the territory.

However, there is not much expectation that either of the aforementioned persons will occupy the station of civil governor. Here the whole tide of popular favor flows in an entire new channel, and should Gen. Kearney appoint a man to the office of civil governor, (who, he says, is to be a civilian) according to the wishes of the populace, Walter Colton is the person who could carry the point beyond all measure. This gentleman, during his short residence here has, by his impartial administration of justice, and his kind and benevolent feelings towards every inhabitant of California, so completely gained the ascendency over the minds of the people, that amongst the natives there would not be one dissenting voice to his appointment.

February 23, 1847 — California is at this moment in a state of anarchy. It is true we have civil magistrates in every town, and they do as much as lies in their power to maintain peace and good order, but as yet there is no protection here of private property out of the towns. Daily complaints of robberies are made to the magistrate of this jurisdiction, but he has no means of enforcing wholesome laws, or carrying his sentences into effect. Daily in-

---

U. S. Navy, having read the Commodore's Proclamation, hoisted the U. S. Flag under a salute in presence of a large concourse of people (*Larkin Papers*, V, 140).

3. The very tall man was probably William H. Russell, sometimes known as "Owl" Russell. He came to California in 1846 and served as ordnance officer in the California Battalion and as Frémont's secretary of state in Los Angeles; instead of gathering names on a petition for himself, he was probably doing so for Frémont, who was rapidly falling from grace. Russell left for the east with his papers on March 23, 1847, and stayed to be a principal witness for Frémont at his court martial. From 1849 to about 1857, Russell practiced law in the San Francisco Bay region.

formation is given as to where many of the most incorrigible characters may be found, but we cannot tell what to do with them after they are taken.

There is no jail fit to hold a man twenty-four hours, if he is determined on making his escape, and here we have nobody to guard the prisoners. Many of the worst characters are aware of this, and consequently continue their depredations with impunity; and things will remain in this state until the Governor, whoever he may be, shall take his seat and introduce such energetic measures as will lead not only to the detection and conviction, but also to the security of those vile depredators.

The farmers have suffered and still continue to suffer severely from the actions of the class of people above mentioned. They do nothing in the world but steal horses, and ride about the country from farm to farm stealing cattle for the sake of the hides, for which article they can always find purchasers as vile as themselves, who will buy them clandestinely at a low price, knowing at the same time that they are stolen property.

Lieut. McLane, of the U.S. frigate Congress, arrived here this afternoon from the town of Angeles, and states that everything at present is quiet down at the south. A great part of the volunteers under Col. Fremont have been discharged, and it is supposed that Commodore Stockton is on his way to Monterey by land in company with Col. Fremont.

Nothing can be more desirable than a meeting between Commodores Stockton and Shubrick, that some regulations may take place for the better security of peace in the future. Every day's delay helps to again unsettle the minds of the natives; and before security can be depended on it will absolutely necessary to use rigorous measures with the law-breaking Californians, by way of punishment for the depredations they are continually committing,

---

1. The Mexican War was unpopular in much of the east, especially in New England. It was denounced as rank militarism and land-grabbing for the benefit of southern slave-holding interests, who were openly calculating how many slave states could be carved from the conquered land. There was serious consideration among northerners whether any territory at all should be taken from Mexico if

and that such punishment may serve as an example for others. Until this is done there will be constant commotions; the authorities will be despised by the Californians, and any restless and worthless fellow will at any time be able to raise a mob; not, perhaps, with any hope or intention of overturning the American Government in California, but for the purpose of plundering undefended individuals residing on their farms at a great distance from the towns, and consequently out of the reach (for a time) of the necessary aid, which will not be requisite after a few examples have been made.

Governor Victoria, (the best governor that ever came from Mexico to California) on his arrival here, began his career by executing the law to the letter, and in nine months after his arrival a thief was scarcely heard of through the country.

February 24, 1847 — In the name of wonder, what is the meaning of all this fuss and bustle about us here in California; or in what is it going to result? Will this country be annexed to the United States of America, or will it not? Some doubts appear to remain, and the question is undecided. Seven-eighths of the inhabitants of California this day believe with me, that it is as easy for the American flag to come down in the city of Washington, as it is that it should ever come down in California; but then we only believe so because we, like most other people, are apt to believe what we wish to be the case; the more especially, as we have good reason to dread the consequences, should the Mexicans ever regain their sovereignty here, which almost all in California are ready to say, *and do say*, God forbid.[1]

There is another strong reason why the U. States is in the present case bound to perform what she has undertaken. She has said, I must have California. The words were hardly spoken

---

such action would upset the precarious balance of power that had existed in the Senate since the Missouri Compromise. Ralph Waldo Emerson said, "The United States will conquer Mexico, but it will be as the man who swallows the arsenic which brings him down in turn. Mexico will poison us."

before we the inhabitants of California heard them, and on hearing them could not refrain from demonstrating our joy, in the hope of being by her freed from the rapacity and caprices of a few individuals who held us in bondage. Should she now abandon us, that joy would be turned into bitter lamentation; because it will not for one moment be supposed by any who are acquainted with the vindictive spirit of our former masters, that they would hesitate or make any scruple about assassinating all those individuals who had expressed the slightest wish to shake off the fetters with which they have been bound for the last twelve years.

Nothing can prevent this disaster but the retention of California by the United States, and the prompt establishment of a settled government under her sanction, and a strict execution of law. Such is the daily and hourly wish of all those persons who hold property. Those who have nothing are the only persons from whom any future dissensions may be expected. But as California has afforded to every man who wished to acquire it, a means of supporting himself and family in an independent manner, those who do not do so may be considered, with a very few exceptions, as a set of worthless men, whose only desire is to support themselves by plundering and cheating the industrious.

As plunder and fraud will not be permitted under the government of the United States with impunity, the result will be one of two things. By a strict execution of justice these delinquents will fall under the iron hand of the law, or they will have to become what they never have been, *honest and industrious citizens.*

The Californians are naturally very docile. Generally speaking, they are very apt to act on the impulse of the moment, without any heed to the future; but the reason is, they have never been taught to look forward for their own benefit. They have been brought up under the government and tuition of vicious and corrupt men, and nothing but example will make them see their folly. Precept will not do it; but as soon as one, two, or three of the worst malefactors have undergone capital punishment, the whole country will be at peace.

Garner's Adobe, Head of Decatur Street on Pacific, Monterey. Cross marks the Serra Landing, but the Serra Oak has been cropped from the original photograph (1887?).

View of Monterey and Remains of Old Fort. From Frémont's *Memoirs*.

Thomas Jefferson Farnham.
By unidentified artist.

The Reverend Walter Colton, First
American Alcalde of Monterey
(Photograph, 1850).

Monterey Pioneers. From a daguerrotype probably taken in 1850. Standing, Left to Right
Talbot H. Green [?], Sam Brannan. Seated, Left to Right: Jacob P. Leese, Thomas Oliver
Larkin, W. D. M. Howard.

"Old Graham the Hunter," Engraved by W. G. Jackman. This romantic portrait was the frontispiece for Thomas Jefferson Farnham's *The Early Days of California: Embracing What I Saw and Heard There, with Scenes in the Pacific*, which was an 1860 reprint of *Travels in California* — including Graham's libelous remarks about Garner.

Custom House, Built 1814, Monterey, California. From photograph taken about 1875.

Ruins of Old Mexican Jail, Monterey, California, 1875. This was the *calabozo* mentioned in the Graham Affair of 1840. Sheriff Garner and Alcalde Colton had their office in this building, and Garner wrote that it was not "fit to hold a man twenty-four hours, if he is determined on making his escape."

February 27, 1847 — The United States frigate Savannah arrived here this morning with Gen. Kearney on board, from San Francisco. Commodore Stockton, with the United States frigate Congress, is still at San Diego, and Col. Fremont, with his followers, in the Pueblo de los Angeles, Capt. Tompkins, with his company of dragoons, is in Monterey, where we hope he will remain.

Disputes begin to run high as to where the capitol of California will be fixed. I have said nothing on that point previous to this, fearing as a resident of Monterey, I might be thought partial; but now the question is on the board, I will venture an opinion, though not with the vain hope that it will have any weight on the subject.

Monterey, then, was chosen by our predecessors for the capitol of California, though perhaps not with the same views or under the same ideas as may now be expressed in its favor. In the first place it has a good harbor, where a hundred or more vessels can lie at anchor well sheltered from any wind that can blow from twenty-eight out of thirty-two points of the compass, and with ordinary good ground tackling. There is at no season any danger to be apprehended from the other four.

Next, it has a more central position as a town than any other part of California, which highly entitles it to the preference of being the seat of government. The first object in all civilized governments being, not the personal convenience of those in command, but the happiness and convenience of the persons subject to the government. Now let us suppose the capitol of California to be San Francisco; only consider what an immense distance those persons would have to travel who live in San Diego, or in the town of Angeles even, to transact their business with the government, and the increased expense and inconvenience they would be obliged to suffer.

In the next place, exclusive of its beautiful harbor, Monterey has a splendid site for the rearing of a large city, and an immense quantity of back ground to support it. All the produce for one hundred miles south of Monterey that is intended for exportation, must come here, as likewise that of thirty miles north from this place. Then, again, the principal commerce in California, one way or another, runs through this channel; and finally, the climate is far superior in Monterey to that of San Francisco. There are no fevers and agues as there are there, and all contagious diseases are unknown here.

There is no doubt that San Francisco will be the great commercial point of California, on account of its superior internal resources, and the extent and security (after once entered) of its harbor; but still the picturesque beauty of Monterey, its healthy climate, and the resources and advantages it contains necessary for a large city, always attract the attention of the enterprising emigrant; whilst its commodious and safe harbor, the quantity of native produce brought to its market, and the wealth of its inhabitants, will likewise, at all times, command the attention of the hardy mariner.[1]

---

1. The *North American* commented on Garner's letter in the same issue with the following editorial:

The news from California, and the letters of our Monterey correspondent, of which we publish a second package today, represent that remote conquest, the present Dorado of the American imagination, in a state of comparative tranquillity. There is no actual civil war raging between the numerous rival governors, naval and military, whom the wisdom of the administration despatched thither, to reign over the new acquisition; and the Mexican creoles, after a vain experiment of resistance, seem to have settled down, pacified and reconciled to their fate, which is that of speedy denationalization, if not extinction. Their lands are mortgaged to the foreigner; they are too indolent and powerless to redeem them either with the gold of labor or the iron of war; and every day, almost, witnesses the increase of Americans by a new horde of adventurers landing from ships, or descending the precipices of the Sierra Nevada.

The country, in fact, appears to be already Americanized; and Speculation, snapping up town-lots as certain prizes in the lottery of fortune, calculates the prospects of cities, and, above all, is exercised in determining the site of the seat of government, — of that mighty city of the imagination, the Tyre or Carthage of the uttermost West, which is to wield the future sceptre of the Pacific. There is something grand enough in the dream of a world of empire, embracing all Oceanica, and the Asiatic and American shores of the South Seas; and many a mind is occupied, at home and abroad, in settling the important question in what country of the West Coast we are to look for the germ of power, and in what neglected nook of that country is to grow up the destined metropolis — whether in American Oregon at the mouth of the Columbia; or in British Oregon, at Nootka Sound, in Vancouver's Island, which the English talk of converting into a great colony; or high up at Sitka, in Russian America; or finally, in California, the Southern land of the vine and orange, which we have just wrested from the hands of the Mexican.

The general question as to the *country* which is to rule the South Sea, is an interesting one; worthy of being made the subject of a future disquisition. At present, we feel prompted by our California letter of February 27, published to-day, to reduce the inquiry within the narrow bounds in which the writer presents it. We can fancy, although he does not so express it, that, in his view, California is to be the happy land, the home of the city which is to give laws to the Pacific. "Disputes begin to run high as to where the capital of California shall be fixed," he tells us. The question is, doubtless, of greater moment in California than in our longitudes. But as it is not without its interest even here, and as our correspondent, notwithstanding his fear of being thought partial to the city of his own residence, has ventured a very decided opinion in favor of Monterey, and upon grounds, too, which, in some respects, do not seem to us so well founded as novel; we make his letter of the 27th the subject of some passing comments.

He supposes San Francisco to be the only rival of Monterey; and he prefers the latter, because it was the site originally selected by the Spaniards for the capital of California; because it has a "good harbor"; because it has "a more central position than any other port of California, which highly entitles it to the preference;" because it is a "splendid site" for a large city, backed by a large territory, of which it is the outlet, extending from thirty miles north to a hundred miles south of the city; and because the climate is far superior to that of San Francisco; in which latter place, he hints, there is the drawback of fevers and agues, while "all contagious diseases are unknown at Monterey."

We can allow many advantages to Monterey; but we confess some surprise at our correspondent's picture of its harbor, which is irreconcileable with the accounts of numerous writers, who represent it as an extremely bad one — in fact, an open and dangerous roadstead. "It is a good harbor," he says, "where a hundred or more vessels can lie at anchor, well sheltered from any wind that can blow *from twenty-eight out of thirty-two points of the compass*; and with ordinary good ground tackling, there is at no season any danger to be apprehended from the other four." Contrast this with the very significant account given by Sir George Simpson, in his *Overland Journey Round the World*. "The harbor, if harbor it can be called, is merely the southern end of the bay, protected from the west by the northerly inclination of Point Pinos. It is sheltered from *only one of the prevailing winds*, the southeastern of the short winter; and so little is it land-locked that in the most favorable state of wind and weather, the whole beach presents nearly as troublesome a surf as the shore of the open ocean. Well was it described by one of the band of Franciscans who first visited it after the days of Viscaino, as "this horrible port of Monterey."

The Bay of San Francisco, on the other hand, a "miniature Mediterranean," is not merely a fine harbor, but one of the finest in the world. A strait of about two miles wide by three long, admits the weary voyager through the rampart of an iron-bound and surf-beaten coast, into a wide expanse of placid waters, a nest of bays, or rather of beautiful lakes, capable of sheltering the navies of the world. The shores are margined by belts of the richest alluvion, from two to six miles wide, the whole hemmed in by amphitheatres of green hills. There are marshes, and, doubtless, there are agues; but insalubrity is no characteristic of San Francisco; which invites, and, if in the hands of the American people, will receive such tributes of immigration as will — perhaps in a brief term of years, not merely adorn its shores with a capital, but plant them with town and cities.

To crown all, the Bay of San Francisco is the embrochure of the only navigable river in California; and it is the outlet of a great valley, by far the greatest in the whole territory. Piercing the western cordillera, known as the Coast Range, the Rio Sacramento, dividing into two forks, the Sacramento proper running to the north, the San Joaquin to the south, opens and waters the whole magnificent valley between the Coast Range and the Sierra Nevada, a valley extending from north to south over more than eight degrees of latitude. This valley, running behind Monterey, far south of that city, and stretching up north to the borders of Oregon, will be the great seat of the population of California. Its commerce will centre on the Bay of San Francisco. Its people will open roads — perhaps railroads — to Monterey, to Santa Barbara, to all the accessible sea-ports, good and bad. But none of these, though fed by the plenty, and enriched by the trade, of the Valley of the Sacramento, can ever expect to grow into the wealth and population which are destined to be the prize of some city, the most favorably planted, on the Bay of San Francisco.

We may add, that of all the numerous ports in Upper California, navigators commend the goodness and security of only two, — the most southern and the most northern, — San Diego and San Francisco.

For all its supercilious tone, the editorial has proved to be a true prophecy. However, at the time Garner wrote, Monterey did have distinct advantages over San Francisco, which in 1847 was a dismal collection of huts shivering under fog and sand-blasted by winds off the dunes. Monterey had prestige, a central location, and remarkable salubrity, but, as the editorial notes, the clinching factor would be San Francisco's magnificent bay and natural access by water to the great interior valleys. The stampede to the northern mines and 1849 gave the coup-de-grace to Monterey's dream of reigning over California in American days as she had during the Spanish ones. Oddly enough, San Francisco never became capital of California at any time, although a handful of lesser known cities share that honor.

MARCH TO OCTOBER 1847

March 1, 1847 — The first great point is at length settled; General Kearny has this day taken command of the civil government of California. That question being decided, we may now hope for a speedy relief from many difficulties under which we have been laboring for some years past.

Another great point is likewise settled — Governor Kearny has determined on making Monterey the seat of government. Having traveled through California from one end to the other since his arrival, he has had an opportunity of observing and forming a good judgment, (without the advice of interested parties,) where the capital ought to be fixed, and his opinion has coincided with that of all intelligent and impartial persons who are acquainted with the country, whether Mexicans, Spaniards, Americans, English, French, or of whatever nation they might be.

Some attempts were made to-day to regulate the streets in the town of Monterey. This is a difficult matter, as each person has built his house on the spot and in the form he thought proper, without any attention to regularity. The front line of one house will run perhaps North and South, and the house on one side adjoining will run Northwest and Southeast, whilst the house adjoining on the opposite side will run a line of Northeast and Southwest, jutting out or standing in several yards. However, after some considerable difficulty, we succeeded in laying off two handsome streets, both of which will form a front line extending in a North and South direction. One of these streets is nine hundred yards long, and the other eleven hundred yards from one extremity to the other. Between these two streets is a scope running the whole length of the streets, one hundred yards in width. This is divided into building lots, which lots were sold under the Mexican government, to different individuals, at different times, and are of various dimensions, from twenty-five to one-hundred yards square. Consequently the two streets now laid off being parallel, there were many small jots and plots of land left vacant within the above scope, and the eagerness with which applications were made to the municipal authority for these remnants, is a sufficient proof that Monterey is destined to increase rapidly in population, and consequently in improvements and wealth.[1]

For the last twenty or thirty days one or more applications (per day) have been made to the municipal authority for building and cultivation lots. Many of the Naval officers in the United States service are now owners of valuable lots in this town. Amongst others, Commodore Shubrick has honored our public records with his name, as having purchased an elegant building lot near the beach; and adjoining his lot, Commander Theodore Bailey has purchased another lot.

As still further proof of what I have advanced in favor of Monterey, the present French Consul is so much taken with it,

---

1. The first two streets laid out by Colton and Garner were Alvarado and Tyler (formerly Calle de Castro).

2. The purchase of these view lots on what is now the Presidio Bluff overlooking the bay was to be a matter of some embarrassment to the naval officers. Fortifications had already been built higher up the slope, and on January 5, 1848, Gov. Mason had his secretary write a letter to Alcalde Colton asking by what authority public land was sold within the limits of Monterey and what, in actuality, were the limits of the town. He also asked for copies of the deeds to the hill lots.

Colton sent copies, certified by Garner, of the deeds of Shubrick, Bailey, Spence, Little, Talbot H. Green, and James Doyle. Bernard McKenzie claimed land but would not send his deed. All the lots were about 200 yards square with waterfront access.

Lt. Halleck certified on June 20, 1848, that he had warned Shubrick, Bailey, Colton, and Capt. C. Q. Tompkins on January 28, 1847, that the land on Fort hill would be required for defense works, and that he had also reported the sales to Kearny who said that he would forbid them but had forgotten to do so.

that he has declared his intention of sending for his family, and has already purchased two large building lots which he intends to improve the present year, preparatory to the arrival of his family here.[2]

March 3, 1847 — The United States ship Columbus, Commodore Biddle, arrived at this port yesterday evening from Valparaiso. There are now lying in this port the Columbus, the Independence, the Savannah, the Warren, and the Lexington transport a greater force than has ever been seen in any part of California at one time. This display appears to have some considerable influence on the minds of the Californians. It has enforced the idea that the United States are determined to hold this country, and it may be perceived already that some latent sparks for hope which still remained in the breasts of some men, are beginning to be extinguished.

General Kearney has taken his seat as civil Governor, and a constitution for the future government of California is now in press. Commodore Shubrick still has the command of the coast, and as Commodore Biddle has expressed his intention of shortly leaving this coast, it is be hoped that he will not interfere with Commodore Shubrick's arrangements. I have said it is hoped that Commodore Biddle will not interfere, not because we sup-

---

According to Halleck, the sales were invalid because the area had always been used as a fortification.

The land question was complicated by the fact that Larkin had already bought the Presidio of San Francisco. Gov. Mason therefore sent the whole problem to Adj. Gen. Jones for decision. Jones named as investigator William Carey Jones, a lawyer expert in Spanish land titles and a fluent linguist. William Jones, who had been Frémont's counsel at his court martial, arrived in Monterey in September 1849, during the Constitutional Convention and found the archives imperfect and unorganized. Eventually, the government recovered title to the lands, but although blockhouses were built up on the hill and a rough coastal defense, named first Fort Mervine, then Fort Stockton, and then Fort Halleck, occupied the old Spanish *castillo*, they were of little importance as a military post. It was not until 1902, after the Spanish-American War, that the area came back into active use, this time as a camp to house returning troops. At present, the Presidio is the home of the Defense Language Institute, West.

For details of the case of the lot sales and a map of Fort hill, see U.S., President, *Message on California and New Mexico*, pp. 117–176, 617.

pose that Commodore Biddle would do anything wrong, but because a monthly change of commanders must tend greatly to retard the establishment of many territorial regulations which are indispensable to the security of peace.[1]

Commodore Shubrick has been indefatigable in searching out the most important points on which depend the future safety and benefit of the country. That all his operations will be directed to these two objects, the inhabitants of California, whether natives or foreigners, are fully persuaded, and any obstacle that is thrown in his way cannot but be severely felt by every resident here.

Colonel Fremont has received orders from General Kearney to repair immediately to this place with his volunteers, bringing with him from the town of Angeles all the public archives which were sent from here by order of Governor Pico in 1845. On the arrival of Colonel F. at this place, it is supposed that he will immediately retrace his steps to the United States, where, doubtless, his services will be more beneficial to his country than previous circumstances will ever permit them to be in California.

Commodore Stockton was some weeks ago ordered to repair with the Congress to this place. He has not yet made his appearance, and it appears to be the opinion of some persons who have lately arrived from the south that he will sail from San Diego for the United States, without coming here. Should that be the case many harsh feelings will arise: all persons in Monterey who had any money have lent it for the uses of the United States, and it is necessary that their bills should be signed by him before they can be reimbursed; consequently should he leave this coast without signing these bills the lenders will suffer severely. We hope, and firmly believe, he will take this circumstance into considera-

---

1. Com. James Biddle commanded the American squadron blockading the Mexican west coast and out-ranked Com. Shubrick, but he did not disturb him in his command of the north Pacific squadron. Biddle left California in July, 1847.

2. Bancroft (*History of California*, V, 463) says that, as far as naval funds were available, Stockton did pay some $30,000 in claims and that before he left California on June 28, 1847, "Stockton is said to have paid . . . certain claims

tion, and not take any step that may in any manner throw a shade on his hitherto noble and generous character.²

What is the most needful for the speedy progress of California is a large body of immigrants, with some capitalists, and no lawyers. Only keep that destructive race of men called *land sharks* from California, and it will, under the auspices of the United States government, become a great and prosperous country.

March 5, 1847 — The Ex-Governor Alvarado, with several of the most respectable citizens in Monterey, made a visit in compliance with an invitation they had received from Commodore Biddle on board of the U.S. line-of-battle ship Columbus; they were accompanied also, at the express request of the Ex-Governor, by the Rev. Walter Colton, Alcalde of Monterey. Commodores Biddle and Shubrick, with Captains Lavalette, Mervine, Wyman, and all the officers under their command, received the Ex-Governor of California with all the respect and honor due to a person of even a higher class. After having been on board about one hour, he expressed a wish to return on shore, which was granted, and on his leaving the ship, he was saluted by Commodore Biddle with thirteen guns, and in a few minutes more he arrived on shore highly gratified with the reception given to him by these distinguished persons.¹

There are now six U.S. national vessels lying in this harbor; they are the Columbus, the Independence, the Savannah, the Warren, the Lexington, and the Erie; though I am sorry to say we are about to lose sight of four of them tomorrow. We, who live here, will feel severely the loss of their company, particularly that of the Savannah, she having been for a great length of time

---

for which he felt a peculiar personal responsibility," probably those of which Garner speaks.

1. According to the *Californian*, March 13, 1847, the "several respectable citizens" who accompanied ex-Gov. Alvarado were Gen. Kearny, Col. Mason, Juan Malarín, and David Spence. The newspaper counted a salute of eleven guns, but Garner is probably right in noting thirteen; Don Juan Bautista was more of a "diplomatic representative" of an unconquered nation than a mere "charge d'affaire" who is only entitled to eleven guns.

cruising backwards and forwards on our coast. The urbanity, the social and gentlemanly deportment of her officers, with all of whom we are well acquainted, make us feel as though we were parting with some very ancient and long esteemed friends.

The Californians have settled down again on their farms, and agriculture has taken their attention from political affairs; all they appear to wish for now is, that the United States will establish a firm government here, and secure to them their property. They wish for no more changes; they all say they struck a severer blow at the United States than ever they had previously imagined lay in their power, and they have seen the uselessness of what they have done, and all they wish for now is, to live in peace and security.

Although it was late in the planting season when they returned from the war to their respective homes, they have been very active in getting a large quantity of grain sown, and as the prospect for a good season still remains, we have every reason to believe that provisions will be very plentiful this fall. All we want now are immigrants to flock in to California. Only let there be plenty of tradesmen and mechanics among them, and California will flourish.

Commodore Biddle, a few days ago, desired the Rev. Walter Colton, as Alcalde, to make application to him for any good men that might be on board of the Savannah, and who might want their discharge, and they should have it, consequently on enquiry it was found that several good mechanics wanted their discharge, and at the suggestion of Mr. Colton, they obtained it to the number of about twenty or twenty-five.

Every step of this kind is a benefit to this country, being so poor as it is, at the same time that it affords every facility for enriching its possessors, and nothing more is required than a sufficient number of intelligent men to turn those resources each into its proper channel, and thus reap the benefit of them.

March 5, 1847 — The demand for landed property in California has increased beyond credulity; that is to say, for building lots in the towns. Daily, and indeed almost hourly, applications are made for building lots in the different towns. Nay, so great has been the demand of late, that it was found necessary to set aside sufficient land for a jail, a market place, a burial place, and a public square.

The proceeds of the sales of these lots are appropriated to the needful objects of the town. A sort of penitentiary is now building under the superintendance of the Alcalde, Walter Colton, Esq., of whom, by the bye, it will be necessary to say a few words here, that his friends in the United States may have the pleasure of knowing how highly popular he has become, not only in his own jurisdiction, but all over California.

About a week ago, Commodore Shubrick informed Mr. Colton that Commodore Stockton had sent for him to go and join the U.S. frigate Congress, in San Diego. As soon as this was known by the inhabitants, they immediately got up a petition, and in about three hours after they knew the orders of Commodore Stockton, this petition was on board the Independence and in the hands of Commodore Shubrick. The purpose of it was, in the first place, supplicating Commodore Shubrick to countermand the order, stating at the same time their motives, in terms of the highest eulogium, — their satisfaction at the manner in which impartial justice had been administered to each individual who had applied for it; and then by way of strengthening the influence of their petition, they alleged the right they have to demand his stay, at least until the 15th of September this year, on which day he will complete one year from the day of his election; and as this election took place in conformity to a general order issued by Commodore Stockton, they say they have an undoubted right as American subjects (in which light they now consider themselves) to maintain in his office the person they have elected to fulfill it.

This public, voluntary act will go far to annul the expression of a certain officer, who informed Commodore Shubrick two days after the arrival of the U.S. Frigate Independence, that "Mr. Colton had made himself very unpopular by undertaking the defense of unjust causes." What may have been meant by the defense of unjust causes I am not aware, unless the gentleman meant the restoration of property to its rightful owners after it had been wrested from them by unlawful means.

October 4, 1847 — The affairs of California continue tranquil. Now and then a report reaches us of Mexicans having crossed the southern line of the Territory; but these are idle rumours. The Mexicans have enough to do at home. We apprehend no outbreak here, the sober portion of the community would regard such a step as one of frantic folly; and even that restless class which is found in every country would shrink from the idea of its fearful issue.

The wild Indians give us some trouble. They come down from the Tulares, steal our horses and drive them into the mountains, where they kill and eat them. They prefer horse flesh to the finest beeves. We want in California for a few years some four hundred men, well mounted. They would repress any possible tumult, and protect property in the settlements from the depredations of the wild Indians. You send us out huge guns, which are of no more use than so many hollow trees. No instrument of war is of use here, unless it is invested with locomotive qualities.

The Congress, Portsmouth and Dale, are on the Mexican coast. The Preble leaves tomorrow for Panama, where she is to receive Commodore Jones, and then return here. Commodore Shubrick goes at once with the Independence and Cyane to join the Congress and Portsmouth, and will then capture Mazatlan, San Blas, Guaymas and Acapulco. It is likely there may be hard knocks at the latter place; indeed, nothing could prevent this but the fact that a considerable portion of the troops have been sent to the city of Mexico. The Commodore, I believe, intends to garrison Mazatlan. This is by far the most important point on the Pacific. What a stride for our arms — from the Atlantic to the Pacific —

---

1. Colton's *Three Years in California*, p. 20, gives an amusing picture of the plight of eager young American lawyers in California, or at least in Monterey:

   Mexican statutes, which prevail here, permit lawyers as counsel, but preclude their pleas. They may examine witnesses, sift evidence, but not build arguments. This spoils the whole business, and every effort has been made to have the impediment removed, and the floodgate of eloquence lifted. I should be

but what treasures and blood it has cost! Nor is the end yet. Think not of peace; it is an idle dream. There is no discharge in this war. There is no settled government or permanent party with which to make a peace. The leaders are all military chieftains, whose ascendency depends on the continuance of hostilities. Peace would deprive them of their commands and of their subsistance.

Harvests this year are very abundant in California; wheat in the kernel is low, and the grinding commonly high. We want mills. Fortunes might be made by them here. They must, however, be run by steam, for we have but few waterfalls, except in the North. We want also steam saw mills. We have fine forest trees for lumber, and yet boards are fifty dollars a thousand and difficult to get at that; much of the sawing is done by hand. Send us out a dozen good saw mills and men to manage them.

The Rev. Walter Colton is still with us exercising the functions of *Alcalde*. This gentleman has so far gained the confidence and esteem of the inhabitants that as soon as they heard he had made application to be relieved from his Alcaldeship, the whole town of Monterey raised their voices, demanding his re-election or appointment, which was accorded to them, and Mr. Colton has agreed to stay with us until the Congress sails for home.

Should Mr. Colton leave California before the war is over, we should be in but a sorry plight in Monterey. It will never do to let an ignorant man hold the Alcalde's staff in Monterey, after Mr. Colton. The lawyers now here would eat up both Alcalde and client.[1]

October 10, 1847 — The Preble will leave here tomorrow for Panama, where she goes to take in Commodore Jones and return here. This will therefore reach you over the Isthmus.

---

glad to gratify their ambition, but it is impossible. I should never get through with the business pressing on my hands in every variety of shape which civil and criminal jurisprudence ever assumed. I tell them after the evidence has been submitted, the verdict or decision must follow, and then if any in the courtroom desire to hear the arguments, they can adjourn to another apartment, and plead as long as they like. In this way justice will go ahead, and eloquence too, and the great globe still turn on its axle.

Nothing of moment has occurred here since my last. The calm and liberal measures of Commodore Shubrick have tranquilized the public mind, and contributed much to a quiet possession of the country. By this I intend no reflection on his predecessors. Commodore Stockton had to contend with elements which are now at rest. The thunder-clouds which then darkened the heavens, are now only seen here and there in fading masses on the horizon. The war is over; hardly an echo of it lingers faintly among the hills.

Commodore Shubrick leaves here in the Independence on Monday or Tuesday next for the coast of Mexico, where he has ordered the whole squadron. He goes down to capture Mazatlan, Guaymas, San Blas, Acapulco and Tehuantepec. These are important commercial points, and their possession will not be without its effect on the public mind of Mexico, though I doubt if any extent of conquest will secure a speedy and permanent peace. There will probably be some fighting at Mazatlan, and still more at Acapulco, which is defended by batteries of great strength. . . . But Commodore Shubrick is determined on the attack, and on the capture too; you will know the result before long.

The advance party of the emigrant column for the season, is already in California. We have ceased counting their wagons, — and as for the emigrants, you might as well attempt to number the trees which wave over them. These emigrants would have settled the fate of California without any declaration of war with Mexico. They might perhaps have had a little fighting here between themselves and the natives, but their triumph was sure, not only in their courage and skill, but in their over-powering numbers.

Some of your politicians talk of giving up California. Why, you can no more give her up, than you can the soil on which you

---

1. Colton Hall is still one of Monterey's treasured buildings. Begun about March 1, 1847, and finished on March 8, 1849, it was intended for several purposes: the lower floor for a school, the upper for an assembly hall and city hall. A jail with an enclosed patio and whipping post adjoined it. Originally there were no broad twin stairways leading to the second-floor balcony. The two massive wooden columns of the balcony are, by family tradition, said to be the work

tread. You may say she shall go back to Mexico, but she won't go there; she will be a Territory, and then a State, of the American Confederacy, and nothing else. We don't care a fig how you figure it out on your political map; we have figured it out for ourselves, and our work will stand, whatever may become of yours.

Monterey has still Mr. Colton, of the Navy as Alcalde. He tried hard to get off when his year was up, but the people remonstrated, and addressed communications to Commodore Shubrick and Gov. Mason, and so he consented to remain for the present. The citizens have offered to send for his family, but he has decided to return home in the Congress when she goes. His popularity lies in his energy, impartial administration of justice, and the extensive improvements he is effecting in the city. Among these is a large stone edifice, designed for public schools. It is a superb building; the citizens call it Colton Hall.[1]

October 10, 1847 — This season of the year in California is delightful, particularly in Monterey, the heat not being so intense here as it is to the southward of this, neither is the breeze so strong as to make the weather unpleasant.

Commerce is increasing with the population, but we want competition. Although the cent per cent duties are done away with, and the new tariff is not yet in force here, still there are many articles brought here for which an exorbitant price is demanded. Of course, there being no articles of clothing manufactured here, as the population increases the demand will of necessity be greater. If a weaving company could be got up here, who would raise their own wool and get such machinery from the United States as would be requisite, a very short time would serve for a number of enterprising persons in that line of busi-

---

of William Garner (interview with Harry Downie). In contrast to the other old structures of Monterey, Colton Hall is not of adobe but of "chalk rock" (see biographic sketch, note 2 above). The roof was of redwood shingles.

Within six months of its completion, Colton Hall was being readied for the first California Constitutional Convention, which met in its upper chamber from Sept. 1 to Oct. 13, 1849.

ness, to make for themselves immense fortunes, while they would benefit in a very great measure the community at large.

The price of farming lands has not yet increased. It is true there are not many persons yet who wish to sell, and if there were, there are no persons of capital sufficient to purchase land by the three or four leagues, and the time is not yet come when a farmer can divide his land into sections, and sell by the section. Town lots, on the contrary, have increased in value from five hundred to a thousand per cent, and their value continues to increase almost daily. There are no less than twenty-seven new and substantial buildings raising and raised in Monterey this year, exclusive of log houses and shanties. This is no trifling advancement in a place like Monterey, particularly when we consider that until the month of May everything was in a turbulent state. There has been upwards of two hundred log houses and shanties erected in San Francisco, but no buildings equal to those put up in Monterey this year.

But California can never go very fast ahead, until capitalists and manufacturers come into the country, either from the United States or some other part of the world. What signify the many thousands of dollars spent and circulated here by the United States army and navy; as fast as the money falls into the hands of the residents, it is shipped off again for wearing apparel, *pickles* and *sweetmeats*, and the mass of the people are as poor now as they were when no money circulated in the country.

As far as California is concerned, the war is over with the United States. What we now require are the two things mentioned above, machinery of all kinds, and persons who know how to make use of them. These once introduced, and this noble country, already rich in its own resources, must become one of the most flourishing States in the Union.

October 10, 1847 — It is wonderful what resources California possesses for the advancement of the most necessary manufactories. Within a few days past, a mine of potter's clay has been found on the very verge of this town; and yet, if we want a plate, we must wait till it comes from the United States, and then pay at the rate of from three to four dollars for a half a dozen.

Iron mines are discovered almost monthly; still we have to pay in the stores, thirty-six dollars for a quintal of shingle nails, and five dollars for a iron tea-kettle; that is to say, when such a thing can be found for sale. Rod and bar iron fetch from ten to twelve dollars a quintal, and no blacksmith here will work it, unless he can make from six to ten dollars per day.

California is one of the greatest countries in the world for wool. It is raised without the least expense, and with very little trouble. The sheep breed regularly twice a year. Still, a rough-spun and rougher-woven blanket costs from eight to ten dollars, and is rarely to be found even at that price. Consequently, all sorts of cloth must come from the United States, or elsewhere, — woolen manufactories not being at present known in California.

It is well known in the United States, that bullocks' hides in California are worth only two dollars each, when paid for in barter, and one dollar and fifty cents each in cash, and that more than one hundred thousand, on an average, have been exported from this country yearly, for many years past; still we must go barefoot, or wait until some vessel brings us shoes from the United States.

No doubt many of my readers will ask if California has so many resources, why do not the residents supply themselves with all these necessaries of life? A great many persons have emigrated to California from the United States, and among them are many enterprising and industrious men, and some good mechanics and artizans. All this is very true; but there are no capitalists among them, and none in California. Not only so, but they have commonly found other resources. The moment an emigrant arrives in California, if he has a team of his own, or in company with another, he soon learns that with his team, he can make from eight to ten dollars a day, and as long as he can do that, he will not shoulder an axe, or pass a shuttle, although he might make as much or more at either, for the very simple reason that in the first case his oxen do the labor, and in the second, he would have to do it himself. On the other hand, if the emigrant has no team of his own, but can raise by any honest means, thirty or forty dollars, he will turn grog merchant, and often realize from forty to fifty dollars per day.

Civilization is fast advancing in California. The manners of the natives are becoming Americanized very rapidly. Several public balls have been given by the officers of the American squadron, the officers of the U. S. army here, and by citizens. At each of these balls, all the respectable part of the community attend, almost without one exception. The consequence is, that instead of seeing a man get up to dance *fandango* — with three or four yards of chamois leather flying loosely about his legs and heels, which every now and then he would slap with his hands, or have to stop dancing to pull those dirty leathers up from the heels to the knees, to save himself from getting entangled, and thereby falling on his face, and perhaps taking his lady partner with him, — we see respectable sets of natives stand up to dance waltzes, quadrilles, contra dances, Polkas, &c.

Also in their manner of living at home, where formerly you would see (that is to say, where some extraordinary attention was paid to the guest,) a bullock's head placed behind you to sit upon, and another one placed before you to put your plate by way of table, you will now see, not only in the towns, but in the most retired farm houses, a decent table, some chairs to sit upon, and the necessary decent table furniture; and instead of the guest being turned out of the house towards evening or after supper to sleep on the cold ground, he will now, generally speaking, find a comfortable room and bed, of course for nothing. I do not wish to insinuate that the natives of California have ever been wanting in hospitality; on the contrary, there never lived a more hospitable race of people in the world; but their manners were rude and uncultivated, and their customs such as nature taught them.

But a few short months ago, if a man went out to walk with his wife, he would be seen walking on, some eight or ten steps in advance, or in the rear; and if a single man was seen speaking with a single lady in the street, it was thought a sufficient motive for the basest calumny. Now it is not so. Gentlemen and ladies, whether related or not, may be seen daily and hourly walking the streets arm in arm; and if a stranger goes to visit them at their houses, the ladies do not run away, and under false pretences, or no pretence at all, shut themselves up in another room, or fly out of the house, but they will receive company with the same cordiality that visitors are commonly received in all civilized parts of the world.

Some few years back, such a thing as a fire-place in a house was unknown in this country; but now every house that is built has one or more fire-places in it. A man would as soon think of finishing off his house without either door or window, as finishing it without a fire-place. Although the winters are not so severe here as they are in the United States by many degrees, still a fire is as requisite here as there. At all events the late comers find it so.[1]

---

1. Many observers, including William Tecumseh Sherman, complained of the cold, damp houses; see *Home Letters*, p. 110. See also above, Garner's letter of October 1846.

APPENDIX I

Record of Baptism of William Robert Garner[1]

ON THE 7th of the month of June, 1829, after sufficient instruction in the dogma and precepts of our Holy Mother Church, and having received proper permission, I solemnly baptized in conditional form because of a doubt as to an error of [his previous] church, an adult Englishman who pleaded antecedent baptism,—to whom I gave the name of William Robert (son of John Garner or Garna, the mother's name being Anne Margaret[?], both Protestants, he a native of Massingham and she of Norwich, county of Norfolk),[2] 25 years of age; a native of Southampton Street in

---

1. California, Mission San Juan Bautista Archives, *Libro de Bautismos,* I, 268. The following is a literal translation.

2. William's mention of John Garner is revealing. The Reverend John Gardner, D.D., a graduate of Cambridge, was ordained in 1726 by the Bishop of Norwich. He was rector of Great Massingham and vicar of St. Giles, Norwich, from 1731 to 1771. Henry Gardner (John Henry?), William's father, would have been his grandson or grandnephew. In East Winch, a parish adjoining Massingham, the land tax returns for 1777 show a William Gardner, possibly Henry's father or uncle. There was also a Captain Gardner in the Bennett whaling fleet where William served as apprenticeship.

In the Norwich city directory of 1801, Ann Godfrey, milliner, lived at 45 Market Place and Sarah Godfrey, linen draper, at 20 Market Place. Ann Godfrey is not named in subsequent editions.

I have not been able to locate the marriage place of Henry Gardner and Ann Godfrey nor the baptismal record of William Robert Garner in the parish registers of the churches near Southampton Street — St. Paul's, Covent Garden and

the Strand, London, according to his parents, before going to sea where he trained for and served as ship's officer.[3] He abjured his errors before baptism and I admitted him to the Holy Sacrament in the church of this mission. Godfather: Manuel Butrón, corporal of the presidio of Monterey; godmother, Agustina Avila. Witness: Carlos Carino of Fuerte.

[Signed]   Felipe Arroyo de la Cuesta[4]

St. Martin's-in-the-Fields — or in the dissenting chapels of the vicinity. He may have been baptized somewhere in Norfolk because of family connections.

3. The actual word used for "officer" is *piloto*; the best translation in context is "mate."

4. Padre Felipe Arroyo de la Cuesta was often described by travelers. He was a Castilian, born April 30, 1780, who came to California in 1808 and served at San Juan Bautista Mission until 1833. He had the reputation of being a very learned and intelligent man and composed a grammar of the Costanoan language spoken by the Mutsun Indians at his mission.

Alfred Robinson, stopping at the mission in 1831, found the padre infirm in health but relieving the tedium by having the Indian children dance and play their games before him. In his love for the classics he had christened the children with heroic antique names: "Ciceros, Platos and Alexanders were to be found in abundance" (Alfred Robinson, *Life in California, During a Residence of Several Years in that Territory* [New York, 1846], p. 140).

Captain Beechey describes him as hospitable, good-humored, learned, and an ingenious inventor: he had arranged a water clock to ring a bell and wake him at any stated hour (Frederick Beechey, *A Narrative of a Voyage to the Pacific and Beering's Strait to Cooperate with the Polar Expeditions . . . in the Years 1825, 26, 27, 28* [London, 1831], p. 41). Padre Arroyo de la Cuesta died at Mission San Inés on September 20, 1840.

APPENDIX II

Deposition of Isaac Graham and Related Documents in the
Garner v. *Farnham* Libel Suit

Deposition of Isaac Graham

THE deponent, Isaac Graham, being duly sworn, deposes and says that sometime in the month of February, 1840, one William Garner, the plaintiff in
the case, was at the deponent's house at Natividad near the Salinas Plains
in Alta California and then and there spoke of a passage made by himself
and other convicts from England to the penal colonies on the Island of
New Holland. And that during his conversation that time, Garner boasted
much of the favors of a very special character which were shown him by his
fellow passengers the convict women on board said ship, confessing himself
to have been a convict. Whereupon this deponent inquired of him the nature
of the crime for which Garner was thus sentenced to New South Wales,
when the said Garner replied, "By God, that is telling" and boastingly related how he escaped from the colony of convicts to which he had been
sentenced.

And this deponent says that Garner further stated that on a certain occasion after his arrival among them, fifteen of the convicts in that country,
himself included, conspired to seize a vessel then lying in port and to make
their escape in her, but that fearing the plot might fail, he himself informed
the authorities of it and his companions in the undertaking were executed.

And this deponent further says that the said Garner mentioned with satisfaction the following circumstances connected with this event, to wit: that one of the said fifteen had previously thereto informed the person in charge of them of some misbehavior of his; on account of which he was flogged, and while being flogged he cried and made much ado as if greatly injured by the blows inflicted on him. And that the said individual who had thus informed against him did remark to those who stood to witness Garner's sufferings on that occasion, with an expression of malicious pleasure, "How the villain murmurs!". And when the said individual was about to be executed as aforesaid, Garner repeated to him these words "How the villain murmurs," thereby obtaining a triumph and victory over his foe at the moment when he was passing to Eternity.

And this deponent further says that Garner at the conversation aforesaid declared that his instrumentality in causing the convicts to be executed gained him great favor with the authorities over him in the penal colony which ultimately enabled him to make his escape therefrom in the following manner. He succeeded by various stratagems in getting aboard an American vessel then lying in port in a cask and was stowed away by the sailors 'til the vessel had put to sea. When she had been three days out, Garner appeared on deck. Whereupon, the commander of the vessel laid to several hours and calling his officers together had much conversation with them about putting back to deliver him up, but eventually prosecuted his voyage without returning.

And this deponent further says that at the same conversation at his house the said Garner also confessed that when he came to California he was landed at Santa Barbara in company with two others who together with him had raised a mutiny on board the vessel that brought them to that place. And that he himself was sentenced to the chain gang and was chained to labor with a negro by the name of Joe on the public works in the said town as a punishment for his mutinous conduct aforesaid.

And this deponent further says that in the year 1836 during the revolutionary movements which elevated Don Juan Bautista Alvarado to the governorship of Alta California, he acted in the capacity of Captain in the revolutionary forces and was for a time stationed with his company at the *cuartel* in Monterey — that the said Garner was a member of this company — that many of the Mexicans of the country were at this time removing their families and effects on board the vessels lying in the harbor preparatory for their leaving for Mexico. And that Garner, knowing that considerable sums of money had been deposited in the said vessels made a proposition to seize upon the vessels, throw the women and children overboard and sail for Texas.

That this deponent, having reprimanded Garner for such an inhuman and piratical intention and having placed a guard upon the beach with orders to protect the vessels against any such attempt, believes that many innocent lives were saved from Garner's barbarous intent to destroy them. And yet this deponent was informed and believes that Garner tried to form a party of sufficient strength from the company to execute his intent even though opposed therein as aforesaid.

And this deponent further says that in the month of April, 1840, himself and many other foreigners resident in Alta California were arrested on the false charge of unlawful designs against the people and government of the said company and sent to Mexico, that this deponent and several others were arrested on that occasion on the night of 6th of April, 1840, at his distillery at Natividad near the Salinas Plains, that the said Garner, plaintiff, was at the said distillery in the afternoon of that day and before night set in, left, saying that he was going to San Juan mission and saying that "the time of some people in this country would be short." That Garner returned to the distillery near one o'clock of the night accompanied by General Jose Castro and others when the events occurred which are related in a work entitled *Travels in California (etc.)*, by Thom. J. Farnham and published by Saxton and Miles, Broadway, New York, in which book the circumstances of my said arrest are more fully set forth.

And this deponent further says that after being fired on in his bed, those who came to arrest him dragged him to a neighboring hill, and while they were thus conveying him, the said Garner rode up and said to him, tauntingly, "Now you are buggered" and other words showing that he rejoiced at the approaching death of this deponent — and after this deponent's captors had made some unsuccessful attempts to kill him and were standing around him with fixed bayonets pointed at him, Garner said to the General, "This is not what you promised me you would do," whereupon the General whipped Garner with his sword blade and contemptuously said to him, "Turn your coat, do you?" and ordered him to be bound. And this deponent further says that afterward, when he was leaving his premises on his way to prison in Monterey, he saw Garner and one other enter his this deponent's house; and soon after heard noises proceeding from the breaking open of his trunks in which was deposited $3,700 in specie. And this deponent further says that he did not see Garner afterward until he noticed him riding by the prison in which this deponent was confined in Monterey, and was surprised to see him well clad and well mounted; for he had always theretofore been poorly clad and, in his appearance as well as his character been a mere vaggabond.

Signed: Isaac Graham

This is to certify that Farnham waited seven days at San Jose for Dr. James Stokes, attorney for Garner, and since he did not come, the under-

signed alcalde assigned James W. Weeks as such attny to witness the taking
and swearing of above deposition. September 1, 1847.

John Burton
Alcalde, Pueblo San José de Guadalupe

Signed: James W. Weeks
attny for said Garner[1]

To consider Isaac Graham's accusations point by point is an
instructive exercise. The first, and apparently the one that most
aroused the ire of William Garner, was the matter of his supposed
confession of conviction, transportation to, and depravity in the
penal settlements of Botany Bay and his escape from there to
California.

When Graham first made the charge to Farnham in 1840, he
was certain that Garner had turned state's evidence and saved his
neck at the expense of those deported. The epithets of "traitor,"
"robber," and "vagabond" therefore came naturally to Graham's
lips, but why he should have called his enemy "a runaway Botany
Bay convict" is uncertain.

Graham had a fertile imagination and a reputation as a liar,
but his knowledge of the world beyond the mountains was far
too limited to supply such a circumstantial tale as he told in his
deposition. As a master of innuendo and exaggeration he had few
equals in California, but he took care to build his air castles from
a reasonable base.

There is little doubt that Garner, in the days before 1837, when
he drank with the hard set at Graham's new distillery did relate
tall stories of his life at sea and the wonders he had seen. He

---

1. Monterey County Archives, XIII, 761–781. A copy made by Garner is in XIV,
1–5.

2. George Mackaness, *Blue Bloods of Botany Bay: a Book of Australian Historical Tales* (Sydney: Collins, 1953), and Lloyd L. Robson, *The Convict Settlers
of Australia* (Victoria: Melbourne University Press, 1958), cite many books and
pamphlets dealing with the distinguished characters, bushrangers, and notorious
convicts which were popular reading fare in the British Isles between 1794 and the
1830's. The exploits of Matt Brady and the twelve convicts who seized a boat and
began a two-year reign of terror in June 1824 were long told in song and story.

probably had served as apprentice on an outbound whaler carrying convict freight to Botany Bay and received "favors" from some of the women as Graham said he boasted of. That such promiscuity was an open scandal of the life aboard convict transports has already been mentioned. Small wonder, then, that Garner referred to it.

As a South Seas sailor, he had certainly heard horrendous tales of life in the penal camps, and when the jug went round and Graham narrated his adventures among the trappers and Indians, it is entirely likely that Garner also obliged with tales of blood and slaughter. The stories need not have been true; Garner was far better read than any of his companions, and the account Graham gives of The Convict's Revenge and The Convict's Escape sounds suspiciously like extracts from a "penny dreadful." [2]

Besides, Graham swore that Garner confessed this most secret, shameful, and damaging intelligence to him in February 1840. If, as general opinion ran, the two men had quarreled in November, 1836, and were no longer friends, it is scarcely to be credited that Garner, who had a reputation for being close-mouthed, would have placed such a weapon in the hands of a man he did not trust. [3]

Graham came back from exile thirsting for revenge against Garner, yet for seven years after he told the Botany Bay story to Farnham, he had never repeated it in Monterey or in the logging camps. Job Dye heard Graham curse Garner with all stops out, but he never knew the word "convict" applied to Garner until he saw it in the book. All the old residents who testified swore that they had never heard that Garner was an escaped convict until they read Farnham. Graham himself, in the deposition and

White, *Early Australian History*, pp. 91–92, lists seven important ships captured by transportees in the penal colonies before 1824. Besides these, many evasions were made in small boats. However, escapes by sea were much rarer than by land; in fact, the history of the penal colonies was one long saga of escapes and attempted escapes.

3. Colton, *Three Years in California*, commenting on Garner's secretiveness, cites his discovery of gold in the Sierra Nevada before the discovery at Sutter's Mill and says, "His keeping the discovery a secret proceeded . . . from an eccentricity of character" (p. 369).

claim for damages that he gave before John Black at the American consulate in Mexico City on May 4, 1841, avoided the word.[4] Five out of seven of Farnham's witnesses do not mention it. That Graham and his henchman Morris were the only persons in all California to treasure this delicious bit of scandal for seven long years is hardly likely.

There was, however, an authentic Botany Bay man among Graham's fellow exiles: Bill Anderson, an exoverseer, according to his own statement. It is possible that Graham gathered from Anderson's tales of the miseries of convict life that the worst that could be said of an Englishman was that he was a transported felon. The analogy with his own situation as an exile was obvious; only a short flight of imagination was necessary to put Garner into a similar one in Australia.

Both Graham and Morris believed that Garner had come to California from the penal colony; they so testified in their early depositions. When they learned that he had been an apprentice aboard the whaler, a recalculation of Garner's age became necessary and Anderson was brought forward to say that he had seen children among the prisoners at Botany Bay. Garner's supposed convict record could thus be made to predate his apprenticeship to Mr. Bennett.

The shortest term of penal servitude was seven years, the next lightest was fourteen years. If Garner had been sent out as a thirteen year old, his term (barring further penalties for local misdeeds) would have ended when he was twenty. But at twenty, Garner's apprenticeship aboard the *Royal George* was about to expire, according to the unimpeachable testimony of Watson and

---

4. Doyce Blackman Nunis, Jr., *The Trials of Isaac Graham*, App. I, p. 112.

5. The *Census Returns of Settlers in New South Wales* and the Criminal Book, *Letters, etc., Regarding . . . Removal of Convicts . . . to Await Transportation Overseas* show three from London jails, one from Oxfordshire, and one from Bedford. Not one of these men fits William Robert Garner's case. The Archives of the New South Wales Principal Superintendent of Convicts and the *Sydney Gazette* list a William Gardner, transported for life in 1814 in the whaler *Baring*, "Born in America, 42 years of age, eyes hazel, hair black, height 5 feet, 5 inches." Another, or possibly the same, "William Gardener, Oxfordshire, 5 feet 5 inches, hazel eyes, brown hair, dark yellow complexion," listed as a runaway on

McKinley. He had served at least five years after having begun his career before fifteen years of age.

It is inconceivable that Mr. Bennett, owner of a dozen whalers, would have signed as apprentice a fourteen or fifteen year old of bad character, an escapee from the vicious society of the hulks and road gangs. An apprentice was not an ordinary man before the mast. He was in training to be an officer or trusted company agent. He had to be recommended by responsible people. Furthermore, it was made almost impossible for transported felons to return to the British Isles after serving their sentence. No free passage home was given, and pay was minute.

The fact of Garner's apprenticeship alone would have destroyed Farnham's case. It is evident that Graham, on whom Farnham leaned for all his information, had not known that Garner had not been a mere seaman until Watson and McKinley gave their testimony. Research now shows how far Farnham had been led astray.

There are five transported prisoners named William Garner, Gardner, or Gardener listed in the British Home Office Records from 1814 to 1824. All of these men were at least twelve years older than William Robert Garner, and the descriptions do not suit the tall, lanky, blond, blue-eyed Californian.[5] In addition, despite intensive search of the documents in the Mitchell Library, no mention can be found of the episode reported by Graham: the plot of the fifteen desperados to gain their freedom, their betrayal and subsequent execution. As for Garner's supposed escape on an American vessel, the *Australian Almanac* for 1824 does not show any American ship arriving or departing in that year.[6]

January 12, 1824, when he was fifty years old, is noted as having arrived on the *Lord Sidmouth*. No date for the ship is given, but it made voyages in 1819, 1821, and 1823. The third William Gardener or Gardner also came on the *Baring*, transported for seven years in 1814. He was then aged fifty and died in 1834. In 1820 John William Garner, sentenced to life, aged twenty-nine, came on the *Neptune*. William Garner, a Bedfordshire farmer, was fifty years old when he was transported for seven years in 1822. He arrived at Botany Bay in the *Princess Royal* in 1823. (Poor fellow, he had probably poached the squire's rabbits or stolen a sheep; crimes only slightly more serious were punishable by death.)

6. The last point is not particularly strong. Whalers generally gave their last

The evidence is persuasive; William Garner was not at any time a Botany Bay convict. That Farnham would have found it impossible to sustain his charge is certain, and with the credibility of Graham's testimony damaged on this crucial issue, the other accusations would have collapsed.

It will be noticed that Garner brought suit against Farnham for only the "runaway Botany Bay convict," "vile fellow," and "vagabond" libels. He did not challenge the allegation that he had been implicated in the arrest of the undesirable aliens in 1840. What he would have said to the additional accusation in Graham's affidavit that he was an inciter to piracy, mutiny, murder, and robbery among the *rifleros* on the beach at Monterey in 1836 may be imagined. The charge came as a surprise, but it was apparently such arrant poppycock that Garner wasted little time refuting it.

Graham's friends John Burton, alcalde of San Jose, and Henry Wood backed him up on this defamation by swearing in their depositions (taken in Burton's office) that "much excitement prevailed among the said company in consequence of an attempt on the part of one Garner, the plaintiff in the case, to seduce certain members of our said company to aid him in seizing a vessel then lying in the port . . . and turn pirates." Wood said that Captain Graham stationed him on the beach with a guard of men to prevent it.[7]

If "much excitement prevailed," Farnham, desperate for unprejudiced, first-hand witnesses of it, could not find one of the original twenty-five *rifleros* except the hostile Graham, Burton, and Wood to swear that Garner was the cause. Neither Burton nor Wood declared that he actually heard Garner make the proposition. Wood was told of it by Graham. Burton said he heard "whisperings" and asked Garner what he was plotting. Garner having answered, "Nothing," Burton

---

port of call when reporting, not their home port. Nor were they always adverse to escaping convicts. It was not uncommon for stowaways to be smuggled off by sympathetic sailors, and some captains were known to kidnap convicts when short-handed. Graham's story had only one flaw: according to the records, the main actor

heard that the said Garner was trying to raise some men for the purpose of seizing a vessel lying in the port of Monterey, belonging to one *Agire* [written in different ink] having on board, *as was reported* [different ink], about $100,000 cash, this deponent charged him with such designs, whereupon the said Garner replied, "Well, what of that?" and this deponent replied, "It is piracy, and where can you go with your illegal booty? The men-of-war will hunt you." Whereupon the said Garner replied, "We'll go where we please."

Burton said that he reprimanded Garner and reported him to Graham who placed a guard under Henry Wood on the beach with orders to kill Garner if he attempted to board the vessel.[8]

Charles Wolter, captain of the *Sonora* (*Leonora,* according to Bancroft), whose ship was anchored in the port at the time, testified for Garner:

I was acquainted with many persons connected with the said revolution among whom was Mr. Garner. I was master of the ship *Sonora* during the said revolution and upon an occasion while the said vessel was lying in the harber of Monterey, and when I left the ship and came on shore, I was prevented from returning to the vessel by a party of foreigners, commanded by Captain Graham. My vessel was seized. I heard [*knew* crossed out] that it was true that my vessel was about to be seized by Captain Graham and Hinckley. I did not see Mr. Garner but heard that he was in the corps of Americans under Graham.

I never heard that a movement was contemplated to obtain possession of my vessel and turn it to a pirate by an independent party in the town. There was not at this time any women or children on the *Sonora.* There was no money on the ship, nothing but hides and tallow. There was no boat launched from the beach, to my knowledge, to take possession of the ship. There were no boats, except those belonging to two American vessels lying in the bay. The government had no boats lying here at that time.

The witness refused to give his opinion as to Graham's veracity under oath. All I know is that Mr. Garner is a hard-working, honest man and has been as long as I have known him.[9]

Wolter told the facts concerning his own ship. He did not bother to tell what was common knowledge about the role played

---

in it could not have been the former apprentice who landed from the *Royal George* at Santa Barbara with four witnesses on November 16, 1824.

7. Monterey County Archives, XIII, 741–743, 745–747.

8. Ibid., pp. 745–746.   9. Ibid., pp. 725–726.

by the other ships in the revolution because the idea of piracy must have appeared ridiculous to him. The truculent Commodore Edmund Kennedy of the United States Navy, after attempting to browbeat Governor Gutiérrez on behalf of American smugglers, had sailed from Monterey three days before Alvarado and Graham arrived in town in 1836. At that moment he was slowly cruising the California coast with his squadron. The harbor was full of whalers and traders: the *Sonora* (Captain Wolter), the *Leonidas* (Captain Aguirre), the *Clementine* (Captain Handley), the *Don Quixote* (Captain Hinckley), the *Carolina* (Captain Steele), and the *Europa* (Captain French). They all had arms and ammunition aboard.

In fact, this is the reason Graham put a guard on the beach and closed it to the public. It was not to prevent mischief but to carry out his own operations. On November 2, the day before the revolutionary forces rode into town, Governor Gutiérrez, defending the presidio, asked the two Mexican vessels, the *Sonora* and the *Leonidas*, to send him all the armed men they could spare. Before Captains Wolter and Aguirre could comply, the *rifleros americános*, arriving on November 3, immediately took possession of the beach so that they might get the supplies of muskets, powder, cannon balls, and lances promised to them from the ships of their secret American allies, Captains Hinckley and Handley. For this reason Wolter was prevented from going out to his ship.

The presidio yielded on the morning of November 5. The siege had lasted one day and two nights. On news of the governor's surrender the *Don Quixote*, *Clementine*, *Carolina*, and *Europa* overawed the two Mexican vessels, forced them to haul down their colors, then dressed ship and fired cannon salutes to the jubilant rebel forces. Captain Hinckley actually sent his ship's band of music to lead the victory parade on the same day.

Governor Gutiérrez, his staff, and some discontented Mexican colonists were put aboard the *Clementine*. About seventy per-

10. George Tays, "Revolutionary California: The Political History of California During the Mexican Period, 1824–1846," Ph.D. dissertation, University of California, Berkeley, 1932. Governor Gutiérrez's report to the Mexican minister

sons, some of them women and children, sailed for Mexico on November 9, 1836. The *Leonidas* followed her shortly with a few more Gutiérrez adherents.[10]

Gutiérrez, a Mexican, had made himself unpopular with many of the northern Californians. There were some shots fired in the air when he and his officers were put aboard. Alvarado, Vallejo, and others say that the reason that the Mexicans were sent out to the *Clementine* soon after their surrender was to protect them from outrage and robbery by Graham and his unruly company. Since Garner acted as a sort of aide-de-camp to General Castro and Alvarado according to all reports, he was probably more in sympathy with their attitude than with that of the irresponsible *rifleros*.

If piracy were in anyone's mind, never was there a less profitable occasion for it. The returning settlers had come to California under the abortive *Hijar-Padres* colonization scheme of 1834, but they had been bitterly disappointed in receiving neither mission lands nor political office from the jealous Californians. They had started with few possessions and had already lost a good part of those in the wreck of the transport *Natalia* in Monterey harbor, December 21, 1834. Those who were giving up and going home to Mexico were destitute. The Gutiérrez faction certainly was not allowed to leave with its pockets bulging. So much for the mythical $100,000 cash that figures in the stories of Burton and Graham.

According to Wolter, Graham had some intention of commandeering the *Sonora*. He may have looked upon it as a legitimate prize of war and suggested to Garner, a fine seaman, that it be sailed to another port and its cargo of negotiable hides and tallow be sold to pay the troops. He may simply have wanted to use the ship to take his men southward on campaign. Since Garner and Wolter were acquainted, the former's refusal to fall in with Graham's design may have led to the coolness that developed between the two men. It was at this time that Garner with-

---

of war from shipboard off Cape San Lucas, Baja California, November 30, 1836, was not seen by Bancroft but is quoted in full by Tays. It is particularly explicit on the part played by the American ships in the revolt.

drew from the *rifleros* and resumed his normal business. In any case, Graham had to wait over a month before the *Clementine* returned from Mexico and Captain Handley consented to transport his company to El Cojo, west of Santa Barbara.

José Ábrego, a merchant and an active member of Alvarado's rebels, testified that Graham was a "quarrelsome and desperate character. . . . Subsequent to the revolution of 1836, public sentiment pronounced Garner and Graham to be enemies. It is said that an altercation occurred between them and I know that they were not upon speaking terms after that time."[11]

That neither man explained why they had quarreled can only be counted in Garner's favor. He was known to be discreet; Graham was notoriously loudmouthed. If the reason for the split had been disreputable for Garner, Graham would have blazoned it to the world long before he made his deposition in 1847. He would surely have poured it into Farnham's ear in 1840 when he found no word vile enough to describe his opponent. Farnham, obviously, had never heard of the piracy charge until Graham made his affidavit. He did not mention it in his book — and he left out nothing that would degrade the adversaries of the exiles.

It is of more than passing interest to note that the depositions of Graham, Burton, and Wood were all given in Alcalde Burton's office at San Jose within a space of three days. Isaac Graham led off with the accusation of piracy, among other things, on September 1, 1847.

He had ridden thirty-five miles over rugged mountain trails to give his testimony before Burton when his residence at Zayante was but seven easy miles from his proper alcalde at Santa Cruz. He did not make the long journey to avoid an unfriendly magistrate at the nearer town. Alcalde Blackburn had previously pleaded with Colton for him in the matter of the estate of Henry Naile, Graham's murdered partner. The reason Graham made the trip is obvious from the documentation.

Two days later, after listening to Graham's deposition, both Burton and Wood gave their support to the piracy item and men-

11. Monterey County Records, XIII, 713–714.

tioned not a single additional point. The legal terminology, the presence of Farnham, and the absence of the signature of Charles White — the alcalde's clerk — seem to indicate that Burton allowed Farnham to draw up the paper from Graham's dictation. Captain Aguirre of the *Leonidas,* the intended victim of the supposed attempt, was living in Santa Barbara; Farnham did not list him as a witness.

Under the circumstances, the testimonies of Graham, Burton, and Wood bear clear signs of collusion. However, since the issue of piracy was not pertinent to the suit, it would not have been considered at the trial except as proof of the "vile fellow" charge. Even then, if the point depended on Graham's word against Garner's, the result would have been disastrous for Farnham.

The third accusation — that Garner deliberately betrayed Graham and his associates to General José Castro and caused their capture at the Natividad distillery — has already been mentioned. The evidence is conclusive that somehow William Garner, the intimate friend of the general, did give information which supported the arrests.

What that information consisted of has never been divulged. Contrary to Farnham's flat statement in his book, Garner never gave oral or written evidence at the preliminary hearing of the prisoners in Monterey. The Mexican government, when it dismissed the case against the exiles, chided Alvarado for not providing such proof of the plot. Nor, in after years, did Garner ever explain or excuse his conduct. In the eyes of the community his course had been honorable. No friend dropped him, and his business affairs and his career prospered.

Deposition of Romana Sánchez

Exactly what transpired between General Castro and Garner in 1840 has never been satisfactorily described. Neither man left a statement. The motives that inspired Garner, the influences brought to bear upon him, the circumstances that led to his action have only been guessed at. The key may lie in a seemingly trivial and misinterpreted document which, matched with the sequence of events and the character of the actors in them, brings all the distorted picture into focus.

To unmask this mystery, it is necessary to go back a few paces. After Padre Suárez del Real's April 3, 1840 letter about the plot had given Governor Alvarado the excuse he sought to expel the troublesome foreigners, the governor sent a note on April 5 to General Vallejo at Sonoma. In it he outlined the perilous situation and told how Castro had been ordered to gather his forces and arrest all illegal aliens. He did not name the ringleaders in the plot; all knew who they were likely to be: the dissatisfied chiefs of the *rifleros* of 1836–1837.

General Castro's first care was the quick and silent capture or elimination of "Captain" Graham. While the tough mountain man remained free, an attempt to round up the other malcontents was dangerous and likely to lead to bloody reprisal. Fortunately for the government, Graham's establishment was far from any of his friends and lay open to a surprise attack. Garner, however, living only about a mile away, would have to be decoyed from the vicinity and secured first. He was Castro's friend, but in the event of an uproar he might flee and spread the alarm among the loggers.

San Juan Bautista, thirty-four miles from Monterey, was a weary day's ride over muddy April trails and across swollen streams. Castro did not leave Monterey until April 5. He may have timed his journey to stop overnight at Garner's house or with the Butróns, for during the morning of April 6, according to Graham in 1840, the general, Garner, Angel Castro, and Felipe Butrón passed his distillery a couple of times. General Castro told Graham that he was marching to San Francisco to depose General Vallejo as commandant general.[12] Graham, Garner, and the others had no reason to disbelieve him; California politics consisted largely of such back-stabbing.

---

12. T. J. Farnham, *Travels in California*, p. 78.

Castro, of course, was doing nothing of the kind. He was spying and covering for the movement of troops coming to arrest the men at the still. Later, in private, he asked his old and trusted ally Garner if he, Graham, and the *rifleros* would support him if he not only ousted Vallejo but Alvarado as well. He was assured that they would welcome the opportunity: in fact, they had often talked of turning the governor out by themselves. Castro then told the Englishman of the governor's fear of the intentions of the unruly foreigners and of the junta's proposal to gather them all in. He flattered Garner by promising to protect him and further his fortunes, but the question of when the blow would fall was left dangling, allowing Garner to assume that all depended on the outcome of the contest with Vallejo. At the end of their talk General Castro asked Garner to come to his home in San Juan Bautista that night to lay plans for the campaign. He then rode up the *carreta* road through Crazy Horse Canyon to the ranch of Antonio María Castro at Aromas, eleven miles away.[13]

Although he and Graham were no longer friends, Garner could not shrug off this threat to his old companions-in-arms. He rode back to Graham's distillery later in the afternoon of April 6. He wanted to warn but not to enrage him to the point of a general muster of the turbulent *rifleros* against what might simply be windy blustering. Pretending to be drunk on whiskey, in Graham's words, Garner "said significantly that the time of some people would be short; that Jose Castro had received orders from the governor to drive the foreigners out of California, or to dispose of them in some other way." Because Garner could not give him even a tentative date for this expulsion, Graham paid no attention to him. He "had heard the same threat made a number of times within the past year, but it resulted in nothing."[14]

Garner was still apprehensive, for he was no fool, nor did he sneer at all Mexicans as gabblers and cowards. He made one more effort before leaving to meet Castro. James Meadows, one of those exiled, stated that Garner told the sneering group at the saloon,

13. Serrano, "Appuntes," p. 65; de la Torre, "Reminiscencias," pp. 88–90.
14. Farnham, p. 78.

"If you hear of me falling off my horse between here and San Juan, look out for yourselves," and that a man did come with that message but that Graham ignored it.[15]

Garner left the distillery late in the afternoon and rode over the Gavilán hills to San Juan Bautista. He did not know that General Castro had long hours before sent a vaquero galloping from Aromas to Monterey with two letters. One was to José María Covarrubias, secretary of the prefecture, ordering that arrests be made in the San Jose area; the other told Alferez Joaquín de la Torre to bring twenty soldiers from the presidio and some militiamen to Graham's house about midnight.[16]

The plan was well laid. Garner would be out of the way in San Juan Bautista, Graham would suspect nothing even if he heard the cavalry ride by, and the distillery would serve as a rendezvous when Castro came back from San Juan Bautista to lead the attack.

For Castro now had additional and substantial evidence for the wholesale arrests. Garner was a witness from the very ranks of the *rifleros*. He had said that he, Graham, Morris, Naile, and others had spoken of overthrowing Alvarado. It was of little moment that all this had been cheap barroom bravado, maudlin recitations of fancied wrongs, nor that it had taken place a year or more before. Castro had a reason for quick action, all the reason that public opinion needed.

When William Garner swung off his horse and entered Castro's house on the plaza about dark, he found the general in a fever of excitement. Here the testimony of old Romana Sánchez and Mariano Macario Castro, the general's uncle, who were living in the same house, provides some revealing views. They were the only persons to tell what took place in San Juan Bautista on the night of April 6–7. Both, although they contradicted each other

---

15. Meadows, "Graham Affair," p. 5.

16. Archives of California, Departmental State Papers, San Jose, V, 32. The letter to Covarrubias (Aromas, April 6, 1840) tells him to go to San Jose and arrest the foreigners there while Castro does the same at Natividad. The letter is incorrectly translated in Bancroft, *History of California*, IV, 11n., and lacks the very important place of origin.

often, were consistent in declaring that word had just been received by General Castro that Graham and his gang were going to follow and kill him in the morning. Romana declared, but would not swear — and Mariano later said that her statement was full of errors — that Garner brought the news and insisted that the general arrest Graham that very night.

Garner could hardly have brought Castro news: the general had already sent for troops to secure Graham at least seven hours before Garner arrived at San Juan Bautista. And if Garner had planned a treacherous attack on Graham, why should he have gone to the man everyone knew he disliked to warn him, not once but twice, of the impending assault? Romana "remembered" that Garner showed Castro a copy of Graham's plan of assassination.[17] Besides the fact that Graham was illiterate and that the existence of such a plan is hardly credible, who is more likely to have had a written description of seditious plots, ideas and schemings: Garner, or the general who had just come posthaste from a junta where the threat of revolt by the foreigners had been explicitly outlined and exactly such a description sent to General Vallejo on April 5? And why, in Romana's tale, should Garner labor to convince Castro to arrest Graham when that was nothing less than Castro's full intention and what he had told Garner that very afternoon he had official orders to do?

Romana Sánchez's deposition, unwitnessed and unsigned, given before Garner's enemy and Farnham's witness, Alcalde John Burton, is an incredible document. The old lady either got it completely backwards, or her testimony was tampered with, or it is a malicious perjury. Only by use of an heroic measure can it be brought to make sense: if read in reverse, that is, putting General Castro's name where Garner's appears in the original, and vice versa (as indicated by italics), it is completely consistent

---

17. This is odd, for Henry Bee said that Graham could neither read nor write in 1837. The signature on his deposition in 1847 is laboriously traced and there is no letter written by him in the old archives. Every letter signed by Isaac Graham was written by somebody else. It is possible, of course, that Morris could have written the plan seen by Romana, but why should he if he was to be one of the cutthroats?

with Castro's timetable and strategy. It then furnishes the key to Garner's actions at Graham's capture.

General Castro told Garner that Isaac Graham and all the other foreigners in Alta California had conspired to put him, Castro, to death and do other deeds of violence against the people and laws of the country. He insisted that they [sic] immediately seize all the foreigners and exile them or otherwise dispose of them except the three following: James Forbes, present British consul, Captain John Burton and another carpenter.

And this deponent says besides that Garner replied that he should write a letter to Graham calling him before his presence where Castro could have the opportunity to accuse him of the criminal intentions to his face, but Castro refused to meet Graham in such a manner, but assured Garner that the attack on him was to take place that very night. And this deponent says that at nightfall, Garner and the General and the others left the house where she resided and after some hours returned, and after they returned, Castro did everything imaginable to induce Garner to go to the distillery of Graham to arrest Graham and Morris and the other foreigners and Garner refused to go at night, saying that it was not honorable to do it that way, but Castro showed Garner what he said was a plan written for the assassination of the general and for doing all sorts of treasonable acts against the people and the government of Alta California, and he said that he was to be assassinated that very night and that Graham was to be the leader of these foreigners who were to do the deed. And this deponent says, that after long persuasion and presentation of the foregoing reasons, Garner consented to go to the distillery.[18]

As Esteban de la Torre said, "Castro was never famous for military genius nor bravery, but he certainly was for a first class intriguer." It is clear that the general, play-acting, stressing the present danger and terrible conscquences of a revolt led by Graham, finally won Garner's reluctant consent to a midnight raid. The Englishman must have imposed his conditions: no killing, fair trials for those accused, and secrecy about his own involvement in the affair. Romana says that Garner asked "to have his hands tied and to be treated like a prisoner" when Castro and the posse brought him with them to Graham's distillery.

Mariano M. Castro, who, when brought before Colton, re-

18. Monterey County Archives, XIII, 755–759.

pudiated the testimony he had given Farnham, was positive on one point. He said that he advised the general to surround the distillery and, in the morning, call on Graham to surrender. "Some persons advised one thing and others another. Mr. Garner said that it would not be prudent to do as the deponent advised as the party inside the house would be sure to make resistence." [19]

The Graham Charges

Garner's intention was to avoid bloodshed, for Graham was a crack shot, and within his walls there were at least three or four men to back him. If any Californian had been killed, Castro and Alvarado would have been assured that a murderous plot existed and a bloody battle with the foreigners at Graham's place might have ensued. As it was, the impetuous Joaquín de la Torre almost ignited the fuse when he called on Graham to deliver himself in the name of the Nation and immediately battered down the door.

According to what Joaquín told his brother Esteban and Florencio Serrano, Graham grabbed his pistol and fired; the ball cut through Joaquín's cape without harming him. Pointblank, Joaquín fired both his horse pistols at Graham, but in the hard ride from Monterey the wadding had worked loose and the bullets had fallen into the bottom of the holsters. Graham's shirt, chest, and stomach were burned by the explosions, but he was more frightened than hurt. The rest of the startled sleepers in the shack either scrambled out through the flimsy walls and ran away or exchanged wildly ineffective shots with the posse. Fortunately, although Naile received a painful sword cut in the leg in the melee, no one was seriously wounded. Graham and the others were quickly subdued. [20]

Albert Morris, the eccentric employee at the still, escaped cap-

---

19. Ibid., p. 783.
20. Serrano, pp. 65–66; de la Torre, pp. 92–93.

ture by crawling out a hole at the back of the bunkhouse and hiding in the willows along the creek. He eventually gave himself up and was exiled with Graham as one of the ringleaders in the supposed plot. He was devoted to Farnham, to whom he believed he owed his life. (Morris was the prisoner over whom Farnham vowed to fling the American flag at the trial in Monterey in 1840, and Farnham supported the exiles through their darkest hours with money and encouragement.)

Morris now did what he could to help his benefactor, but besides echoing Graham's Botany Bay convict story, he had little of value to contribute. He claimed that while the guns blazed and the posse was breaking in the door of Graham's house "he heard Garner encourage the assailants in their evil work and advise them to set the house afire." No one else heard this, not even Graham. When it is remembered that the attack took place between one and three A.M. in the wet and foggy dark, that there was considerable shouting and firing, and that Morris, half-naked, was fleeing for his life into the brush, it seems probable that he was mistaken. He had not told Farnham of it in 1840.

Graham also touched up his earlier recital in *Travels in California*. With Morris and Mariano M. Castro, he declared that Garner was on a hill at a distance from the house with General Castro. Joaquín de la Torre scornfully told Florencio Serrano that the general very prudently kept himself a long way from the fight on pretext of guarding Garner. Graham says Garner was tied up at Natividad; Romana Sánchez said he left San Juan Bautista in bonds.

When the fracas started, then, Garner was a bound prisoner and kept from the scene of action. Morris's recollections are at best faulty, if not mere reflections of his loyalty to Farnham. Graham says that when he was brought struggling before the general and hemmed in by bayonets, Garner taunted him. No one else recalls this, and it is most unlikely to have occurred. Had Garner turned state's evidence, it is scarcely reasonable that he would have boasted of it to Graham while he himself sat roped to his horse. Graham at that moment was powder-burned from de la Torre's pistols, his resistance had aroused intense excite-

ment, and he was in imminent danger of death. It is far more
believable that if Garner called out at all, it was to advise him to
give up and go along quietly or they would all suffer.

In doing this, Garner may indeed have commented bitterly,
"Now you are buggered," but in quite a different sense from that
insinuated by Graham. Garner, who had listened for years to
Graham's bombast and foofaraw, now saw to what a pass such
loose talk had brought all the foreigners in California. If he had
phrased it more elegantly, Graham might have heard, "You
and your brave talk! You have raised this storm and you are the
first to be caught in it — and by the Mexicans you have always
so despised!"

Garner's other comment, as reported by Graham: "This is not
what you promised me you would do," was addressed to General
Castro. Graham construed it as a promise to kill him. It was
obviously just the opposite, a promise *not* to harm Graham and
his friends exacted from Castro by Garner during the argument
in Castro's home. That Graham, Naile, Morris, Bill Barton, and
John (Jonathan?) Smith were fortunate to escape with their
lives after having opened fire on the legal authorities can only
have been due to some previous agreement among the members
of the posse.

The same distortion of motive is evident in Graham's statement
that Castro sword-whipped Garner for betraying the Americans.
Incapable of believing that Garner would protest his ill-treatment,
the battered prisoner jumped to the conclusion that the flat of
the blade was aimed at the Englishman because he had "turned
his coat" on his former cronies. Castro was not known for such
quixotic displays of chivalry. To punish a friend for loyally supporting him against an enemy would have appeared ridiculous
to him. But the whole episode may be a simple transposition. In
1840, Graham did not mention Garner's presence at the fight,
and claimed that he was the one struck over the head with the
sword and ordered shot.

Graham accused Garner of entering his house and stealing his
money. Mariano M. Castro, testifying before Colton and Hartnell and presumably telling the truth this time, said that General

Castro appointed him guardian of the property at the distillery until the alcalde of San Juan Bautista arrived and took charge.

Being asked if while he remained in charge of the distillery Garner had at any time been there, he answered "No, that he had not." If he had heard that Garner had gone to the distillery at any time and broken open any trunks or taken any thing away from the said premises, he answered "Not while he was in charge, nor did he ever hear that before or after he had done so." [21]

The soldiers searched Graham's effects for incriminating papers and undoubtedly stole some articles while they were at it. The one thing they would not have found in any quantity was money. Some years later, Morris told how, after fleeing to the hills near Santa Cruz, he surrendered to Antonio Buelna and was taken to Monterey. His escort obligingly consented to go there by way of the still so that he might get some clothing and money. Naile was lying inside suffering from a cut on his leg. No one else was to be seen. The room had been ransacked. Morris got some clothing but Naile could give him no money. It was buried, according to the usual custom, and Naile was in too much pain to dig it up. Neither did Naile, in that narrative, mention Garner's name.

William Garner as robber was a flight of Graham's vindictive fancy. He forgot that he had already sworn that General Castro put Garner in bonds up on the hill. He also forgot that in Mexico in 1840 he had told Farnham that his money was safely buried at Natividad and that he had told his captors he had none for "I was determined they should never enjoy it." [22]

In 1847 Isaac Graham charged Garner with stealing $3,700 in specie from him, contradicting the statement he had made seven years before to Farnham. It is most unlikely that he had any such sum in the first place. If Graham had actually hoarded that amount, he would have possessed one-twentieth of all the cur-

---

21. Monterey County Archives, XIII, 783.
22. T. J. Farnham, p. 80.
23. Larkin, *Chapters in the Early Life of Thomas O. Larkin, Including his*

rency in California. Hartnell estimated in 1844 that there was not $60,000 to $70,000 in hard cash in the entire country. Thomas O. Larkin's home, the most elegant and expensive one built during this period and the admiration of all California, cost $3,843.03 (including land, labor, material, imported furniture and rum for raising the rooftree).[23]

In June 1840 Larkin estimated Graham's loss at a very generous $19,000. On December 31, 1840, José María Jimenes, the Mexican minister of the interior, wrote to Alvarado, "Mr. Lawrence Carmichael has a claim for $7,380 . . . The claims of the other prisoners are much less." On May 4, 1841, when it was clear that the government would have to abandon its case against him, Graham determined to make Mexico suffer for it. He lodged a claim with the American consul in Mexico City for $36,094 plus pay at $1,500 a month since his arrest. After returning to Monterey, Graham recalculated the figures. He sent to Secretary of State Daniel Webster a brazen claim for $36,000 in property damage, $50,000 for loss of health and time, and $1,500 a month pay for the profits he had lost in business while absent in Mexico! This for a crude homemade still and a few kegs of rotgut whiskey! Graham owned no other valuable property except his rifle and pistols, a racehorse, cows, and a few saddle ponies, some hides he may have taken in trade, and some uncollected debts. By 1844 he had reluctantly scaled it down to $72,500 for loss of property and $1,500 a month for loss of time. This bill the secretary was happy to forward to Mexico, but there, needless to say, it perished of neglect.

In the end, through sheer persistence, the unexpected acquisition of California by American forces and the advocacy of Commodore Thomas ap Catesby Jones in Washington, Graham did eventually bilk the United States, not Mexico, out of $38,125 on his claims. In the treaty of Guadalupe Hidalgo after the Mexican War, a somewhat shamefaced United States paid Mexico

Experiences in the Carolinas and the Building of the Larkin House of Monterey, ed. Robert J. Parker (San Francisco: California Historical Society Special Publication No. 16, 1939).

$15,000,000 for territory taken and agreed to settle all claims decided and pending against her, a gesture which cost another $3,250,000. Isaac Graham's bill wobbled through on the last day of the claims commission's existence, April 15, 1851.[24]

Despite wild rumor, there is no proof that anyone else got more than the $250-$300 each that the British consul at Tepic advanced them. As the caustic Bancroft remarked, "If each of those adjudged to have been illegally exiled could have received $500 in compensation for his losses, it would have been a better use of his time than any one of their number was likely to have made in California." [25]

Poor Morris, who never owned more than the clothes he stood in, had a claim for $30,000 in damages when he died indigent in 1871. He bequeathed this "pie-in-the-sky" to bewildered relatives and friends who promptly accused each other of hiding it away. They might just as easily have hidden a wisp of fog.[26]

The last charge against William Garner: that "in his appearance as well as his character (*he had*) been a mere vagabond," "a vile fellow", was the easiest of all to disprove. His twenty-three years of work as a lumberman and rancher, his service to the community, his honest dealing and full payment of debts brought him quick support from the old responsible businessmen of Monterey. Larkin, Hartnell, Abrego, Francis Job Dye, Stokes, Watson, McKinley, Esteban Munras, Juan Malarin, Charles Wolter, Talbot Green, Moses Schallenberger and others stood shoulder to shoul-

---

24. *Larkin Papers*, I, 68–69: Graham's letter of claim, March 24, 1842. Vallejo, XXXIII, No. 68: Naile ordered to sell distillery and Graham's effects and leave California within two months after May 2, 1840. Since Naile was unable to travel, he was allowed to stay, but he either sold the equipment or let the shacks and articles revert to Butrón in lieu of rent. Nunis, pp. 36–41, has definitely put to rest the question of payment on Graham's claim. He has followed it in all its meanders to final settlement in National Archives, Record Group 76, *Records of Boundary Claims and Arbitrations: Claims vs Mexico, November term, 1848*, vol. II, Cases No. 59 and 250, "Awards," Washington, D. C.

Incidentally, Commodore Jones, who received part of Graham's award for steering it through the commission, seems to have been as untrustworthy as his client. In 1851 he was convicted of speculating in gold dust with navy funds and was suspended from the naval service for five years with loss of pay for two and one-half years. Bancroft, *History of California*, VI, 265n.

25. Bancroft, IV, 41.

der for him. His record for truthfulness, industry, honesty and citizenship was so immeasurably better than that of Graham and his associates that in 1885 Bancroft gave his opinion in Garner's favor largely on this basis.[27]

Mason Letter on Ricord

Hdqt, Tenth Military Department
Monterey, California   November 5, 1847
Sirs:

I acknowledge per the receipt of your letter of the 29th ultimo and its enclosure, asking me to effectuate the power you exercised in commanding the parties, Garner vs Farnham, to appear before you and a jury at San Luis Obispo on the first Monday of January next and requesting me to communicate that fact to the Alcalde and people of that district.

You have, as I remarked to you in conversation on the 28th ultimo, misconceived the powers with which you were clothed in the case abovementioned. One of the parties having applied to me for a change of venue, on the ground of alleged partiality on the part of the Alcalde, etc., I referred the application to the Alcalde, before whom I thought the initiatory steps should be taken and sent the application by the party who made it.

I understand he never delivered it but threw it into the fire. I then received a communication from the Alcalde asking, with the concurrence of both parties, that a special judge should be appointed to try the case. This, I understand to be an agreement or compromise between the parties, upon the question of change of venue.

---

26. Albert Ferdinand Morris, "The Journal of a Crazy Man," ed. Charles Camp, *California Historical Society Quarterly*, 15:1, 2.

27. Those who knew Graham best, liked him least. Farnham, Hastings, Wilkes, etc., scarcely knew him at all or found in his brutal contempt for Mexicans an echo of their own intolerance. Many reputable Americans and the Californians painted unflattering pictures of him. He eventually alienated every old friend except the weak-willed Naile. Benjamin Davis Wilson ("Some Facts About Isaac Graham and John Sutter, by a Pioneer of '41," 1877, MS, Bancroft Library) knew Graham in New Mexico in 1832 and stated, "He was noted for being a bummer, a blow-hard and a notorious liar without an atom of honesty in his composition."

It seems clear that but for the full-blown partisan publicity given to the exiles of 1840 by the advocates of Manifest Destiny, Isaac Graham would have gone down in history as one of the most disreputable figures in California's past.

You were appointed to hold a special court to try the case, and by reference to that appointment, you will find that it did not clothe you with any power beyond those possessed by the Alcalde of Monterey. Had he changed the venue, he could not have followed the case to another jurisdiction and then tried it, even if there had been no objections raised against him, which caused the change of venue to be made; and so neither can you, had you possessed no powers over the case beyond his. You stand in regard to the case *exactly* in his place, possessing neither more nor less powers than he did. I therefore cannot give the notification to the Alcalde and people of San Luis Obispo that you ask; the cause must be tried before the civil magistrate of the district or jurisdiction to which it is taken. I think it would be establishing a bad precedent, and treating the Alcalde of San Luis Obispo with a marked slight and disrespect, to send a person into his district to hold a special court upon no other ground than that a neighboring Alcalde had been objected to, and the venue changed from one district to another.

The parties having already been notified, the venue will stand changed to San Luis Obispo for the first Monday in January, 1848.

I will furnish Messers. Garner and Farnham with a copy of this communication.

I remarked the language used in the stipulation entered into by the parties, viz. "and whereas an allegation has been made by the defendant against the impartiality of the said Alcalde, in consequence of which, a special commission has been issued to the Hon. John Ricord for the trial thereof, and full judicial powers over the said controversy conferred upon him co-extensive with the Territory of California." Those gentlemen could not have seen your commission or letter of appointment; it contains no such language as that expressed in the latter part of the quotation, gives no such powers and no such inference can be drawn from it.

I am resp.fully yr obt. ser.

R. B. Mason, Col. *Ist* Dragoons
and Governor of California.[28]

---

28. *Californian*, San Francisco, Dec. 15, 1847.

BIBLIOGRAPHY

Manuscripts

Unless otherwise noted, in the Bancroft Library, University of California, Berkeley.

Archives of California. Vols. XV–XX. Provincial State Papers and Departmental State Papers (Bencia) Military, 1767–1846.

Bancroft, Hubert Howe. Reference Notes, 1874–1890.

Bee, Henry J. "Recollections of the History of California." 1877.

California. Mission San Juan Bautista Archives. In custody of the pastor, Father George McMenamin.

———. Mission Santa Barbara. Archivaum Provinciae. Santa Barbara.

———. "Transcript of the Proceedings . . . José Abrego, et. al., Claiments, vs. the United States, Defendant, for the Place named 'San Francisquito.'" Land Case 247SD.

Carriger, Nicholas. "Autobiography." 1874.

Castro, Manuel de Jesús. Correspondence and Papers: 1830–1863.

Chamberlain, John. "Memoirs of California Since 1840." 1877.

Coronel, Antonio Francisco. "Cosas de California." 1877.

Dawson, Nicholas. "Reminiscences, California in 1841." n.d.

Ezquer, Ignacio. "Memoria de cosas pasados en California." 1878.

Gomez, Vincente Perfecto. "Lo que sabe sobre cosas de California." 1876.

Graham, Isaac. Deposition. Monterey County Archives, XIII, 761–781.

Great Britain, Public Record Office, Home Office Records. "Census Returns of Settlers in New South Wales, 1814–1824; and Criminal Book: Letters, etc., Regarding . . . Removal of Convicts . . . to Await Transportation Overseas, 1814–1824." London.

Guerra, Pablo de la. Letters and Papers. Various dates.

Loomis, Elisha. Journal: Hawaii, 1824–1826. University of Hawaii, Honolulu. On film in Bancroft Library.

Mason, Richard Barnes. Correspondence and Papers, 1847–1848.

McKinley, James. Family Letters and Accounts, 1837–1849.

Meadows, James. "Statement . . . Respecting the Graham Affair of 1840." 1877.

Monterey County Archives. 16 vols. County Courthouse, Salinas, California. See especially Vol. XIII, for documents pertaining to the *Garner* v. *Farnham* libel suit.

Morris, Albert Ferdinand. "The Diary of a Crazy Man, or An Account of the Graham Affair of 1840." 1871.

––––––. "The Journal of a Crazy Man." [1853?]

National Archives. Record Group 217 (1846–1850). Old Military Records, Social and Economic Records Division. Washington, D.C.

Nidever, George. "Life and Adventures of George Nidever, a Pioneer of California since 1834." 1878.

Norwich Archives. Norfolk and Norwich Record Office. Central Library, Norwich, England.

Rodriguez, Jacinto. "Relation of the Arrest of Isaac Graham." 1874.

Serrano, Florencio. "Apuntes para la Historia de California." 1877.

––––––. "Recuerdos historico de Don Florencio Serrano." 1875.

Torre, Esteban de la. "Reminiscencias." 1877.

Vallejo, Mariano Guadalupe. Documentos para la Historia de California. 36 vols. 1769–1850.

Weeks, James W. "Reminiscences." 1877.

Wilson, Benjamin Davis. "Some Facts About Isaac Graham and John A. Sutter, by a Pioneer of 1841." 1877.

Printed Documents and Primary Sources

Beale, Thomas. *The Natural History of the Sperm Whale . . . To which is added a Sketch of a South-Sea Whaling Voyage . . . in which the author was personally engaged.* 2d ed. London, 1839.

Beechey, Frederick William. *A Narrative of a Voyage to the Pacific and Beering's Strait to co-operate with the polar expeditions . . . in the Years 1825, 26, 27, 28. . . .* London. 1831.

Belcher, Sir Edward, *Narrative of a Voyage Round the World, Performed in Her Majesty's ship Sulphur during the Years 1836–1832.* 2 vols. London, 1843.

Belden, Josiah. *Josiah Belden, 1841 California Overland Pioneer: His Memoir and Early Letters.* Edited by Doyce B. Nunis, Jr. Georgetown, California: Talisman Press, 1962.

Bennett, Frederick Debell. *Narrative of a Whaling Voyage Round the Globe from the Year 1833 to 1836 . . .* London, 1840.

Bidwell, John. *Echoes of the Past: an account of the first emigrant train to California, Fremont in the conquest of California, the discovery of gold and early reminiscences, by the late General John Bidwell. . . .* Chico, California, [19—?]

————. *A Journey to California.* [Missouri? 1842?].

Bloxam, Andrew. *Diary of Andrew Bloxam, Naturalist of the 'Blonde,' 1824–1825.* Honolulu: Special Publication No. 10, Bernice P. Bishop Museum, 1925.

Bowers, William. *Naval Adventures During Thirty-Five Years' Service.* 2 vols. London, 1833.

Brewer, William H. *Up and Down California in 1860–1864.* Edited by Francis Peloubet Farquhar. New Haven: Yale University Press, 1930; 3d ed. Berkeley and Los Angeles: University of California Press, 1966.

Bryant, Edwin. *What I Saw in California: being the Journal of a Tour by the Emigrant Route . . . in the years 1846, 1847.* New York and Philadelphia, 1848.

Carson, James H. *Early Recollections of the Mines, and a Description of the Great Tulare Valley.* Stockton, 1852.

Cheever, Henry Theodore. *The Whale and his Captors . . . as Gathered on the Homeward Cruise of the 'Commodore Preble' from the Sandwich Islands to Boston.* New York, 1850.

Colnett, James. *A Voyage to the South Atlantic and Round Cape Horn into the Pacific Ocean, for the Purpose of Extending the Spermaceti Whale Fisheries. . . .* London, 1798.

Colton, Walter. *The Sea and the Sailor, Notes on France, Italy and other literary remains of Rev. Walter Colton, with a Memoir by Rev. Henry T. Cheever.* New York, 1851.

————. *Three Years in California.* New York, 1850.

Cook, Sherbourne F., ed. "Expeditions to the Interior of California: Central Valley, 1820–1840." *University of California Anthropological Records,* 20 (1962), 151–213.

Cordua, Theodor. "Memoirs of Theodor Cordua." Edited and translated by Erwin G. Gudde. California Historical Society *Quarterly* 12 (1933), 279–311.

Derby, George. *Report of the Secretary of War Communicating, in compliance with a Resolution of the Senate, a report of the Tulare Valley, made by Lieutenant Derby.* Senate Executive Document No. 110, 32d Cong., 1st sess. Washington, D.C., 1852.

Farnham, Eliza Woodson. *California Indoors and Out: or, How We Farm, Mine and Live Generally in the Golden State.* New York, 1856.

Farnham, Thomas Jefferson. *Travels in California and Scenes in the Pacific Ocean.* New York, 1844.

Farthest West, The [pseud., Washington Allon Bartlett?]. "California in 1846." *The Friend,* Oct. 15, Nov. 16, Dec. 1, 1846; Reprinted several times.

Frémont, John Charles. *Memoirs of My Life: Including in the Narrative Five Journeys of Western Exploration, During the Years 1842, 1843–4, 1845–6–7, 1848–9, 1853–4.* vol. I. Chicago and New York, 1887.

Garner, José. "Obituary of William R. Garner — A Pioneer of 1826 — Sketch of his Life." *San Jose Pioneer,* April 27, 1878.

Golder, Frank A. *The March of the Mormon Battalion from Council Bluffs to California, Containing the Journal of Henry Standage.* New York, 1928.

Hartweg, Karl Theodor. "Journal of a Mission to California in Search of Plants." Horticultural Society of London *Journal,* 1, 2, 3 (1846–1848).

Hastings, Lansford W. *The Emigrants Guide, to Oregon and California, containing scenes and incidents of a Party of Oregon Emigrants; . . . and A description of California. . . .* Cincinnati, 1845.

Hooker, Sir William J., and G. A. Walker Arnott. *The Botany of Captain Beechey's Voyage; Comprising an Account of the Plants Collected by Messrs. Lay and Collie, and other Officers of the Expedition, during the Voyage to the Pacific and Bering's Strait, performed in Her Majesty's Ship Blossom . . . in the Years 1825, 26, 27 and 28.* London, 1841.

Hutton, William Rich. *California, 1847–1852; drawings by William Rich Hutton, reproduced from the originals in The Huntington Library, with an introduction by Willard O. Waters.* San Marino, California: The Huntington Library, 1942.

————. *Glances at California, 1847–1853; Diaries and Letters . . . with a Brief Memoir and Notes by Willard O. Waters.* San Marino, California. The Huntington Library, 1942.

————. "Two Letters on Post-Conquest Monterey." Monterey History and Art Association Quarterly *Noticias . . .* 5 (June 1961).

Janssens, Victor Eugene August. *The Life and Adventures in California of Don Agustin Janssens, 1834–1856.* Edited by William H. Ellison and Francis Price. San Marino, California: The Huntington Library, 1953.

King, Dr. William S. "The Medical Topography of Monterey, California, (1852)." Senate Executive Document 96, 34th Cong., 1st sess., 1856. Reprint. Monterey History and Art Association *Noticias . . .* 10, 11 (Dec. 1966, March and June 1967).

Kotzebue, Otto von. *A New Voyage Round the World, in the Years 1823, 24, 25 and 26.* 2 vols. London. 1830.

Larkin, Thomas Oliver. *The Larkin Papers: Personal, Business, and Official Correspondence of Thomas Oliver Larkin, Merchant and United States Consul in California.* Edited by George P. Hammond. 10 vols. Berkeley and Los Angeles: University of California Press, 1951–1964.

———. "Mineral Lands in California." House Executive Document No. 1, vol. I. 30th Cong., 2d sess. Washington, D.C. 1848–49.

Lloyd's Register of Shipping. London. Yearly from 1804–1834.

Lyman, Chester A. *Around the Horn to the Sandwich Islands and California, 1845–1850.* Edited by Frederick J. Teggert. New Haven: Yale University Press, 1924.

Mason, Richard Barnes. "Correspondence with United States Adj.-General Jones on the extent and effect of the Gold Discovery (1848)." House Executive Document No. 1, vol. I. 30th Cong., 2d sess. 1848–1849.

Moerenhaut, Jacques Antoine. "The French Consulate in California: 1843–1856: The Moerenhaut Documents." Edited by Abraham P. Nasatir. *California Historical Society Quarterly*, 12, 13 (1933, 1934).

———. *Jacques A. Moerenhaut: The Inside Story of the Gold Rush.* Translated and edited by Abraham P. Nasatir. San Francisco: Special Publication No. 8, California Historical Society, 1935.

Nuttall, Thomas. *The North American Sylva.* . . . 2 vols. Philadelphia, 1865.

Ord, Angustias de la Guerra. *Occurrences in Hispanic California.* Edited by William Ellison [translated by Francisco Price]. Washington, D.C.: Academy of Franciscan History, 1956. A translation of Mrs. Ord's dictation to Thomas Savage in Spanish, the original manuscript of which is in the Bancroft Library.

Robinson, Alfred. *Life in California, during a residence of several years in that territory.* New York. 1846.

Rojas, Arnold R. *California Vaquero.* Fresno, California: Academy Library Guild, 1953.

Sandels, G. M. Waseurtz af. *A Sojourn in California by The Kings Orphan . . . who visited California in 1842–1843.* Edited by Helen Putnam Van Sicklen. San Francisco: Grabhorn Press, 1945.

Sherman, William Tecumseh. *Home Letters of General Sherman.* Edited by Mark Anthony DeWolfe Howe. New York: Scribner's, 1909.

———. *Memoirs of General W. T. Sherman.* 2 vols. New York, 1875.

Smith, Jedediah Strong. *The Travels of Jedediah Smith; a Documentary Outline, including the Journal of the Great American Pathfinder.* Edited by Maurice S. Sullivan. Santa Ana, California: The Fine Arts Press, 1934.

Stewart, Charles S. *Journal of a Voyage to the Pacific and a Residence in the Sandwich Islands during the Years 1822, 1823, 1824 and 1825.* . . . New York, 1828.

Swan, Jack. "Monterey in 1843 — By a Pioneer." *Monterey Weekly Herald*, 1874–76.

Thomes, William H. *On Land and Sea: California in 1843, '44, and '45.* Boston, 1884.

United States. President. *Message . . . on the Subject of California and New Mexico.* House Executive Document No. 17. 31st Cong., 1st sess. Washington, D.C., 1850.

————. Senate. *Reports on Explorations and Surveys to Ascertain the most practicable and economical route for a Railway from the Mississippi River to the Pacific Ocean . . . Made in 1853–6.* Executive Document No. 78, vol. VII. 33d Cong., 2d sess., Washington, D.C., 1857.

————. War Department. *Reports of explorations and surveys, to ascertain the most practicable and economical route for a railroad from the Mississippi River to the Pacific Ocean.* 12 vols. Washington, D. C., 1855–60.

Voyage Through the Islands of the Pacific Ocean, A. Dublin, 1824.

Whitney, J. D. *Geology: Report of Progress and Synopsis of the Fieldwork from 1860 to 1864.* Geological Survey of California, vol. I. Philadelphia, 1865.

Wilkes, Charles. *Narrative of the United States Exploring Expedition during the years 1838, 1839, 1840, 1841 and 1842,* vol. V. Philadelphia, 1845.

Wise, Harry A. *Los Gringos, or An Inside View of Mexico and California.* London, 1849.

Wood, William Maxwell. *Wandering Sketches of People and Things in South America, Polynesia, California, and other places visited, during a cruise on board of the U.S. ships Levant, Portsmouth, and Savannah.* Philadelphia, 1849.

Secondary Sources

Bancroft, Hubert Howe. *California Pastoral: 1769–1848.* San Francisco, 1888.

————. *History of California.* 7 vols. San Francisco, 1884–1890.

Baur, John E. "California Crops That Failed." California Historical Society *Quarterly*, 45 (1966), 41–68.

Burcham, Levi Turner. *California Range Land; an Historico-Ecological Study of the Range Resource of California.* Sacramento: State Printing Division, 1957.

California. Division of Mines and Geology. *Mineral Commodities of Califor-*

nia; *Geologic Occurrence, Economic Development and Utilization of the State's Minerals.* San Francisco: Bulletin 176, 1957.

Cleland, Robert Glass. "Larkin's Description of California (1846)." Historical Society of Southern California *Annual* 10, part 3 (1917): 70–74.

Church, Albert Cook. *Whaleships and Whaling.* New York: W. W. Norton, 1938.

Clowes, William L. *The Royal Navy; A History, from the Earliest Times to the Present.* 7 vols. London: S. Low, Marston, 1897–1903.

Commons, John Rogers; David J. Saposs, Helen L. Sumner, E. B. Mittleman, H. E. Hoagland, John B. Andrews, and Selig Perlman. *History of Labor in the United States.* 4 vols. New York: Macmillan, 1918–1935.

Cook, Sherbourne F. "Aboriginal Population of the San Joaquin Valley, California." *University of California Anthropological Records,* 16:31–78.

Cowan, Robert Granniss. *Ranchos of California; a list of Spanish Concessions, 1775–1822, and Mexican Grants, 1822–1846.* Fresno, California: Academy Library Guild, 1956.

Craig, Donald M. "Ghosts and Gold in Old Monterey." Monterey History and Art Association Quarterly *Noticias . . .* 9, 10 (Dec. 1965–Sept. 1966).

Crampton, Charles G. "The Opening of the Mariposa Mining Region, 1849–1859." Ph.D. dissertation, University of California, Berkeley, 1941.

Cullum, George W. *Biographical Register of Officers and Graduates of the U.S. Military Academy at West Point, New York.* 2 vols. New York, 1868.

Dakin, Susanna Bryant. *The Lives of William Hartnell.* Stanford: Stanford University Press, 1949.

Dakin, William John. *Whalemen Adventurers; the Story of Whaling in Australian Waters and Other Southern Seas. . . .* 2d rev. ed. Sydney: Angus & Robertson, 1938.

Heitman, Francis Bernard. *Historical Register and Dictionary of the United States Army from its Organization September 29, 1789 to March 2, 1903.* 2 vols. Washington, D.C.: Govt. Printing Office, 1903.

Hertzog, Dorothy Allen. "Isaac Graham: California Pioneer." Master's thesis. University of California, Berkeley, 1941.

Hoover, Mildred Brooke; H. E. and E. G. Rensch. *Historic Spots in California.* Rev. by Ruth Teiser. Stanford: Stanford University Press, 1948.

Judd, Gerrit Parmele, IV. *Dr. Judd, Hawaii's Friend; a Biography of Gerrit Parmele Judd (1803–1873).* Honolulu: University of Hawaii Press, 1960.

Klose, Nelson, "Louis Prevost and the Silk Industry at San Jose." California Historical Society *Quarterly* 43:309–317.

Larkin, Thomas Oliver. *Chapters in the Early Life of Thomas O. Larkin, Including his Experiences in the Carolinas and the Building of the Larkin House at Monterey.* Edited by Robert J. Parker. San Francisco: California Historical Society Special Publication No. 16, 1939.

Mackaness, George. *Blue Bloods of Botany Bay; a Book of Australian Historical Tales.* Sydney: Collins, 1953.

Mumford, E. Philpott. "Early History of Cotton Cultivation in California: Researches Among the Old Spanish Manuscripts." California Historical Society *Quarterly,* 6 (1927), 159–166.

Mulder, William, and A. Russell Mortensen, ed. *Among the Mormons: Historic Accounts by Contemporary Observers.* New York: Knopf, 1958.

Nunis, Doyce Blackman, Jr. *The Trials of Isaac Graham.* Los Angeles: Dawson's Book Shop, 1967.

Richards, William. *History of Lynn.* 2 vols. Lynn, England, 1812.

Robson, Lloyd L. *The Convict Settlers of Australia,* . . . Colton, Victoria: Melbourne University Press, 1965.

Rowland, Leon. "Isaac Graham, Swashbuckling Soldier of Fortune." *Santa Cruz News,* 58 (Aug. 1, 1936), 7.

Sudworth, George B. *Forest Trees of the Pacific Slope.* Washington, D.C.: United States Department of Agriculture, 1908.

Tays, George. "Revolutionary California: The Political History of California During the Mexican Period, 1824–1846." Ph.D. dissertation, University of California, Berkeley, 1932.

[Walton, W. H. F., and Curtis, E. E.?] *Handbook of Monterey and Vicinity.* San Francisco, 1875.

White, Charles. *Early Australian History: Convict Life in New South Wales.* Bathurst, Australia, 1889.

INDEX

Note: Italic numbers have been used for illustrations.

Abbatt, William, *Magazine of History*, 2

Ábrego, José: quoted, 50, 222; discovers quicksilver lode, 60; forms Santa Clara Mining Co., 60; buys Garner estate, 80; identified, 222; supports Garner, 234

Acapulco, Mexico, 200, 202

Acedo, José Antonio, lawsuits against, 37 and n.

Admiralty: British, 6; Court of, Monterey, 60

Admittance, Garner auctions, 60

Agriculture, 96–97; possibilities for, 98–100, 102, 158, 176; dependence on Indian labor, 127; low rate of production, 127–128; production exaggerated in pamphlets, 130–132, 132–133 n.; 1847 harvest, 198, 201. *See also* Soil

Aguirre, José Antonio, 219, 220, 223

Alcaldes, 174; powers, 55, 56, 236; duties described, 177; inability to enforce law, 185–187. *See also* Colton

Alder, 139

Alisal (Salinas), 129n.

Alisal, Rancho, silver found on, 133 n.

Alvarado, Juan Bautista, 34, 42; leads revolt (1836), 22; becomes governor, 23; grants Garner citizenship, 24; orders arrest of *Rifleros Americános*, 24–25; Garner held at house of, 26; sells Mariposa to Frémont, 42n.;

Farnham on, 45n.; nominated to Legislature, 178; saluted, 197; cited, 221; plan to depose, 225–226, 229

Alvarado, Martina Castro de, 42 n.

Alvarado family: political struggles, 21

Alviso, Nicolás, 18 n.

Amador, María Ignacia, Garner wrecks house of, 30

Ambrís, Padre Doroteo: subscription for, 40–41; asks for reprieve for Indians, 48

America, Americans. *See* Immigrants; United States

Amestí, José: contract with Garner, 20; vouches for Garner, 24; lawsuit, 47

Anderson, Bill: witness for Farnham, 49; testimony, 50; knowledge of penal colonies, 216

Apples, 94

Araiza, Francisco, acts as *hombre bueno*, 31

Aram, Capt. Joseph, goes to diggings, 63–64

Argüello, Santiago, nominated to legislature, 178

Arroyo de la Cuesta, Padre Felipe: baptizes Garner, 17–18, 209–210; transferred, 18 n.; biographical sketch of, 210 n.

Arroyo Seco (Tassajara Hot Springs), silver deposits, 113 n.

Artellán, Pedro (Pierre), buys house from Garner, 41